Living Japanese

生きた日本語

生きた日本語
さまざまな言葉、さまざまな生活

Living Japanese
Diversity in Language and Lifestyles

KAREN COLLIGAN-TAYLOR

Conversations with Native Speakers
Ceil Lucas, SERIES EDITOR

Yale University Press   New Haven and London

Publisher: Mary Jane Peluso
Development Editor: Brie Kluytenaar
Production Editor: Ann-Marie Imbornoni
Production Controller: Karen Stickler
Marketing Manager: Timothy Shea

Cover designed by Sonia Shannon.

Printed in the United States of America.

Library of Congress Cataloging-in-Publication Data

Colligan-Taylor, Karen.
Living Japanese, diversity in language and lifestyles = [Ikita Nihongo, samazama na kotoba, samazama na seikatsu] / Karen Colligan-Taylor.
    p. cm. – (Conversations with native speakers)
System requirements for accompanying DVD: NTSC.
ISBN-13: 978-0-300-10958-0 (pbk. : alk. paper)
ISBN-10: 0-300-10958-X (pbk. : alk. paper) 1. Japanese language--Textbooks for foreign speakers--English. I. Title. II. Title: Ikita Nihongo, samazama na kotoba, samazama na seikatsu.
 PL539.5.E5 C65 2007
 495.6'82421--dc22

                                                                2006048314

A catalogue record for this book is available from the British Library.

The paper in this book meets the guidelines for permanence and durability of the Committee on Production Guidelines for Book Longevity of the Council on Library Resources.

10 9 8 7 6 5 4 3

Contents

Acknowledgments

Many thanks to:

Yale University Press, for providing funding for the project; Mary Jane Peluso, Publisher, for supporting its cultural orientation; and Brie Kluytenaar, Mary Pasti, Ann-Marie Imbornoni, and Tim Shea for their thoughtful assistance.

Ronald Reed, videographer, and Patrick Harris, digital engineer, at Gallaudet University Media Services, for their fine technical work.

Ceil Lucas, Series Editor of *Conversations with Native Speakers*, for inviting me to participate in this innovative series. The series also covers Italian, French, Spanish, and Arabic.

Kyōko Selden, Harumi Befu, Matsumoto Kentarō, Hisamatsu Mikio, Kusuoka Yasushi, Taniguchi Yōko, Susan Matisoff, Yuri Itoh, Yoshiko Matsumoto, Mark Selden, Sumi Colligan, and Mike Taylor for their considerable time and excellent editorial suggestions at various stages of the manuscript. I am responsible for any errors and for balancing differing viewpoints.

Ishii Kazuko, Umezaki Kunitomo, Katō Masako, Matsuda Motoko, Kusuoka Yasushi, Matsumoto Kentarō, Taniguchi Yōko, Odajima Mamoru, Sachi Yoshio, MORI Sōya, Mary Anne O'Neil, and Judy Hauck for special contributions to the DVD and text.

Matsumoto Masa, Matsumoto Keiko, and Ishii Kazuko, for their warm hospitality.

Sasaki Yasuko, for playing the theme music, and Yamazaki Mayumi, for her lovely singing.

Narita Kazuyo, for sign language interpretation.

The Shisendō, Kyoto, and the Shiga Prefectural Lake Biwa Museum, for on-site photography; and the many wonderful people who opened their residences or places of work to our film crew.

Most of all, my sincere thanks to the participants, the real authors of this text, and to their families: Abe Nobuko; Imai Haruka; Ishii Kazuko; Umezaki Kunitomo and the Aioi Kendō Club; Endō Rie; Odajima Mamoru; Kada Yukiko; Katō Sadamichi; Katō Masako; Kusuoka Yasushi; Sasaoka Yumiko; Sasaki Chikako; Sasaki Yasuko; Sasaki Yoshisato; Sachi Yoshio; Satō Mayumi; Shizuka Yaeko; Shinohara Akira; Suzuki Furoten; Taniguchi Yōko; Nakagawa Shōgakkō; Nakajima Masahiro; Narita Kazuyo; Hashimoto Midori; Hori Shūkō and family; Matsuoka Yoshie; Matsuda Motoko; Matsumoto Keiko; Matsumoto Kentarō; Matsumoto Masa; Miyata Tsuneo; MORI Sōya and family; Yanagisawa Tomoko; and Yamazaki Mayumi.

心から感謝申し上げます

Introduction

Objectives and Organization

    The DVD and text *Living Japanese: Diversity in Language and Lifestyles* 『生きた日本語——さまざまな言葉、さまざまな生活』 are designed to hone Japanese listening comprehension and speaking skills at the intermediate and advanced levels through the medium of unscripted interviews. The conversations focus on twenty topics in Japanese culture and society. Students have the opportunity to develop an extensive vocabulary while gaining familiarity with conversational Japanese. The DVD and text may be used as primary or supplementary materials in Japanese classes or as review materials by individuals who wish to maintain or enhance their language skills. *Living Japanese* may be used as well in classes with an emphasis on Japanese culture and society, through the presentation of diverse elements and viewpoints. While the conversations reflect individual perspectives and are not intended to provide a definitive view of the topics, they provide a valuable springboard for further research and discussion.

    Living Japanese will facilitate implementation of the "Standards for Foreign Language Learning" established by ACTFL (American Council on the Teaching of Foreign Languages). Students will develop *communication* skills by using the DVD to improve listening comprehension; by building vocabulary; and by discussing the topics and the style in which they are presented. Their understanding of Japanese *culture* will deepen as they listen to diverse perspectives on the culture of everyday life as well as broader social institutions and issues. They will perceive elements of culture in conversational style. The DVD permits students to visualize cultural practices and products. Discussion questions encourage students to make cross-cultural *comparisons*. Some questions require that students interview native speakers at their school or in the larger *community*, and students are encouraged to invite native speakers to take part in discussions of the DVD topics. Students may make *connections* with knowledge gained in other disciplines, bringing new perspectives to class discussion and new methodologies for framing or analyzing specific issues on the DVD. Likewise, viewpoints presented by the Japanese speakers will help students evaluate aspects of their own lives, as well as topics presented in different disciplines, from another cultural perspective.

To students:

As you watch and listen to the DVD you will find that the speakers, aged seven to seventy-five, will gradually become familiar as they reappear in different lessons, sharing their thoughts, experiences, and feelings on a wide spectrum of topics. The speakers are drawn from diverse professions and come from many different parts of the country. We begin with topics related to everyday living: the family; the house and its environment; architecture; household crafts; organic farming; eating habits in a busy society; views of marriage; women and work; and personal experiences at the elementary, high school, and university levels. The second half of this text introduces the speakers' views on familiar topics such as *anime, manga, kendō,* and related pastimes and artistic disciplines, as well as less widely discussed issues such as ways of seeing and valuing the natural world, environmental education, and the Buddhist doctrine of the essential interrelatedness of all things. In Lesson 14 two speakers present moving recollections of childhood experiences, and in Lesson 15 a professional singer and a pianist perform the two songs on which the music used in the beginning of the DVD and the lesson openings is based. In the final two lessons the speakers discuss linguistic diversity within the Japanese language. Recurrent themes are highlighted by cross-referencing related lessons or segments within lessons; recurrent themes are also the subject of many discussion questions.

Preceding each transcription is an English introduction intended to place a specific topic in a broader cultural context, to provide further discussion by one or more speakers, or to provide background information about the speaker relevant to the topic. The transcriptions are followed by extensive vocabulary and grammar notes so that you can dispense with hours of dictionary work and focus on listening. Phonetic readings of *kanji* are provided throughout. Each lesson ends with discussion questions, providing you with the opportunity to articulate your own views, drawing on the vocabulary and expressions introduced in each lesson. Expressing ourselves becomes easier when we have models of natural speech.

A list of references and suggested readings follows the main text. To protect the privacy of the participants many names have been changed and place-names withheld.

The Transcriptions

The transcriptions are verbatim recordings of every word spoken by the speaker. When several speakers appear in one lesson, the responses of each speaker are given a specific number (Speaker 1 is Segment 1; Speaker 2 is Segment 2). If a speaker's conversation is extensive, it is broken into short segments for easy listening (Segments 1.1, 1.2, 1.3). If there is only one speaker who addresses a series of questions about the topic, each question is given a separate segment number. Time codes corresponding to the DVD recordings are given for every segment in the text so that you can listen to a segment repeatedly until you hear each word.

In most cases you will not hear the interviewer ask the question. Questions are highlighted as follows in the text: $\boxed{\mathbf{Q}}$. At each question, pause the DVD and read the question aloud. In this way *you* will become the interviewer.

Although you are listening to spontaneous interviews rather than two-way conversations, you will find many of the elements present in natural everyday discourse.

Elements of Conversational Japanese

Reviewing basic elements of conversational Japanese will help you avoid some confusion from the outset. Specific word usage is addressed in the vocabulary notes following the transcriptions.

Word order

Word order is flexible, often deviating from the standard "subject, object, verb." An inversion occurs when the speaker withholds important information until the end for emphasis. Examples:

少しの差に敏感ですね、女性は。 (They're) very sensitive to subtle differences, women are.

そういうコミュニケーション作(づく)りができればいいなと思っているんですけれど、

家(いえ)を通(とお)してですね。 (An architect:) I'd really like to be able to facilitate that sort of

communication—through the medium of the house.

Ellipsis

      Ellipsis is the omission of a word or phrase necessary for a complete syntactical

construction, but not necessary for understanding. In Japanese conversation, almost any

element in a sentence may be omitted: the subject, the predicate, or various particles

such as を and が. Listeners are able to fill in the missing items for themselves. In the

following examples the topics and the particles を and が are understood in context:

パン＊買いに行ったんです。　（を）

決(き)められたところ以外(いがい)に当(あ)たる時(とき)＊あるんですね。　（が）

 （About *kendō*:) There are times when (the bamboo sword) lands on other than the

designated places.

Contractions

      One of the most common contractions is って、representing either と or という。

どちらか<u>って</u>いうと	どちらか<u>と</u>いうと
・・・<u>って</u>ふうに	・・・<u>という</u>ふうに
日本の家屋(かおく)<u>って</u>のは	日本の家屋<u>という</u>のは
職人(しょくにん)さんの仕事<u>って</u>のは	職人さんの仕事<u>という</u>のは
必要(ひつよう)がある<u>って</u>思います	必要がある<u>と</u>思います

Other common contractions:

大事なことだと思ってます	大事なことだと思って<u>い</u>ます
住んでる	住んで<u>い</u>る
使ってらっしゃる	使って<u>い</u>らっしゃる

ですけども   ですけれども

かくりじょうたい   かくりじょうたい
隔離状態にする<u>ん</u>もよくない   隔離状態にする<u>の</u>もよくない

はたら
働 きに行かなく<u>ちゃ</u>いけない   働きにに行かなく<u>ては</u>いけない

わす
忘れ<u>ちゃう</u>   忘れ<u>てしまう</u>

なっ<u>ちゃう</u>   なっ<u>てしまう</u>

かん
感じるようになって<u>くん</u>ですね   感じるようになって<u>くるの</u>ですね

ひょうじゅんご か   か
標 準 語化されて<u>くん</u>だ   標準語化されて<u>いくの</u>だ

<u>Filler words</u>

    By "filler words" we mean 間投詞、 literally "words thrown in between."
かんとうし

These include utterances such as あ、ああ、あの、あのう、うん、ええ、ええと、
こう、その、そのう、ね、ま、and まあ. Most people filter out the filler words as
they listen to a conversation, focusing on the meaning. As language learners, you will
want to avoid these fillers, in the same way you would avoid excessive use of "um" and
"uh," or "like" and "you know," in English. However, from a linguistic point of view
these fillers can be interesting, as they each have their own nuance. A linguist would take
note of the particular environment in which each type of filler is found.

    Filler words may have any of the following functions: they give the speaker time
to think; they make the speech less direct; they express emotion or emphasis regarding
the subject matter; they qualify a statement; they express the speaker's nervousness.
Their use may be habitual, even providing a verbal signature. On occasion, fillers appear
to play a hybrid role, retaining much of their basic meaning (こう、その). The speakers
themselves are not aware that they are using them. The most common filler words have
been reduced in size so that you can practice reading the conversations aloud without
them.

Related to filler words in terms of expressing nervousness or hesitation or giving the speaker time to think are phrases such as 何ですか、何て言いますかね、何てい うんですか —all variations of "What should I say?" or "How should I put it?"

Misspeaking

Often we begin to express something one way and then decide to take a different approach. We may use one word but correct ourselves and use another. In clear instances of misspeaking (言いよどみ), I have placed the rejected word or phrase in parentheses.

Aizuchi 相槌

As you will recall, *aizuchi* are feedback signals letting the speaker know that the listener is paying attention—for example, はい、ええ、うん、そうですか、and それ で？ Head-nodding is an important non-verbal feedback signal. The term *aizuchi* is derived from the rhythmic hammering of blacksmith and apprentice as they forge a sword blade. Interjecting *aizuchi* after key phrases or at the end of sentences helps maintain the rhythm of a conversation. These words confirm the involvement of the listener and encourage the speaker to continue. In our text the longer utterances of the interviewer are placed in brackets {   }, but in order to focus on the speaker's words and keep the sentences uncluttered, most *aizuchi* are not noted.

Speech level and style

Because being interviewed is a somewhat formal occasion, most of the participants tended to speak at a more polite level and in a more formal style than they would if they were off-camera chatting with a close friend. At times the speakers forgot about the camera and spoke directly to the interviewer—in these cases the speech level is more familiar and the style more representative of age and gender. This is especially true of the first speaker in Lesson 14, who reared the interviewer. In some instances, the speaker was quite conscious of a DVD audience and used polite verb forms on behalf of that imagined audience. In another instance, people in the room with the speaker influenced the speech level. These differences are noted in the individual interviews. Most of the speakers were longtime acquaintances of the interviewer. Some were more accustomed to public speaking or speaking before a camera than others.

Communication

Communication involves so much more than words—sincerity, proper etiquette, an interest in learning the other person's viewpoint or cultural background, listening, adjusting to a different rhythm, and reassessing one's expectations. Obviously we can't approach our neighbors or visit another country and expect people to do and think as we would. While you develop your language skills, don't forget to open your heart and mind!

Using the DVD and Workbook

To the instructor:

The terms "intermediate" and "advanced" are still rather fluid in Japanese instruction. An "intermediate" course at one school might be an "advanced beginning" course at another. You may wish to use selected lessons and segments within lessons according to your students' interests and ability. (Each lesson is followed by a complete vocabulary list.) Or, you may wish to use all of the text as primary or supplementary course material. This will give students the opportunity to think about recurrent themes and to consider one topic in light of another. The grammatical patterns used are not complex; they are patterns generally introduced by the third year of language study. What may be new to students are elements of conversational Japanese, as well as vocabulary specific to a given topic. Students must also adjust to language spoken at natural speed and to variation in speech according to region and individual characteristics. Whether you use these materials over one semester or one academic year, you may wish to incorporate these suggestions:

❖   Ask the students to read the introduction and vocabulary notes for the segments you wish to cover before coming to class. You may wish to designate vocabulary the students should memorize. Students should have a personal copy of the DVD so that they can watch it multiple times on their own.

❖   View the lesson or segment as a class. This is an important review, even if students have watched it in advance. Pose basic content questions, and have the students listen again in order to pick up key information without looking at the transcript.

❖   Go over the transcript with the students, highlighting grammar, word usage, and elements of conversational Japanese. You may wish to test listening comprehension by providing selections from the transcript in which key words or expressions have been left blank. Have students complete the selections as they listen to the DVD in class. It is useful to play the selections at least twice.

❖   Proceed to the suggested discussion questions. Many of these questions involve native speakers at your school or in your community. Some of the questions require students to think about the topic in their own personal or cultural context. Answering the questions and discussing the topics will prepare students for responding to similar questions in Japan. These, or your own questions, may be used as composition topics, and you may wish to have students develop a topic further as an oral or written report.

To independent learners:

Form a study group of individuals who have returned from prolonged stays in Japan. Invite native speakers to join your group in watching the DVD and discussing the content. Have fun!

第1課　家族構成

Families in Transition

How will a falling birthrate and burgeoning elderly population affect Japanese family size and structure? A few statistics will help us appreciate the rapid change in Japanese households. According to the Ministry of Health, Labor, and Welfare 厚生労働省, the average family size in Japan is declining steadily: 2.82 people in 1995; 2.7 in 2000; and 2.61 in 2005. The average family size in Tokyo is 2.14. The Bureau of Statistics 統計局 reports that, nationwide, 58.4 percent of households consist of a nuclear family, and 27.6 percent are one-person households. However, families of three generations are still common in some rural and semi-rural prefectures. In 2000, half of persons aged sixty-five and over lived with relatives, mainly with the families of their children (Sugimoto, 175). This is one aspect of Japanese family structure that differs from that in other industrialized countries, although this may change as Japanese elderly opt for senior homes with nursing care.

In 2005 Japan's birthrate fell to 1.25 births for each woman of child-bearing age, far short of the 2.08 necessary to maintain a population of 127,780,000 (Bureau of Statistics, April 2006 estimate). Compare this with figures worldwide: the average woman in a wealthy country bears 1.6 children, while in a poor country the figure is 2.9 (Cohen, 50). The fall 2005 census suggests that Japan's population may have peaked earlier than expected, at 127,790,000 (Bureau of Statistics, December 2005 final estimate). By 2030 the population is expected to decrease by ten million. This phenomenon is not unique to Japan. By 2050 significant population loss is expected to occur in most of the more economically developed countries (Cohen, 50).

Worldwide, old people began to outnumber young people in the year 2000 and this trend will continue. With 20 percent of the population at age sixty-five or older, Japanese society is aging more quickly than any other society in the world, leaving fewer

1

wage earners to support each retired person. Japan now wrestles with the question of whether to encourage immigration of workers to bolster its economy and sustain its population. The government is also exploring a variety of reforms to make the workplace more attractive to women, to extend the working years, to increase childcare, to expand social services for the elderly, to provide training programs for unemployed socially disengaged youth, and so on, in order to create a more family-friendly society with increased work opportunities. However, these ideas for reform have been implemented slowly at best. And thus far there have been no significant measures to expand an immigrant population which currently stands at less than 1 percent.

Taniguchi Yōko, a Ph.D. candidate in cultural anthropology, begins this series of conversations by discussing her own family structure and changes in Japanese family structure in recent years. Taniguchi lives in a metropolitan center, while the other speakers live in bedroom communities or semi-rural prefectures. In the interviews below, note especially the phenomenon of older children living at home. Is this practice becoming more common elsewhere?

Segment 1　東京都在住の大学院生の話　　TIME CODE　0:00:00

Segment 1.1

Q　家族構成について教えていただけますか。

私 の家族は、あのぅ、六人家族です。で、東京に住んでいます。で、六人
の、あのぅ、構成をいうと、え、私 の母方の祖父母、それから 私 の両親、
そして 私 の 弟 （の）、と 私 と六人です。それと、あと、犬も住んでい
ます。

{で、日本では、六人家族は一般的ですか。}

昔 は一般的だったんですけども、現代の、特に東 京の生活の中では、ま
ぁ、六人家族は非常にまれです。

Segment 1.2 　　　　　　　　　　　　　　TIME CODE　0:00:40

Ｑ　じゃ、日本の一般的な家族というのは、どんな家族ですか。

（一般的）日本で一般的な家族と言われるのは、大体、お父さん、お母さ
ん、子供、子供が一人か二人かによって違うんですけども、三人から四人
の核家族が非常に、まぁ、いわゆる一般的で普通の家族と言われる 形 だと
思います。それと、あと、あのぅ、昔 は、まぁ、何十年も前なんですけど
も、昔はその六人家族というのも日本の家族として非常に一般的でした。
でも、あのぅ、私の六人家族とまた違う点は、私の家族は私の母の、あの、
祖父母と一緒に住んでいるという点で違います。で、まぁ、一般的、昔 の
一般的の六人家族は父親の両 親と、あの、同居するという 形 が、まぁ、一
般的でした。

Segment 1.3　（続<ruby>き<rt>つづ</rt></ruby>）　　　　　　　　　　TIME CODE　0:01:25

私の家族についてもう一つ付け<ruby>加<rt>くわ</rt></ruby>えたい<ruby>点<rt>てん</rt></ruby>があります。私<ruby>六人家族<rt>ろくにんかぞく</rt></ruby>という

ふうに言ったんですけれども、私はもう二十八、さきお話ししましたが、

<ruby>弟<rt>おとうと</rt></ruby>は<ruby>二十五歳<rt>にじゅうごさい</rt></ruby>で、もう<ruby>成人<rt>せいじん</rt></ruby>している、まぁ、<ruby>大人<rt>おとな</rt></ruby>になっている子供が、ぁ

の、<ruby>親<rt>おや</rt></ruby>と<ruby>同居<rt>どうきょ</rt></ruby>しています。で、それは、まぁ、日本では、それ<ruby>最近<rt>さいきん</rt></ruby>でも、ぁ

のぅ、あまり<ruby>珍<rt>めずら</rt></ruby>しいことではないんですけれども。というのは、私はまだ、

あのぅ、まぁ<ruby>大学院<rt>だいがくいん</rt></ruby>で<ruby>勉強<rt>べんきょう</rt></ruby>している<ruby>学生<rt>がくせい</rt></ruby>で、まぁ、<ruby>奨学金<rt>しょうがくきん</rt></ruby>をもらいながら、

<ruby>家<rt>うち</rt></ruby>から大学に<ruby>通<rt>かよ</rt></ruby>うのが<ruby>一番経済的<rt>いちばんけいざいてき</rt></ruby>にも、ぁの、<ruby>交通<rt>こうつう</rt></ruby>の<ruby>面<rt>めん</rt></ruby>でも、まぁ、<ruby>便利<rt>べんり</rt></ruby>だ

ということで、<ruby>便宜上<rt>べんぎじょう</rt></ruby>、あのぅ、<ruby>生活<rt>せいかつ</rt></ruby>しています。で、<ruby>弟<rt>おとうと</rt></ruby>も、あの、

<ruby>二十五歳<rt>にじゅうごさい</rt></ruby>で<ruby>就職<rt>しゅうしょく</rt></ruby>したんですけれども、あのぅ、<ruby>月<rt>つき</rt></ruby>の<ruby>内<rt>うち</rt></ruby>、<ruby>半分以上<rt>はんぶんいじょう</rt></ruby>は<ruby>国内<rt>こくない</rt></ruby>で

<ruby>出張<rt>しゅっちょう</rt></ruby>しているので、あのぅ、まぁ、<ruby>東京都内<rt>とうきょうとない</rt></ruby>で<ruby>部屋<rt>へや</rt></ruby>を<ruby>借<rt>か</rt></ruby>りるというのは、

<ruby>非常<rt>ひじょう</rt></ruby>に、まぁ、<ruby>物価<rt>ぶっか</rt></ruby>も高いですし、<ruby>光熱費<rt>こうねつひ</rt></ruby>もかかるという、まぁ、<ruby>経済的<rt>けいざいてき</rt></ruby>な

<ruby>理由<rt>りゆう</rt></ruby>が<ruby>一番大<rt>いちばんおお</rt></ruby>きいんですが、まぁ、そういう<ruby>理由<rt>りゆう</rt></ruby>で、あのぅ、まぁ、<ruby>今<rt>いま</rt></ruby>は<ruby>親<rt>おや</rt></ruby>と、

あのぅ、<ruby>生活<rt>せいかつ</rt></ruby>していますが、まぁ、あと<ruby>何年<rt>なんねん</rt></ruby>かして、もうちょっと<ruby>貯金<rt>ちょきん</rt></ruby>した

ら<ruby>自分<rt>じぶん</rt></ruby>で<ruby>生活<rt>せいかつ</rt></ruby>を<ruby>始<rt>はじ</rt></ruby>める。あるいは、私も<ruby>弟<rt>おとうと</rt></ruby>も<ruby>結婚<rt>けっこん</rt></ruby>したら、ぁの、<ruby>家<rt>いえ</rt></ruby>を出

て<ruby>独立<rt>どくりつ</rt></ruby>した<ruby>生活<rt>せいかつ</rt></ruby>をするというふうに<ruby>考<rt>かんが</rt></ruby>えています。で、こういうことは、

ま、日本では、まぁ、<ruby>最近<rt>さいきん</rt></ruby>では、<ruby>特<rt>とく</rt></ruby>に<ruby>今<rt>いま</rt></ruby>あまり<ruby>珍<rt>めずら</rt></ruby>しいことではないです。

Segment 2 TIME CODE 0:02:45

三人の女性の話。大学を卒業、現在働いている。

Q 自分の家族構成について話してくださいますか。

(遠藤さん) 私は今、ええと、父と母と私と三人暮らしです。で、兄がいる
んですが、結婚して、まぁ、一つの家庭を作って外に出てしまったので、
現在は三人で暮らしています。

(今井さん) 私の家は五人家族です。両親と弟と祖母がいます。祖父
は去年亡くなりました。その前は、はい、六人で住んでいました。

(橋本さん) 私は、ええと、今は三人です。父と母と私で住んでいます。
で、前は姉が一緒に住んでいたんですが、今はお嫁にいってしまって、今
は三人です。

Segment 3 ある経済学者の話。 TIME CODE 0:03:33

家族は四人です。まず私と妻、それから娘が二人おります。娘は、上の
娘は年は十歳です。下の娘は二歳です。年がまだ小さい娘です。

Segment 4　ある農家の方の話。　　　　　TIME CODE　0:03:51

今現在、私の家では、あの、夫婦、私の妻と、両親と子供二人、まあ、六人で生活しております。農家は家族は普通多いのが普通です。で、昔から助け合って生きていくということになるわけで、仕事をそれぞれ分担してやっております。あのう、大きな仕事は私たち夫婦がやるわけですけど、まあ、おじいさん、それからおばあさんも、あのう、野菜の手伝い、細かい仕事がたくさんありますので、あのう、大変助かっております。

Segment 5　ある禅寺の住職の話。　　　　　TIME CODE　0:04:37

お寺の住職、私が住職で、え、私の家内、ええと、私の母親、おばあちゃん、それと私の子供が四人、おります。ええ、長男が、一番の上の男の子、高校生一年生になります。二番目が女の子、長女で、中学三年生になります。ええ、三番目、四番目は男の子で小学校四年生と小学校の二年生になります。ちょっと多い方ですね（笑）。

Segment 6　山里に住む子供たちの話。　　　　　TIME CODE　0:05:24

Write your own transcript! Note the familiar suffixes used when the children refer to their grandparents and older siblings. What do we learn about family size in this mountainous district known for its forest products?

単語と<ruby>文法<rt>ぶんぽう</rt></ruby>ノート **Vocabulary and Grammar Notes**

Title

<ruby>家族構成<rt>かぞくこうせい</rt></ruby>　　family structure

Segment 1

（に）<ruby>在住<rt>ざいじゅう</rt></ruby> する　to live, reside (in, at)

Segment 1.1

<ruby>母方<rt>ははかた</rt></ruby>の　　on the mother's side

<ruby>祖父母<rt>そふぼ</rt></ruby>　　grandparents

<ruby>両親<rt>りょうしん</rt></ruby>　　parents

<ruby>一般的<rt>いっぱんてき</rt></ruby>な　　general, usual, ordinary

<ruby>非常<rt>ひじょう</rt></ruby>に　　extremely

まれ　　rare

Segment 1.2

X と言われる　　that which is called X (言われてる　→　言われている)

いわゆる　　so-called

<ruby>普通<rt>ふつう</rt></ruby>の　　the usual, common, ordinary

<ruby>母の祖父母<rt>そふぼ</rt></ruby>　　the speaker meant to say 母方の祖父母 as in Segment 1.1

<ruby>同居<rt>どうきょ</rt></ruby>する　　to live together; to live, stay (with a family)

Segment 1.3

<ruby>付<rt>つ</rt></ruby>け<ruby>加<rt>くわ</rt></ruby>える　　to add

成人する <small>せいじん</small>	to become an adult; to come of age
親 <small>おや</small>	parent(s)
最近 <small>さいきん</small>	recently
珍しい <small>めずら</small>	strange, unusual
大学院 <small>だいがくいん</small>	graduate school
奨学金 <small>しょうがくきん</small>	scholarship
通う <small>かよ</small>	to attend; to commute
経済的に <small>けいざいてき</small>	economically
交通の面 <small>こうつう めん</small>	from the standpoint of transportation
便利な <small>べんり</small>	convenient
便宜 <small>べんぎ</small>	convenience; 便宜上 for convenience' sake （便宜のため）
就職する <small>しゅうしょく</small>	to find work, employment
出張する <small>しゅっちょう</small>	to take a business trip
東京都内 <small>とうきょうとない</small>	within Tokyo
物価 <small>ぶっか</small>	prices
光熱費 <small>こうねつひ</small>	lighting and heating expenses; cost of light and fuel
理由 <small>りゆう</small>	reason
貯金する <small>ちょきん</small>	to save money

独立した生活　　　an independent lifestyle

Segment 2

暮らす　　　to live; 三人暮らし three of us living together

嫁　　　bride; 嫁に行く　to get married

Segment 3

Our speaker, MORI Sōya (his preferred Romanization), is a member of the Japanese Deaf community, communicating in Japanese Sign Language (JSL). We hear him through the voice of his interpreter, Narita Kazuyo. Over 95 percent of the Japanese Deaf community understand standardized JSL, although they also use local JSL. News programs are televised using standardized JSL. According to MORI, there are essentially two major dialect versions of Japanese Sign Language: Tokyo JSL and Kansai JSL. The latter originated at the Kyoto School of the Deaf, founded in 1878. JSL and American Sign Language (ASL) are totally unrelated, and both are full-fledged languages with their own rich vocabulary and unique grammatical structure. To understand Japanese, English, JSL, and ASL is to know four different languages. To learn more about sign language, see Lesson 10, Segment 3, and Lesson 19, Segment 3. The unifying organization for the Japanese Deaf community is the Japanese Federation of the Deaf 全日本ろうあ連盟 (JFD), with two main offices, one in Tokyo and one in Kyoto.

経済学者　　　economist

妻　　　wife

娘　　　daughter

おる　　　おります humble polite for います

Segment 4   Our speaker discusses organic farming in Lesson 5.

<ruby>農家<rt>の う か</rt></ruby>	a farm household; a farm family; a farmhouse; a farmer
<ruby>夫婦<rt>ふ う ふ</rt></ruby>	husband and wife
<ruby>野菜<rt>や さ い</rt></ruby>	vegetable(s)
<ruby>手伝い<rt>て つ だ</rt></ruby>	help, assistance
<ruby>助かる<rt>た す</rt></ruby>	to be helped out (of a difficulty); to find (something) to be helpful; to escape death

Segment 5   To learn more from the head priest, see Lesson 18.

<ruby>禅寺<rt>ぜんでら</rt></ruby>	a Zen temple
<ruby>住 職<rt>じゅうしょく</rt></ruby>	the head priest (of a Buddhist temple)
<ruby>家内<rt>か な い</rt></ruby>	my wife
<ruby>長 男<rt>ちょうなん</rt></ruby>	eldest son
<ruby>長 女<rt>ちょうじょ</rt></ruby>	eldest daughter

Segment 6

<ruby>郊外<rt>こうがい</rt></ruby>	suburbs

Related Themes: The issue of the elderly population is brought up in Lesson 3; lack of successors in farms and family businesses is mentioned in Lessons 4 and 5; issues of family structure and communication come up in Lessons 3 and 6; the later marriage age and declining birthrate are discussed in Lesson 7; the issue of women and work is addressed in Lesson 8; and some issues affecting children are brought up in Segment 3.1 of Lesson 3, Lesson 6, Segment 1 of Lesson 9 and again in Lesson 17.

話し合いましょう

1）自分たちの家の家族構成について話し合いましょう。

2）家族のあり方は、職業、収入、宗教、結婚年齢、教育水準、人口密度など、さまざまな要因によって規定されます。自分の故郷では、どのような家族構成が一般的でしょうか。また、その構成に影響を与えているものは何でしょうか。

あり方	the way it is; the way it should be
職業	occupation
収入	income
宗教	religion
結婚年齢	age at marriage
教育水準	level of education
人口密度	population density
要因	primary factor

規定する   to regulate; to determine; 〜される   (passive)

影響を与える   to influence

3）日本では家族構成の変化が社会や経済の構造に対して、さらには未来のあり方に対して多大な影響を及ぼしつつあります。日本における家族構成の変化、とりわけ少子化や高齢化といった現代的な問題とその対策に関して調べ、話し合いましょう。

変化	change
構造	structure
未来	the future
多大な	great, considerable
影響を及ぼす	to influence, have an effect on
〜つつある	to be in the process of
とりわけ	especially, above all, in particular
少子化	having fewer children
高齢化	aging
現代的な問題	contemporary problems, issues
対策	solutions
調べる	to investigate, inquire into

第2課　　生活環境

Homes and Their Surroundings

Our choice of living place is dictated by many considerations—convenience for commuting to work or school, budget, local culture, proximity to nature, and so on. A place works on us, contributing to who we are, and we, in turn, affect our place through our interaction with our local environment and community. Katō Masako, Odajima Mamoru, and Miyata Tsuneo introduce us to their living environment, providing three very different perspectives on home.

Katō, who lives several hours outside Tokyo by train, takes us on a tour of her suburban home, explaining the function of each room. The average suburban home in her area is about 40 *tsubo* 坪 (1,440 square feet), says Katō, explaining that one *tsubo* is the equivalent of two *tatami* mats. Her home is 50 *tsubo* (1,800 square feet) and also differs in that it has a spacious yard. Although she grew up in Tokyo, Katō prefers the slower pace of life and proximity to nature in her current setting. A breeze comes off nearby mountains and circulates through the residential district. Rain sinks into the earth, nourishing the garden and forested hills. She can hear the silence of night and see the stars. After three months in a Tokyo apartment, Katō's daughter decided to make the long daily commute to college rather than give up her quality of life in the suburbs. Katō, a cooking instructor, often shares delicacies with her neighbors. She is also well versed in traditional medicine and is always willing to help a neighbor.

One way suburban neighbors keep in touch is through participation in a neighborhood group, *tonari gumi* 隣組. Katō's group includes fifteen households. Regional notices are passed from one house to the next by relay. Of course, they could be mailed to each house, but the relay system encourages neighbors to stay in contact. Households participate in semi-annual neighborhood clean-up activities. The groups participate in festivals for local shrines and deities. In Katō's region, festivals are held for O-Fudō-sama and O-Jizō-sama. Festivals used to be held twice a year, but today they are held once a year in autumn. The neighbors will prepare special food to offer to the

13

deities, after which the group will enjoy a meal together. In the past, neighborhood groups were in charge of funerals and would help the bereaved family. But today, says Katō, most people hire a funeral parlor instead of burdening their neighbors.

A retired videographer for nature programs, Odajima Mamoru lives in a sparsely populated area on the edge of wilderness in Hokkaido. His hobby is making canoes and teaching his wife's college students how to canoe. He also conducts annual surveys of brown bear in Hokkaido. In his conversation on the DVD Odajima refers to the brief lifetime of most homes. During the booming economy of the late twentieth century many Japanese seem to have discarded an appreciation of well-crafted items designed for long use. Today few people buy and renovate an existing single family home, 中古住宅. If they can afford a home, they want a new one. Mass-produced homes are not built to last, nor are they maintained by their owners. In fact, most contemporary houses hold up for little more than twenty years. At resale the home has no value, so the valuable land is sold, the house is demolished, and a new one is built. This scrap-and-build housing policy is one reason Japan is now the world's largest importer of timber, much of it coming from rapidly vanishing forests in Southeast Asia. Odajima and his wife are an exception to the scrap-and-build trend. Before they built their new house they lived next door in an abandoned restaurant; that building is now being remodeled by Odajima to serve as a private natural history museum.

Miyata Tsuneo, an organic farmer, describes his home and land as a place of work. His current house does not look at all like the old family home. During the period of rapid economic growth beginning in the 1960s, farmers sold some of their land for factories or housing projects. They used the profits to replace old homes that had, to their credit, stood up for several generations. On the DVD he tells us how a farmer's house is also an important locus of production.

Segment 1   郊外にある家の案内   TIME CODE 0:06:12

Segment 1.1   庭、玄関

我が家に、ぁのぅ、皆さんようこそいらっしゃいました。今、これから、ぁのぅ、私の家の周り、それから家の中をご案内させていただきます。

私の庭から見える、ぁのぅ、周りの景色なんですけれども、ぁのぅ、周りは山に囲まれて、今大変美しい、ぁのぅ、新緑の時期です。私の庭は、ぁのぅ、周りが全部バラが植わってますね。そのバラの下は芝生なんですけれども、日本は大変雨が多く湿度が多いために芝生よりも雑草の方が元気です。ですから、芝生と雑草との、毎日、戦いをして、草むしりが大変な仕事になってます。

どうぞ、玄関にお入り下さいませ。日本の玄関はまず、ぁのぅ、スリッパがおいてある家が殆どです。で、玄関から中に入る時には必ずそのスリッパを履いて、ご自分の履いてきた靴を脱いでいただきます。

Segment 1.2　こたつの部屋、神棚　　　　　　TIME CODE 0:07:30

どうぞ、もう（ひと）少し奥に入ってください。そこは、ぁのぅ、玄関から一番近い部屋です。六畳ほどありますけれども、畳敷きです。真ん中に、ぁのぅ、冬の寒さのために、また、家族が団欒するための掘りごたつという、普通のこたつよりも中が、ぁのぅ、くぼんでまして、そこに足を下ろせる形のこたつというの（を）が家にはあります。そしてそこは普段家族が、

あの、そこで食事をしたり、朝ごはん食べたりということで、大変くつろぐ部屋になってます。

その神棚というのは、ぁのぅ、私たちの生活が平和でありますようにという願いが、（みまもって）神様が見守ってくださるという意味合いでその神棚を設けている人も多いようです。ただ現在は、その神棚、神棚のない家も多いと思います。

Segment 1.3　ダイニングルーム、お仏壇　　　　TIME CODE　0:08:34

そしてどうぞ、次のダイニングルームの方にお入りください。この部屋は、亡くなった主人が、ぁのぅ、大変、その火の好きな人で、そのためにどうしてもそのマントルピースを作ってほしいということで、マントルピースを中心に家の設計をしました。で、私の家ではよく主人がお客様を連れてきましたので、そこでお客様と集う場所でもあるし、また、時にはここで家族が食事する場所でもあるし、一番ここは使い勝手がいい部屋だと思います。

で、このダイニングルームの、ぁの、集う部屋に、人が来るのが大好きだった主人のお仏壇があります。ですから、お客さんが来たり、家族がこ

こで楽しい話をしていると多分聞いていてくれるんだといつも安心しています。

Segment 1.4　台所　　　　　　　　　　　TIME CODE 0:09:33

で、次は台所なんですけれども、ぁのぅ、あまり広くはありません。ただ、私一人がそこに立っていますと、いろんなものが、ぁのぅ、すぐに取れるので、大変便利に使っています。このスペースの台所にしては大きな冷蔵庫がおいてあります。この冷蔵庫は、私が、ぁのぅ、調理をしたり、保存食を作ったり、それを保存していくためにはどうしても大きい冷蔵庫が必要なので、それで、ぁのぅ、こちらに、ぁのぅ、場所の割には大きい冷蔵庫をおいています。

Segment 1.5　客間、床の間　　　　　　　TIME CODE 0:10:07

この部屋は、ぁのぅ、客間なんですけれども、普段は私たちの家族としては生活をしてない部屋です。その中に床の間の横に押入れがありますけれども、この押入れというのは、ぁのぅ、お布団が現在たくさん納まっています。その布団類というのはお客さんのためのお布団です。そして正面に床の間というのがあります。その床の間の空間というのは、神様がそちらに宿っている、神様見えないですけれども、神様がそこにいらっしゃる

空間として日本ではとても大事にしています。そして、そこに掛け物があ

りますけれども、その掛け軸というのは、昔は、その仏画をかけていたそ

うです。しかし今、ぁのぅ、仏教の信仰というのは日本人の感覚の中から

大変薄れてきましたので、ぁのぅ、美術的な美しい絵を描いた掛け物とか、

その字のことが多いように思います。

Segment 2   野生の自然に囲まれた家   TIME CODE 0:11:10

Segment 2.1

私は、ぁのぅ、日本の北の、まぁ、端にある北海道という島に住んでいるん

ですけれども。その中の、ぇ、やや北にある、まぁ、オホーツク海に面した

網走という町に住んでいます。そして町の中心からは十五キロほど離れ

ています。で、家の東側と北側は湖に面しています。湖までの距離

は二百メートルぐらいありますけれども、殆どそちら側は一年中人の動

く様子が見られない、まぁ、いわゆる自然の景色で、まぁ、それがとても気

にいってそこを選んだわけですけれども。ええ、ま、冬は湖が凍ります。それから海の水が入ってくる湖なんで、ええ、ま、アザラシが冬になると来たり、それからその湖までの間のウェットランドですね、湿原のようなところには、ぇ、タンチョウが、ジャパニーズクレインと言われているタンチョウですね、タンチョウが来たり、それからオジロワシが繁殖していたり、それから、まぁ、キツネが時々姿を見せたり、それからシカなんかも見られるという、まぁ、家の中からそういった野生の世界を覗きみること、垣間見ることができる、そんな場所に住んでいます。

Segment 2.2   TIME CODE 0:12:37

家は最近新しく建てたわけですけれども、一番その家を建てる時に考えたのは、まずその暖房を少なくすることを考えました。それから家が今は日本では三十年とか、せいぜいまぁ二、三十年でですね、若い人たちはだめになってしまうような家を建てるんですね。で、それはたいへん今環境の問題から言っても、木を無駄遣いしているということで、できるだけ私たちがまぁ死んだあとも子供なり、その先まで使えるように、一応百年ぐらいもつといわれているメーカーの家を建てました。ですから、考えたことは、一つは長く無駄にならないように資源を使うこと、そして暖房のような、その資源もできるだけ少なくすること。

Segment 3 生活及び生産の場である家　　　TIME CODE 0:13:34

Segment 3.1

Q 宮田さんの家とそのまわりの環境を紹介してくださいますか。

私の家は、ぁのぅ、農家です。まぁ、四百年ぐらいたっているでしょうかね。それ以上かもしれません。カシの木が四百年か五百年ぐらい立っているということですから、ぁのぅ、お墓の様子からしてもそのくらいここにずっと住んでいると思います。今ある家は、この家は、ぁのぅ、三十年ぐらい前に新築したものです。

Segment 3.2　（続き）　　　　　　　TIME CODE 0:14:03

この前の家ですと、やはり農家は大きい家がたくさんありましたけど、ぁの、家の中でも養蚕を飼って、そこが生活の場所であると同時に生産の場所でもあって、蚕を飼うことをやっていたわけですね。…大人の指ぐらいの大きさに虫が成長します。で、このくらいになってくると、もう

たくさんの桑を食べるわけです。で、夜中ももちろん食べているわけですから、夜中に、ぁのぅ、蚕が桑を食べる音がちょうど雨が降ってきたようなざわざわざわざわした音がするんですね。で、家の中が蚕でいっぱいになっちゃうわけで、寝るところも本当に畳の上の、まぁ、狭いところでやっと寝るような、そういうようなこともありました。

Segment 3.3   TIME CODE 0:15:04

Q 後ろにあるカシの木はご神木というふうに考えてもいいでしょうか。神木ということを説明していただけますか。

ぁのぅ、大きな木に、例えば百年だとか二百年立った木は、ぁぁ、人間でいえば、やっぱり、ぁのぅ、相当年を取った木になるわけです。で、そうすると昔の人たちはそういう大きな木には、まぁ魂が宿るという、人間と同じような人格がそこにあるというふうに考えていたんだと思います。それで、大きい木を大切にしたのでしょう。で、家のもそういうことでいえば、四百年、五百年立っていると言われていますので、ぁのぅ、もう、本当に、ぇぇ、神様がいるということになるんだと思いますね。｛ええ｝で、まぁ、神社だとかお寺というものは、そういう大きな木が、ぁのぅ、たくさんあるわけですけど、｛はい｝そういう中の、特に大きな木は、ご神木として大切に祀られていると思います。

単語と文法ノート

Title

<ruby>生活環境<rt>せいかつかんきょう</rt></ruby>   living environment

Segment 1   We meet Katō Masako again in Lesson 6, where she discusses contemporary food culture. Note the level of formality as she welcomes you, an imagined audience, into her home.

<ruby>郊外<rt>こうがい</rt></ruby>   suburb

<ruby>案内<rt>あんない</rt></ruby>   a tour

Segment 1.1

<ruby>庭<rt>にわ</rt></ruby>   garden, yard

<ruby>玄関<rt>げんかん</rt></ruby>   front entryway

<ruby>我が家<rt>わ が や</rt></ruby>   我が＝私の、自分の my own; our own; one's own. Cf. 我が国、我が子。我が家 means 私の家、often contracted to わたしんち。我が家 is used on formal occasions. Often 家 is used alone to indicate 私の家。

<ruby>周り<rt>まわ</rt></ruby>   surroundings

<ruby>案内<rt>あんない</rt></ruby>する   to show around, give a tour of

          案内させていただく。You will recall that (さ)せていただく literally means "to receive the favor of letting one do." I will receive the favor of your allowing me to show you around. ＝   Please let me give you a tour (of the house).

景色 (けしき)	scenery
囲む (かこ)	to surround; 囲まれる (かこ) (passive) to be surrounded
新緑の時期 (しんりょく じき)	season of spring greenery
バラ	rose (flower)
植わる (う)	to be planted with; the intransitive form of 植える
芝生 (しばふ)	lawn
湿度 (しつど)	humidity
雑草 (ざっそう)	weeds
戦いをする (たたか)	to wage battle
草むしり (くさ)	weeding （〜をする）
置く (お)	to place; 置いてある (お) are placed. Transitive verb てある describes the state resulting from an action. The verb has been done (for a specific reason). (Slippers have been set out so that guests can use them.)
殆ど (ほとん)	almost, nearly; hardly (with a negative)
履く (は)	to put on, wear (footwear, trousers)
脱ぐ (ぬ)	to take off (clothing, shoes); 脱いでいただきます (ぬ) (Verb ていただきます to have someone do something for you; polite form of Verb てもらいます)

Segment 1.2

こたつ	a low table with a heating element underneath to keep one's feet and legs warm; a quilt between the table top and the table frame hangs down to keep the sitter snug and warm.
神棚	a household Shintō altar (Cf. Lesson 18, Segment 1.1)
畳敷き	covered with *tatami* mats
団欒する	to sit in a family circle and chat pleasantly; to enjoy one another's company
掘りごたつ	a sunken *kotatsu*; a low table draped with a quilt and placed over a cavity in the floor so people can sit on the floor and hang their legs down. In the past there was a *hibachi* in the cavity, and the legs were warmed by a charcoal fire; the interviewer had such a *kotatsu* as a child and burned holes in many a pair of socks. Today, one generally finds a heating element under the table top.
くぼむ	to become sunken; くぼんだ、くぼんでいる to be sunken
足を下ろす	to let down one's legs; 下ろせる is the potential form.
平和でありますように	平和 at peace ＋ であるように that it be this way
願い	a wish, hope, entreaty
神様	god; anything awesome may be considered a *kami*, a spirit, a god. (Cf. Lesson 18)
見守る	to watch intently; to watch over and protect

意味合い　　　　　　reason　仔細、理由 ; nuance, background

設ける　　　　　　　to provide

Segment 1.3

仏壇　　　　　　　　a (family) Buddhist altar (Cf. Lesson 18, Segment 1.1)

亡くなる　　　　　　to die, pass away

マントルピース　　　a mantelpiece

設計　　　　　　　　a plan, a design

連れてくる　　　　　to bring (people, animals)

集う　　　　　　　　to gather, get together 集まる

時には　　　　　　　ときとして at times; occasionally

使い勝手がいい　　　very handy, flexible in its use

Segment 1.4

台所　　　　　　　　kitchen

〜にしては　　　　　for; considering;

　　　　　　　　　　このスペースにしては　　　for this size space

冷蔵庫　　　　　　　refrigerator

Xが置いてある　　　Cf. Segment 1.1, above. (A large refrigerator has been

　　　　　　　　　　placed there—for the reasons indicated.)

調理をする　　　　　to cook, prepare; 料理をする

保存食 （ほぞんしょく）   preserved food

場所の割りに （ばしょ の わ）   for/considering the space

(see above,　このスペースにしては)

Segment 1.5

客間 （きゃくま）   guest room

床の間 （とこ の ま）   an alcove raised slightly above floor level

押入れ （おしいれ）   closet with *fusuma* (papered sliding doors) for storage of

bedding, etc.

布団 （ふとん）   bedding; 布団類 （ふとんるい） bedding: quilts, mattresses, etc.

納まる （おさ）   to be stored inside

正面 （しょうめん）   the front

宿る （やど）   to reside in

空間 （くうかん）   space

掛け物 （か もの）   hanging scroll

仏画 （ぶつが）   Buddhist picture/painting

かける   to hang

仏教 （ぶっきょう）   Buddhism

信仰 （しんこう）   faith; belief

感覚 （かんかく）   senses; feeling; sensibility

薄れる　　　　　　　　　to fade

美術的な　　　　　　　　artistic

絵を描く　　　　　　　　to draw a picture

字のこと　　　　　　　　(matters of) writing

Segment 2　　Odajima Mamoru speaks to us again in Lessons 12 and 20. Segue photos for Segment 2 courtesy of the speaker.

野生の自然　　　　　　　wild nature

囲む　　　　　　　　　　to surround; X に囲まれた (passive)

　　　　　　　　　　　　to be surrounded by X

Segment 2.1

端　　　　　　　　　　　the edge; border; extremity; tip

島　　　　　　　　　　　island

やや　　　　　　　　　　a little; slightly

オホーツク海　　　　　　Sea of Okhotsk

X に面する　　　　　　　to face on X; to look out toward X

X から(distance)離れている　　to be (such and such a distance) from X

湖　　　　　　　　　　　lake

距離　　　　　　　　　　distance

様子　　　　　　　　　　appearance

気<ruby>気<rt>き</rt></ruby>に<ruby>入<rt>い</rt></ruby>る   to like

<ruby>選<rt>えら</rt></ruby>ぶ   to select

<ruby>凍<rt>こお</rt></ruby>る   to freeze up

アザラシ   an (earless) seal

<ruby>湿原<rt>しつげん</rt></ruby>   a marsh; a wetland

タンチョウ   red-crowned crane; Japanese crane (*Grus japonensis*)

オジロワシ   white-tailed eagle (*Haliaeetus albicilla*)

<ruby>繁殖<rt>はんしょく</rt></ruby>する   to breed

キツネ   fox

<ruby>姿<rt>すがた</rt></ruby>   figure; form; shape

シカ   deer

<ruby>覗<rt>のぞ</rt></ruby>き<ruby>見<rt>み</rt></ruby>る   to peer/peep/peek at

<ruby>垣間見<rt>かいまみ</rt></ruby>る   literally: to peer through an opening in a fence. A term

often found in Heian-period (794-1185) literature, this verb describes the actions of men who would find an opening in a fence or blind through which to view a woman in whom they held some interest. The verb suggests that one secretly peers through an opening into a special or forbidden world.

Segment 2.2

<ruby>建<rt>た</rt></ruby>てる   to build, construct

<ruby>暖房<rt>だんぼう</rt></ruby>   heating

せいぜい	at the very most, at best
(time reference)で	in/within; 二、三十年でだめになる　to go bad (fall apart) within twenty to thirty years
環境の問題	an environmental problem
無駄遣いする	to waste
Noun なり	なり indicates that one example is mentioned from a number of similar possibilities. Cf. Lesson 13, Segment 4: 魚なり何なり。
一応	tentatively; for the time being
資源	resources

Segment 3　　Miyata Tsuneo describes his work as an organic farmer in Lesson 5.

及び	and, as well as
生産の場	a place of production

Segment 3.1

家	house; family
農家	a farmhouse; a farming family; a farmer　(We are a farming family, and we've been doing this for some 400 years, maybe even longer . . .)
カシの木	an oak tree (genus *Quercus*)
墓	grave
〜からしても	or even judging from (the look of the graves)

新築する   to build, construct   （新築の newly built）

Segment 3.2   Cf. Lessons 12, 13, on 里山.

養蚕   sericulture (raising of silkworms to produce silk)

蚕   silkworm

飼う   to raise

指   finger

虫   caterpillar; bug

成長する   to grow

桑   mulberry (tree); silkworms eat the leaves of mulberry trees

ざわざわ   sound of falling water or rustling leaves or grasses

いっぱいになっちゃう   ＝   いっぱいになってしまう

やっと   at last; finally; with difficulty; barely

Segment 3.3   Cf. Lesson 11, Segment 2.1, animism; Lesson 12, Segment 1.2 鎮守の
森 ; and Lesson 18, Segment 2.

神木   a sacred tree

相当   かなり

年を取る   to grow old; 年を取った old

魂   soul; spirit

宿る
<ruby>宿<rt>やど</rt></ruby>る   to reside in, dwell in

<ruby>人格<rt>じんかく</rt></ruby>   character; personality

<ruby>大切<rt>たいせつ</rt></ruby>にする   to take good care of; <ruby>大切<rt>たいせつ</rt></ruby>な important; valuable; precious

<ruby>神社<rt>じんじゃ</rt></ruby>   (Shintō) shrine

<ruby>寺<rt>てら</rt></ruby>   (Buddhist) temple

<ruby>祀<rt>まつ</rt></ruby>る   to deify; to worship

祀られている(passive) to be worshipped

Related Themes: For a discussion of Japanese architecture see Lesson 3. For a look at urban apartment housing, see Lesson 10.

話し合いましょう

１）自分の<ruby>住<rt>す</rt></ruby>まいを<ruby>紹介<rt>しょうかい</rt></ruby>しましょう。

２）<ruby>職場<rt>しょくば</rt></ruby>と<ruby>住居<rt>じゅうきょ</rt></ruby>とが<ruby>一緒<rt>いっしょ</rt></ruby>になっているのは、<ruby>農家以外<rt>のうかいがい</rt></ruby>にどのような<ruby>職業<rt>しょくぎょう</rt></ruby>があるでしょうか。<ruby>具体例<rt>ぐたいれい</rt></ruby>をあげてください。

<ruby>住居<rt>じゅうきょ</rt></ruby>   residence, house

<ruby>以外<rt>いがい</rt></ruby>の   other than

<ruby>具体例<rt>ぐたいれい</rt></ruby>   concrete example

3）家を建てる、あるいは家を買う時、どのような場所を選びますか。ま
た土地、眺め、気候、隣人などの環境面、さらには建築物の設計や材料、
さらには冷暖房、庭、家族構成などを考慮に入れたとき、どの条件を
一番大切にしたいですか。

眺め	view
気候	climate
隣人	neighbor(s)
環境面	environmental aspects
建築物	a building, a structure
設計	a design
材料	materials
冷暖房	cooling and heating
考慮に入れる	to take into consideration
条件	condition

第3課　　　ある建築家の話
だい　か　　　　けんちくか　　はなし

Reflections of an Architect

Shinohara Akira, the head of an architectural design and construction firm, grew up in a large farmhouse used in silkworm cultivation 養蚕農家.
ようさんのうか
Though he was initially attracted to modern commercial building design, his interests gradually shifted to residential architecture and the way people live. The turning point in his career came when he was invited to restore a farmhouse belonging to the family of a childhood friend. In Shinohara's native prefecture most of the farmhouses involved in sericulture had been built in the Meiji period (1868-1912), when the silkworm industry flourished. By the time Shinohara's friend grew up, the house was much in need of repair and the family had dispersed. Because his own family was so big, says Shinohara, he often spent days at a time at his friend's house, where there was more room for neighborhood children to get together. The opportunity to restore a place where he had played as a child and the knowledge that it would now be passed on to future generations gave him much happiness. When the restoration was complete, the family gathered for a reunion and told stories of the old days. Shinohara realized that as people live in a place it acquires a certain warmth. It is a medium in which is etched the family history. Eventually it takes on a life of its own.

In the process of restoring the farmhouse, Shinohara became familiar with the quality of the old timbers and construction methods and reached a new appreciation of features that have come to characterize Japanese architecture. In the prewar days, he says, Japanese homes generally were made of natural materials—domestic timber for pillars and beams, stones for the foundation, handmade paper, or *washi*, for the *shōji* and *fusuma*. Roofs might be either thatched or covered with tile, but they were all sloped to shed rain, in hipped, hipped and gabled, or gabled styles. A distinctive feature of the roofs was their long eaves, to protect the house from rain and summer heat. Below the eaves was the *engawa* 縁側, the "hem" of the house. Sometimes the *engawa* lie within the house,
えんがわ

behind glass doors but outside of the living space proper. In either case, belonging to neither the inside nor the outside, the *engawa* is a bridge between the two. *Shōji* let in a soft light while affording privacy. The *fusuma* may be closed to divide rooms, but are generally left open, creating a sense of spaciousness and providing ample room for family and guests. Air flows through the house, and the living space merges gently into the garden.

Much has changed in today's mass-produced homes. Gone are the wide eaves and the *engawa*. The garden has been replaced with a carport, and the *tokonoma* has given way to the entertainment center. It used to be that the outer walls had cracks and crevices letting in fresh air or winter cold. Dealing with some discomfort built our character, Shinohara asserts. Today the house is tighter and is warmed or cooled to an even temperature, providing a steady state of comfort. For each thing we gain, he observes, there is something we lose: 建築というのは、何かを得る代わりに何かを失う。 He explains that a house made from high-quality timbers can be restored; if it is taken down, the natural materials will biodegrade. People once had a sense of the life in wood and stone, he says. Today lightweight plastic, aluminum, and other manufactured materials make house construction easier and less expensive, but the warmth of natural materials is lost. Modern housing is not built to last and is not likely to be restored or passed on to future generations. When the house is taken down, many of the manufactured materials will not biodegrade.

When people buy a modern manufactured house, adds Shinohara, they are confronted with the finished product. They have no sense of the process of creation, of the materials and personalities involved. Their appreciation is diminished: いい製品がドンと目の前に現れると、たしかに便利さになったんですけれども、その過程がすべて見えなくなったがために、そのありがたさが薄れているのかなと。

Land is expensive, so small row houses are built for nuclear families. Individual rooms are separated by fixed walls and doors. Often there is little place for the family to gather, let alone entertain guests or provide for grandparents. There is no space for the eye to wander, the air to flow, for communication to take place. Family and social relations begin to degenerate.

To learn more, visit Shinohara at his office and then join him on a tour of a newly completed residence, clearly beyond the financial means of the average family. In this residence Shinohara has attempted to retain many of the attractive features of the traditional Japanese house while providing for modern energy performance. All rooms on the first floor are open to each other.   They were designed in a barrier-free manner so that the couple could enjoy the home into their old age. To make the kitchen a more social space, Shinohara added an oblong *kotatsu* between the kitchen and living room. When we arrived at the house, mother and daughter were seated there in conversation.

In back of the home is a small factory that has been in the owner's family for several generations. Here fabric is woven for kimono and accessories, and also for more contemporary products such as hand bags, cushions, and wall hangings. The owner's fine eye for textile design has been applied to the planning of his garden. Within a small area, the plantings, rocks, and collection of stone lanterns 石灯籠 impart a sense of space and diversity, providing a peaceful milieu for relaxation or contemplation. Below, Shinohara explains elements of design in this house and then moves to a more general discussion of the implications for social relations of the typical modern dwelling.

Segment 1   TIME CODE 0:16:13

Q 小さい時の体験が今の仕事に影響を及ぼしているでしょうか。

はい。あのぅ、私は、あのぅ、昔（大家族）九人兄弟の一番下に育ちまし

たんで、まぁ、最大、一番大人数がいた時は十三人の家族と一緒に、ええ、

暮らしてましたですから、やっぱりそこには、まぁ、私みたいに小さいの

からそれからおばあちゃんとか、そういう形でずっとその年代、各、バ

ランスよくと言いますか、あのぅ、暮らしたわけですね。だから逆に家そ

のものは、その全部そこはコミュニケーション[の場で]、自分の個のとい

うの、自分のものという所有物というのは、そういう場所は一つもなかっ

たんですけど、全部がオープンスペースという形だったんですね。そこで

育ちましたんで、どうしても私はやっぱり広い、私が設計するのは広い

一部屋を皆が、大勢の方が集まれるようにという形の作品が比較的多い

です。

Segment 2

Q 今日は篠原さんが設計なさった家をお訪ねしておりますが、この家の

設計についてお話しくださいますか。

Segment 2.1　　　　　　　　　　　　　　　TIME CODE　0:17:18

この地形を見せていただいた時に、やっぱり道路と近いんで、これを表に出してしまうと圧倒的な、こう威圧感を与えてしまうと、それをなくすためにセットバックをさせて、で、しかも向こうの建物は一段下げてやって、で変化をつけさして、ぁのぅ、道路との威圧感を与えないような、という形をまず最初に心がけましたですね。やはり、バランスの問題、周囲とどう溶け込むか、そこでまたその中で、こう庭は、これはご主人でも植木屋さんと一緒にやっているんですけれども、非常にそういう面ではバランスがいいということですね。

Segment 2.2　　　　　　　　　　　　　　　TIME CODE　0:17:57

それと、もう一つ、日本の家屋ってのは、どちらかっていうと夏向きという、本来はですね、ぇぇ、夏向き、これも見ても分かるんですけれども、非常に眺望がいいと、というと中と外、それの境界が、本当は日本の家屋というのはそんなにないんですね。ですから、ぁのぅ、座敷から見て、（外を）外を見ると…非常に外との一体感をはかって広がりを出しているわけですね。

Segment 2.3　　　　　　　　　　　　　　　TIME CODE　0:18:23

まあ、このご主人は非常にその、ぁのぅ、周囲というか、その友達付き合いというか、それも大切にされる方なんで、で、別の棟にその囲炉裏がある

んですけど、やっぱり囲炉裏って、まぁ、西洋もそうだと思うんですけれ

ど、暖炉があるっていうのは火を見ることによって落ち着くわけですね、

人間は、｛そうですね。｝そこを囲むと。それとやはり火の温かみとい

うものが感じられるということですね。そこで、ぁのぅ、来てくれた方を

歓待するというような、そういう使い方を、ぁのぅ、別棟はなっているんで

すけど。

Segment 3

Q　建築によって見えてくる社会問題についてお話しいただけますか。

Segment 3.1   TIME CODE　0:18:59

まぁ、私が感じるのは、子供部屋ができたがために閉じこもりですか、ぁ

のぅ、人と接触しないで、そこで自分の空間の中でぇぇ想像力だけを伸ば

してしまうと。やっぱり人とすり合うというか、そういう機会がすごく減

ってしまっているんじゃないかなと。それが、一つは社会現象になって

いじめる、ぁのぅ、逆に人を殺してしまうというような極端な例にまで

発展しているんじゃないかなと。

Segment 3.2　　（続き）   TIME CODE　0:19:33

まぁ、前にも出ましたが、大家族が崩れてですね、みんな個の時代になっ

てきてるんで、なかなかこぅ大きな建物ができにくくなっていること…

高齢になってくるとやっぱり弱い存在になるわけです。そういうものが

家族の中で分かっていたのがだんだん隔離されるようになってしまったが

ために弱い人が分からなくなってきたんじゃないかな。だから、いじめな

んかもそうなんですけれど、弱いものを徹底的にいじめてしまうと。やっ

ぱり、あの子は、私なんかは親に、あの子は、ぁのぅ、ちょっと障害を持

っている方なんか、障害を持っているんでかわいそうな子なんだよとい

う形で、かわいそうな子だってのは、保護してやらなくちゃだめなんだ

よという意味も含まれていたと思うんですね。

Segment 3.3　（続き）　　　　　　　　　　　TIME CODE　0:20:15

だけどそれが、これから日本が急速に高齢化されるわけなんで、そのへ

んの問題が非常にこれから出てくるんだろうなと。ええ、まして、じゃ、

一人暮らしのお年寄りがいた、じゃ、だれが面倒を見るのだと、というよ

うなことも含めてですね。だからと言って、みんなお年寄りだけ集めて

隔離状態にするのもよくないんじゃないかなと。やっぱり小さい子供さん

が遊んでいる姿を見られる、やっぱりそれで元気が出てくるということ

なんで、やはり、できれば、世代間がずっとこう共生ができるというん

ですかね。ぁのぅ、身近にそういうものが眺められるような、そういうコミ

ュニケーション作りができればいいなと思ってるんですけれど、家を通し
てですね。

単語と文法ノート

Title

けんちくか
建築家   an architect

Segment 1

たいけん
体験   personal experience

えいきょう　およ
影響を及ぼす   to influence; to have an effect on

そだ
育つ   to grow; to be brought up

にんずう
人数   number of people

Verb, adjective (plain form) んです/のです。 This pattern often follows an
                          explanation in conversations. It adds emphasis to the
                          speaker's words, and is similar in use to わけです. Nouns
                          and adjectival nouns are followed by なんです。 んです
                          approximates the English expression "the thing is that."

やっぱり   （やはり）you see, as I (you, she) thought or said; as
                          expected; also, likewise; still, all the same; after all. Here,
                          what follows やっぱり conforms to or arises from the
                          situation described before it. This term is used frequently
                          in conversations.

く
暮らす   to live

年代
<ruby>年<rt>ねん</rt></ruby><ruby>代<rt>だい</rt></ruby>   age rank, age class

<ruby>各<rt>かく</rt></ruby>   each, every; the speaker appears to use this term in the

sense of <ruby>各々<rt>おのおの</rt></ruby>、<ruby>各自<rt>かくじ</rt></ruby>、それぞれ   each; respectively

Verb (plain form) わけだ   See notes for Lesson 5, Segment 1.1.

<ruby>逆<rt>ぎゃく</rt></ruby>に   conversely

<ruby>個<rt>こ</rt></ruby>の   （<ruby>個人<rt>こじん</rt></ruby>の）private, belonging to an individual

<ruby>所有物<rt>しょゆうぶつ</rt></ruby>   possession

<ruby>育<rt>そだ</rt></ruby>つ   to grow up, be brought up. Cf. <ruby>育<rt>そだ</rt></ruby>てる to bring up, raise;

育てられる to be brought up, raised (passive).

<ruby>設計<rt>せっけい</rt></ruby>する   to plan, design

<ruby>集<rt>あつ</rt></ruby>まる   to gather;   集まれる to be able to gather (potential)

<ruby>作品<rt>さくひん</rt></ruby>   work, product

<ruby>比較的<rt>ひかくてき</rt></ruby>に   relatively, comparatively

Segment 2.1

The speaker's level of politeness and deference toward the owner of the house we visit
are in part due to the presence of the owner's wife and daughter during the interview.
The speaker is sincerely grateful for the opportunity to design a house that incorporates
so many fine features. However, he notes at the end of the interview (not on the DVD)
that a well-built house does not reflect the work of any one person, such as the architect,
but is the product of a great many talented individuals, including carpenters, roofers, mat-
makers, plasterers, and gardeners. He is thankful to be a member of this architectural
orchestra.

訪<ruby>ねる<rt>たず</rt></ruby>	to visit
地形	lay of the land, topography
道路	road, street
表	the front—here, toward the street
圧倒的な	overwhelming, overpowering
威圧感	feeling that something is overpowering, overbearing
与える	to give, impart
与えてしまうと、	(そう思って/そういうわけで is implied after the comma)
一段下げてやる	to lower (it) by one level
変化	change
心がける	to bear in mind; to be careful to do; to endeavor to do
周囲	surroundings
溶け込む	to blend in with (melt into)
庭	garden
ご主人	here, owner of the house; employer of the architect
植木屋	a gardener (specializing in the care of trees)

Segment 2.2

家屋	a house, a building

ってのは　　　　　っていうのは 、 というのは　that which is called

どちらかっていうと　more often than not

夏^{なつむ}向き　　　　　designed for/oriented toward the summer

本^{ほんらい}来　　　　　originally; fundamentally, essentially

眺^{ちょうぼう}望　　　　　view

　　　　　　　眺望がいいと　(there is a possible omission:

　　　　いうことで or いうのが特徴^{とくちょう}で)

というと　　　　　in other words; what this means is

境^{きょうかい}界　　　　　boundary

座^{ざしき}敷　　　　　room floored with *tatami* mats; a parlor

一^{いったいかん}体感　　　　　sense of unity, integration

X をはかって　　　　aiming at, striving for (a sense of unity with the

　　　　　　　　out-of-doors)

広^{ひろ}がりを出^だす　　　to produce a sense of space, expanse

Segment 2.3

Note the カラオケ equipment at the far end of the room. At the opposite end, by the

door, is a small cooking area. The house owner often prepares handmade noodles from

buckwheat flour, *soba*, for guests. (For more on preparing *soba*, see Lesson16, Segment

1.2.)

周^{しゅうい}囲　　　　　those around him, his friends and acquaintances

友^{ともだちづ}達付き合^あい　　　social gatherings with friends

大切にする	to value, consider important; される honorific of する
別の棟 （別棟）	another building/wing (detached from the main building)
囲炉裏	a hearth constructed in the floor
囲炉裏って	囲炉裏というと/といいますと
西洋	the West
暖炉	a stove, a fireplace
落ち着く	to relax
囲む	to surround (here, sit around)
温かみ	warmth
感じられる	to be felt (the warmth of the fire is/can be felt)
歓待する	to entertain; to cordially receive

Segment 3.1

子供部屋	child's or children's room
閉じこもり	shutting oneself up/in; confining oneself to one's room
接触する	to come in contact with, associate with
空間	space
想像力	imaginative power, imagination
伸ばす	to extend

すり合う　　　　　　to interact with (people)

機会　　　　　　　　opportunity

減る　　　　　　　　to decrease; 減っている is decreasing

じゃないかなと　　　ではないのかなと思います
　　　　　　　　　　I wonder if it isn't the case that

社会現象　　　　　　social phenomenon

いじめる　　　　　　to bully, treat harshly

逆に　　　　　　　　conversely, on the contrary (instead of mingling with

　　　　　　　　　　people, on the contrary, they bully or even murder them)

殺す　　　　　　　　to kill

極端な　　　　　　　extreme

例　　　　　　　　　example

発展する　　　　　　to develop

Segment 3.2

大家族　　　　　　　large/extended family

崩れる　　　　　　　to fall apart, collapse

個の時代　　　　　　age of the individual

高齢　　　　　　　　an advanced age　(Cf. 高齢化社会　an aging society)

弱い存在　　　　　　a weak (form of) existence; a vulnerable state of being

隔離する   to isolate, separate

隔離されるようになってしまったがために

                             as a result of having become isolated/separated

いじめなんか   things like bullying

徹底的に   thoroughly

保護する   to protect

やらなくちゃ   やらなくては（ならない or いけない）

含まれている   to be included in

Segment 3.3

急速に   rapidly

高齢化される   to be turned into (a society of) people of advanced age

まして   still more (even more so, take the case of . . .); not to

                             mention . . .

一人暮らしのお年寄り   an elderly person living alone

面倒を見る   to look after, take care of

〜を含めて   including

隔離状態   isolated situation, condition

姿   form, appearance

世代間   the different generations

共生する   to live together（共に生きる）

身近に　　　　　　　　　　close by

眺める　　　　　　　　　　to look at, watch（眺められる、potential form of verb）

コミュニケーション作り　creating communication

できればいいな　　　　in this case Verb ばいい　may be considered as

　　　　　　　　　　　Verb したい．な or なあ following the pattern

　　　　　　　　　　　Verb ばいい often expresses the idea "I wish that . . ." but

　　　　　　　　　　　in this case it may be used simply as a sentence softener or

　　　　　　　　　　　to modulate the rhythm of the sentence.

家を通して　　　　　　　through the medium of the house

Related Themes: For another perspective on the breakdown of communication, see Lesson 6. For an introduction to four other types of living environment, see Lesson 2 and Lesson 10, Segment 1.1.

話し合いましょう

１）それぞれ、自分の故郷、あるいは、現在の居住地域において一般的な家屋の形態は、そこで生活する人々の人間関係に影響を与えると言えますか。逆に、その地域に特有の人間関係が家屋の形態に影響を与えているということはありますか。

故郷　　　　　　　　　　hometown

居住地域　　　　　　　　the region in which one resides

形態　　　　　　　　　　form, shape

人間関係   human relations

逆に   conversely

特有の   special (to); characteristic (of)

2）自分の国では、通常、庭はどのように利用されていますか。家屋と庭とは、どのような関係にあるでしょうか。

通常   usually, commonly
利用する   to use

第4課　　職人——桶屋さんの例
しょくにん　　おけや　　れい

Visiting a Cooper

The product of an artisan does not bear the self-conscious signature of its maker. Its quality is born of techniques improved over time and passed on from one generation to the next. Its beauty is enhanced through daily use by the discerning consumer. By the Edo period (1603-1868) we find artisans representing a great variety of trades, including the blacksmith, silversmith, lacquerer, dyer, sake-brewer, sawyer, plasterer, thatcher, tiler, mat-maker, paperer, and cooper—many of whom still play a role in contemporary society. For centuries many types of craftsmen wandered the country as itinerant workers, taking their tools with them. Eventually the more successful might become established in a town, serving customers who came to their shops or going to the homes of customers to perform their work.

Suzuki Tsutomu tells us about the business of the cooper, *okeya*, a crafter of wooden tubs and buckets. *Oke* ranged from wooden bathtubs to a variety of buckets for hauling water, washing clothes, pickling vegetables, serving rice, and so on. The *okeya* also made bath accessories such as the *furoisu,* a small stool. Suzuki uses the same kind of wood used by his ancestors—*hinoki* (*Chamaecyparis obtusa), sawara* (*Chamaecyparis pisifera*), and *sugi* (*Cryptomeria japonica*). Though frequently called cedars, these trees are in the cypress family. Suzuki obtains his cypress from the forested mountains of the Kiso region in central Japan.

Suzuki's *oke* shop has received prefectural recognition for the manufacture of a local daily-use handicraft ふるさと伝統工芸品 with traditional methods, materials, and
でんとうこうげいひん
tools. In fact, all the tools are also hand-made. None of the *oke* products are signed. Suzuki tells us about how his grandfather decided to open a shop in the town of Kiryū, about changing values in the use of household items, about how *oke* are used today, and about prospects for transmitting this craft to future generations. To supplement his

income from this craft, Suzuki also owns a business with a contemporary line of bath products.

Other crafts that have received prefectural certification in Gumma-ken include straw *noren* (doorway hangings); a variety of handwoven fabrics; pottery; wooden bowls, trays, and storage vessels; *geta*; *tansu* (wooden chests); a variety of baskets woven from bamboo; kitchen knives and other cutting implements; straw brooms; regional *taiko* (drums); *washi* (Japanese paper); and local folk toys. Today the Ministry of Economy, Trade, and Industry (METI) 経済産業省 promotes regional crafts through a certification process and by holding national fairs and competitions. Famous artisans are recognized on a roster. It is possible, however, that the very attempt to preserve handicrafts will turn them into objects of appreciation divorced from everyday life.

Segment 1   TIME CODE 0:21:06

Q どういう理由で桐生に店を開いたんですか。

あのう、私は現在で三代目になります。で、あのう、初代は、あのう、那須、群馬県じゃなくて、栃木県の那須の人でして、で、昔の職人さんというのは、あのう、道具箱一つもって、まあ、それは桶屋の職人さんに限らず、

いろんな職人さんは技術習得のために、ぁのぅ、旅をして歩いたんですけれども、で、いろいろ回って、ええ、まあ、こちら群馬県桐生市というところに来たらば、まあ、昔から言われているように、ぁのぅ、風は強い、けど、雨は少ないし雪は少ないと、ここは住みやすい所かなっていう所がありまして、で、ぁのぅ、桶屋っていう商売は、まあ、その時代に「風が吹くと桶屋が儲かる」という諺があったかどうかは存じ上げないですけども、もしあったとすれば、一番ぴったりの地域だったかなと、うん、ありますね、それは。

Segment 2   TIME CODE 0:22:24

[Q] 桶作りは室町時代から日常生活に関わる日本の工芸の一つですが、現在では「ものを作る」、そして「ものを使う」態度は昔とはかなり違いますね。

基本的に今の世界は、ぁのぅ、捨てるものにたいしてあんまり頓着がない、ぁのぅ、関心を持たない、新しく購入してどんどん捨てていくって、消費社会になってますので、昔はそうじゃなくって、一つのものを購入すると、それを孫子の代まで使う、まあ、あの、ちょっとオーバーな言い方かもしれませんけれども、一つのもの、例えばうちの製造してます、ぁのぅ、桶一つとってみても、一つその桶を作ると自分の時代だけで終わらず、何代

も後まで使えるような、ぁのぅ、生活に必要なものとしてのとらえ方として、

まぁ、そういうふうな形で、ぁのぅ、認識的には、ぁのぅ、今の学生さんには

お分かりいただけるかどうか分かりませんけど、それが、そういうところ

にすごく神経を使ってやってきたのかなっていうところがあります。

Segment 3   TIME CODE 0:23:30

Q 桶の使い方はどういうふうに変わりましたか。

昔は、ま、ぁのぅ、さきほど話した室町時代から出てきたわけですが、

基本的には生活にどうしてもそれはないと困ると、生活必需品で、水廻り

にはどうしてもそれがないと困るっていうふうな形でもって、ぁのぅ、

使用されていたものなんですが、現在は、まぁ、それまでの間、かなりの

年数がありますので、ぁのぅ、一時的にまるっきり殆ど出ない状態がしば

らく続きました。で、この十年くらい前から、ぁのぅ、逆に、感性ですか

ね、ぁのぅ、使う方がその本来の使用用途と違うふうな形でもってとらえ

て、ぁのぅ、使ってらっしゃるって方が多いです。ということは、ぁのぅ、例

えば、ぁの、お風呂で使う湯桶一つとってみても、基本的にはそれは、ぁの

ぅ、お風呂の中の入っているお湯を汲みだして顔を洗ったり頭を洗ったり

するために本来は作られたものなんですが、現在それをマガジンラックに

したり、はい、それから、ぁのぅ、床の間に飾るお花の、まぁ、花瓶の代用

にしたりして使っている方もいますね。

Segment 4　　　　　　　　　　　　　　TIME CODE　0:24:53

Q　お風呂の場合はどうですか。若い人たちは木のお風呂に興味がありま

すか。

ちょっと変わった使い方としては、ぁのぅ、セカンドバス、ぁのぅ、二つ目の

お風呂って形で、まぁ、ぁのぅ、今ですと、ぁのぅ、普通の住宅に、ぁのぅ、

お住みの方は、わりかしユニットバスですとか、それから、まぁ、お

風呂場の中にある浴槽に入ってシャワーを浴びていらっしゃるって方が

殆どなんですが、まぁ、最近若い方で特に目立つのは、ぁのぅ、ベランダに

木のお風呂を持っていって、で、ぁのぅ、日本人の感覚であるお風呂につか

りながら、ぇぇ、徳利の中に入っているお酒をちびちびといただくという

ふうな形が夢だったんですよと、そういうふうに言って、ぇぇ、うちから

お求めになられるお客さんが最近、特に若い人が多いです。｛若い人｝

はい。まぁ、一般的に木のお風呂が一番うちは、ぁのぅ、うちの職人さんが

作っている本数とすると多いです。｛そうですか。｝はい。

Segment 5   TIME CODE 0:25:55

Ｑ　こうした技術をもった職人仕事はこれからも伝わっていくと思います

か。

あのう、職人さんの仕事ってのは、まぁ、いろんな業種で違うと思います

けど、私が存じ上げてる桶の世界の職人に関して申し上げますと、

二十年前からすると職人さんの数が十分の一ぐらいに減っています。

高年齢化で後継者がいないというふうな形で、作る方がそれだけ、もう、

それを残しておこうという感覚をもっている方からするとまことに残念な

ことなんですが、ただ、それを作って生活ができる、作り続けて生活がで

きるような、今、世の中じゃないと思います。…あの、希望とすれば、今

お話ししたように、若い方が、ぁの、ベランダですとか、屋上ですとか、

で、ぁのぅ、ちょっと余裕のあったお休みの時なんかに、あのうね、景色を
見ながら、ぁのぅ、それから夜の星を見ながら、月を見ながら、ぁのぅ、お
風呂に入るっていう感性というのは、私は、できればみなさんがもって
ほしいなと思います。

単語と文法ノート

Title

職人	a craft worker; an artisan
桶	a wooden tub or vessel; 桶屋 a cooper: a person who makes and repairs wooden tubs and casks; the cooper's profession
例	example

Segment 1 The speaker is conscious of you, his audience, and is very polite to the interviewer as well, with whom he is acquainted, but in a more formal capacity than is the case with some other speakers.

開く	to open, start (a shop, a business)
三代目	third generation
初代	the founder
道具	tool(s); instruments; 道具箱 a toolbox
〜に限らず	not limited to X , but . . .
技術	an art; a skill; a technique; technology

習得 (しゅうとく)　learning;　技術習得のために (ぎじゅつしゅうとく)

in order to acquire/learn skills/techniques

旅 (たび)　travel

歩く (あるく)　to walk; 回り歩く to travel, walk from one place to

another

回る (まわる)　to make the rounds

来たらば (き)　when he came to Kiryū (he found out that what he had

heard was true). たら ＝ when, and in this case ば

suggests that coming is a condition for realizing what

follows.

風 (かぜ)　wind

商売 (しょうばい)　business

儲かる (もう)　to find the business profitable; to find that money flows in

諺 (ことわざ)　proverb

存じ上げる (ぞん)(あ)　存じる is a humble form of 知る。存じ上げる is one

step more humble than 存じる。

Segment 2

室町時代 (むろまちじだい)　the Muromachi period (1392-1573); the Ashikaga

shogunate took as its headquarters the Muromachi district

of Kyoto.

日常生活 (にちじょうせいかつ)　everyday life

工芸 こうげい	handicrafts; industrial art
態度 たいど	attitude
基本的に きほんてき	basically
捨てる す	to throw away
に/に対して頓着がない とんちゃく	to have no concern for, be indifferent to
関心 かんしん	concern, interest
購入する こうにゅう	to buy, purchase （買う） か
消費社会 しょうひしゃかい	consumer society
子孫の代まで しそん　だい	down to posterity (children and grandchildren)
製造する せいぞう	to manufacture, produce
とってみる	to take (consider) (X, for example)
終わらずに お	終わらないで お
とらえ方 かた	way of grasping (considering, viewing) something
認識的に にんしきてき	in terms of conscious knowledge or awareness
神経 しんけい	nerves; 〜を使う to pay very close attention to つか

Segment 3

生活必需品 せいかつひつじゅひん	an article indispensable for daily life; necessity of life

水廻り（みずまわり）　家屋（かおく）の中（なか）で、台所（だいどころ）・洗面所（せんめんじょ）など、水（みず）を使（つか）う箇所（かしょ）

places where you would use water in a residence, such as the kitchen and washroom

使用する（しよう）　to use, employ, make use of

年数（ねんすう）　many years

一時的に（いちじてき）　temporarily

まるっきり　まるで、まったく quite, completely

殆ど（ほとん）　almost; nearly まるっきり殆ど出ない状態

a situation in which they were hardly produced at all

状態（じょうたい）　state of things; situation

逆に（ぎゃく）　conversely

感性（かんせい）　sensibility

本来の（ほんらい）　original

使用用途（しようようと）　a use, manner of use

湯桶（ゆおけ）　a bucket to be filled with hot water, used when bathing

汲みだす（く）　to scoop, ladle

飾る（かざ）　to decorate

花瓶（かびん）　flower vase

代用（だいよう）　a substitute; in place of

Segment 4

興味 きょうみ	interest
変わった か	different; novel
普通の住宅 ふつう　じゅうたく	a typical residence
わりかし	colloquial for わりかた　＝　わりあいに、比較的 ひかくてき
浴槽 よくそう	bathtub
目立つ め　だ	to stand out
感覚 かんかく	sensation; here, "aesthetic sense, aesthetic sensual pleasure"
お風呂につかる ふ　ろ	to soak in the bath
徳利 とっくり	a tapered sake flask
ちびちびと	ちびりちびり little by little, in little sips
夢 ゆめ	a dream
うちの	our (affiliated with our business)
本数 ほんすう	the number (of)
〜とすると	in terms of 〜

Segment 5

業種 ぎょうしゅ	a type or category of trade or business
申し上げる もう　あ	humble form of 言う
減る へ	to decrease

高年齢化で	due to the process of aging (of the current artisans)
後継者	a successor
残す	to leave behind　残しておく
感覚	feeling
残念な	regretful
希望	hope;　〜とすれば (if I were to hope for anything it would be that . . .)
屋上	housetop; roof
余裕	spare time
景色	scenery
星	star(s)
感性	sensibility

話し合いましょう

１）自分の家で代々使っている工芸品はありますか。もしあれば、その歴史や用途について説明してください。

代々	from generation to generation
工芸品	a craft product
用途	a use

2）「用の美」という表現がありますが、これは工芸品の場合にはどの
ように解釈すれば良いでしょうか。また、この概念は現代社会において
も未だに通用しうるものだと思いますか。

用の美	the beauty attained through daily use
表現	expression
概念	concept
未だに	still; even now
通用する	to be accepted; to hold true
～うる・える	（得る）auxiliary verb expressing possibility；the negative form is えない.

3）日本の工芸品を一つ調べ、その結果をクラスメイトに発表しましょ
う。

結果	result(s)
発表する	to report　(on one's research)

第5課　　有機農業——ある農家の話

The Neighborhood Organic Farmer

Miyata Tsuneo is a full-time organic farmer. He farms 1.4 hectares of rice and 1.2 hectares of vegetables, for a total of 2.6 hectares, or 6.42 acres. (One hectare is 2.469 acres.) In Japan farms average 2.18 hectares (5.38 acres), which is larger than farms in China, South Korea, and Indonesia, but minuscule compared to the average farm size of 171 acres in the United Kingdom and 436 acres in the United States (ERS). The majority of commercial farmers in Japan are part-time operators, earning much of their income outside the agricultural sector. Three out of five farmers are sixty-five years old or older, and farmland is being abandoned at an alarming rate (Yamashita, 21). Older farmers today lament the lack of successors, while younger ones cannot find a spouse.

In 2003 women accounted for 55.3 percent of the total labor force in agriculture (Gender Equality Bureau 男女共同参画局), although the number of farms owned and operated by women alone is small (ERS). Women may work on the farm while their husbands take urban jobs, and yet women play a minor role in determining local agricultural policy (Gender Equality Bureau). Miyata's wife works full-time on the farm; she is especially busy with deliveries. His elderly parents were of great assistance, as you will see on the DVD, but his father passed away shortly after we filmed. His daughters are not likely to succeed to his profession.

Miyata is able to live close to a subsistence lifestyle. With his diversity of production, including free-range chickens and occasionally pigs, he can support his family in terms of both food and income. Japan's self-sufficiency in food as measured in calories is only 40 percent, although the government plans to raise this to 45 percent by 2015. By comparison, Britain stands at 61 percent and the United States at over 100 percent (Yamazaki, 50). Japan remains self-sufficient in rice production, which is highly subsidized by the state, but there is concern about the multiple consequences of dependence on imported food, including the safety of the imports. Any nation or region must be careful about relying exclusively on imports, for such factors as climate change, decline of soil health, crop or stock disease, or political instability in the exporting nation(s) and reliance on fossil fuels for shipping can result in unexpected cost hikes or cessation of the production or shipment of staple foods.

Discussions on agricultural reform call for reducing farm subsidies (difficult owing to the disproportionate strength of the rural vote), allowing shareholder companies to enter the agricultural business, and concentrating state support on large-scale principal farmers (Richardson). Proponents of large-scale farming hope that if full-time farmers are given assistance to acquire cultivated land as it becomes available, the average farm size will increase and farming practices may become more efficient. However, if holdings are scattered, farmers trying to expand their operations or newcomers wanting to rent land will find that the drive from one spot to another will increase time and cost. With regard to the trend toward larger-scale operations, Miyata comments: "Democracy increased as a result of the liberalization of land after the war. People are forgetting the value of this freedom. Power is returning to the hands of the few."

While the discussion regarding national agricultural reform goes on, some producers find at least a personal solution to these issues in the revival of diversified organic production on the family farm. Consumers have responded to and encouraged this movement through a growing interest in direct purchases from organic farmers. When rice loses its subsidies, it may find new support in the organic market.

Miyata is the youngest son of a farming family. In a society in which the eldest son was expected to inherit the farm, he was the only child willing to take up his father's occupation. His father, a product of postwar agricultural practices, used the full regimen of inorganic fertilizers and agricultural chemicals recommended and sold to him by Nōkyō 農協 (農業共同組合、the Association of Agricultural Cooperatives, known today as JA, Japan Agricultural Cooperatives). Many of these chemicals were imported from the United States and used in Japan long after they had been banned in their country of origin. According to the U.S. Department of Agriculture, Japan still uses seven times as much pesticide per hectare as the United States does (ERS). For the reasons he relates on the DVD, and in the face of bitter opposition by his father, Miyata decided to turn to organic farming, an enterprise in which he has succeeded through study, experimentation, hard work, and innovative methods in direct marketing.

Through diversified farming, Miyata is able to use manure and compost as fertilizer; he rotates crops and grows produce appropriate to the season. *Shiitake* logs are spread out in his bamboo grove. The bamboo is used for poles and farm implements; he also uses it to make a charcoal additive for the soil. "After the war, agriculture became mechanized and farms began to raise only one product. People's lives took the same turn—they are like a monoculture," says Miyata. "People do the same thing every day. They don't balance their lives with outside work. Everything today is tied to economy of scale, to increasing personal wealth. People don't think about the source of their food and the way it is grown. The study of nutrition today is no more than numbers or data. It is divorced from environmental awareness. And yet healthy food comes from a healthy environment, and we can protect the environment through diversified organic agriculture. We mustn't forget that the environment itself is the body's nourishment (環境そのものは体の栄養です)." Miyata's farm nurtures life at all levels—from the microorganisms in the soil, so critical for healthy crops, to the wildlife that flourishes in the absence of agricultural chemicals. His words put pride of culture and respect for life back into agriculture.

Segment 1

Q　宮田さんは、お父さんの世代の農家の方とは違って有機農業をなさっていますが、この転換のきっかけは何だったんですか。

Segment 1.1

それも、転換のきっかけは考えてみるといろいろあるんですけどね、まぁ、三つぐらいに大きく分けることができるかと考えているんですけども。まぁ、何と言っても一番大きいのは自分が健康じゃなかったということでしょうかね。…それで、こう農業をやり始めた時、特に農業をやりはじめてですけど、あのぅ、基礎体力がないわけですね。こう力が体についてこないということで、なんとかこれはパワーの出る体をつけたいというふうに思ったわけですね。健康な人は本当にうらやましかったわけです。みなさん並、力の出る、その体を作りたいなというふうに思って。そしたら、一番初めに食べ物に関心がいくようになったわけですね。食べ物に関心がいって、一番初めはまず添加物なんですね。食品添加物がこんなにも多く使われていたということを知って驚きました。で、しばらく添加物の勉強なんかを始めたんですね。

Segment 1.2 （続き）　　　　　　　　　　TIME CODE　0:28:35

で、その次には農薬問題が当然出てくるわけですけど、で、農薬は大変だ

ということが分かってきたわけです。それでどんどんどんどん、ぁのぅ、

勉強をしていくうちに食べ物というのは、これは、まぁ、ただならないも

のだということが理解できて、それで急速に今度は環境の問題と結びつ

いてきたんですね。で、現在ではもう環境問題と、もう、食べ物の問題

はまったく同一だというふうに考えております。で、それを生産するとこ

ろが、なんと、考えてみれば農業であるわけですから、一番大切な

職業だというふうに自信と誇りをもっているつもりでおります。

Segment 2　　　　　　　　　　　　　　TIME CODE　0:29:25

Q　宮田さんはどんなものを栽培していらっしゃいますか。

私の家では、ぁのぅ、主には田んぼで、米の生産だと思いますね。まぁ、

全体の半分以上が米ということになると思います。で、そのほか、野菜類、

野菜類はたくさんあるんですね。ぁのぅ、そうですね、数えた（場合）だけ

でも数十種類になるでしょうかね。｛そうですか。｝まぁ、みなさんご

存知なのは大根だとか、大根、人参などの根菜類、それからキャベツだと

か、ブロッコリーだとか、まぁ、レタスだとかね、ぇぇ、それに葱だとか、

玉葱、後ろにあるような玉葱だとか、まぁ、（それ）細かいものまで入れ

たら、さらには胡瓜だとか {トマトは?} トマトだとかあるわけですから、細かいものを入れると数十種類ぐらいになるでしょうか。いつも十種類ぐらいは取れるようになっていると思います。で、そのほか、ぁのぅ、葡萄が、葡萄の木を植えてまだ十年までたっていませんですけど、あったり、ええ、鶏もいます。鶏が百五十羽ぐらい。それは、ぁの、ケージではなくて平飼いの、自由に動くことのできる、ぁの、平飼いといいますけど、そういうところで卵を取るためにいるわけですね。さらには、ぁの、椎茸というのがあります。

Segment 3　　　　　　　　　　　TIME CODE 0:31:11

Q　この農作物はどういうふうに販売なさいますか。

で、販売の方ですけど、私の家では、ぁのぅ、有機農産物ということで、ええ、やはりそれをちゃんと理解できる消費者のところへ届くようになっているんですが、ぁのぅ、それにはたくさんの形式があって、グループでお付き合い、自然食品を愛好するグループ、主婦の集まりがあっちこっちにあるわけですけど、そういうところだとか、あるいは、自然食品店をやっている、ぁの、お店であるとか、また個人のお客さんもいるんですよね。個人の人だとか、ええ、まぁ、保育園なんかもあります。そういう、非常にさまざまな形になっています。

Segment 4　　　　　　　　　　　　TIME CODE　0:32:02

Q　アメリカでは家族農業という小規模農業は消えつつありますが、

日本の場合はどうでしょうか。

日本もご存知と思いますが、ぁのぅ、農業は非常に厳しい状況になって

おります。で、日本の農業は、本来自給自足を中心にして戦後まもなく

までは自給自足が中心の農業であったわけです。で、それは家族を

中心にして自給自足をしていくということだったわけですけど、だんだ

ん工業がさかんになって、ま、そっちへ、ぁの、人々が出ていって、工業、

商業がさかんになってきたわけですね。で、そうすると、それから最近

は特に問題なのは、ぁの、外国から自由に農産物が入ってくるようになっ

てきました。特にここ十年ぐらいは、中国からもうたくさんの農産物が

入って、安い農産物が入ってきます。で、その影響を受けて日本の農業

はどんどんどんどん、まぁ、若者はほとんどやらなくなってしまった。ええ、

今年寄りたちががんばってやっとやっているところで、どこでも後継者の

問題は深刻な問題になっております。

Supplementary Passage (not on DVD)

Q　田んぼというのは、自然環境にどういうふうに役立っていますか。

(宮田さん)　日本は、大変雨の降る所です。で、その水は非常に米を育てるのに有効なわけですね。田んぼというのは、水を溜めるわけですから、ダムの役割をします。大雨が降っても、一時に川へ流れていかないわけですから、洪水調整の役割をしているんだというふうに言われています。それは、だれでも分かる通りの一点です。もう一つ大事なことは、水を張ることによってそこに生物が生まれるわけですね。まず、ミジンコがでてきます。ミジンコを食べる虫がたくさんでてくるんですね。で、トンボの幼虫のヤゴだとか、オタマジャクシもたくさんそこにでてきたり、またそれを食べるクモだとかね。で、さらにですね、オタマジャクシからカエルがたくさん発生して増えてきて、当然ヘビもでてくるし、それからそういう虫たちを餌にして、鳥たちもたくさん集まってきます。そこで大きな生態系が起こってくるんですね。で、それを支えるのは水田だというふうに考えております。で、もちろん米の生産は、そこでその大きな生態が起こってくることによって米も、健全な米が取れることになるわけです。

単語と文法ノート

Title

有機農業　　　　　　　organic agriculture

農家　　　　　　　　　farmer; farmhouse; farm family

Segment 1

世代 せだい	generation
転換 てんかん	conversion; changeover
きっかけ	opportunity; chance; start, beginning

Segment 1.1

健康 けんこう	health
基礎体力 きそたいりょく	basic physical strength
力がついてこない	I didn't have any strength

(力がついてくる to gain strength)

わけだ　　　　　　explanatory sentence ending (used frequently by this

speaker).　わけです may mean "the fact of the matter is . . ." or, "the

thing is . . . ." わけです is similar to sentence ending のです or んです

in that it often follows an explanation. It may be used for emphasis or

simply for rhythm and is not always translated. This form is frequently

used in conversation. It follows the plain forms of verbs or adjectives and

the な form of adjectival nouns.

つける	自分のものとする

(I wanted to develop a powerful body.)

うらやましい	be envious of
並 なみ	common; ordinary; average;

みなさん並　just like everyone else

関心 かんしん	interest; concern

食品添加物　　　　　a food additive

驚く　　　　　　　　to be surprised, amazed

Segment 1.2

農業問題　　　　　　agricultural problems or issues

当然　　　　　　　　naturally, as a matter of course

農薬　　　　　　　　agricultural chemicals (pesticides, herbicides, fungicides)

ただならない、ただならぬ means 普通ではない、大変な、容易ならぬ

　　　　　　　　　　Here: something serious, something of an alarming nature

理解する　　　　　　to understand

急速に　　　　　　　rapidly, quickly

結びつく　　　　　　to be linked to

環境問題　　　　　　environmental problems or issues

生産　　　　　　　　production

同一だ　　　　　　　to be one and the same, identical

自信　　　　　　　　confidence

誇り　　　　　　　　pride

つもりだ　　　　　　This pattern is often used to express intention, but in this

　　　　　　　　　　case it means "to believe that," "to feel sure that." It

　　　　　　　　　　expresses our friend's deepest convictions.

Segment 2

栽培する	to cultivate, grow
主に	primarily
田んぼ	rice paddy/paddies
米	rice
全体	the whole (here, his whole farming operation)
野菜類	vegetable products
数えただけでも	just by counting
数十種類	tens of kinds
ご存知だ	you know, you are aware; honorific form of 知っている
大根	Japanese white radish
人参、ニンジン	carrots
根菜類	types of root vegetables
玉葱	round onion
細かい	small. Here the farmer refers to things he grows in small quantities, in season. For example, many people grow tomatoes and cucumbers year-round in hothouses, making extensive use of inorganic fertilizers, herbicides, fungicides, and pesticides—not to mention heating fuel. Miyata grows a small quantity of such produce in season, outside, in the real earth by organic methods.

さらに	その上に、なお further
胡瓜 （きゅうり）	cucumber
取れる （と）	to be produced
葡萄 （ぶどう）	grapes
植える （う）	to plant
鶏 （にわとり）	chicken
羽 （わ）	counter for birds
平飼い （ひらが）	free-range; not caged
卵 （たまご）	eggs
椎茸、シイタケ （しいたけ）	*shiitake* mushrooms

Segment 3

農産物 （のうさんぶつ）	agricultural products
販売 （はんばい）	sales, marketing
消費者 （しょうひしゃ）	consumer
届く （とど）	to reach, be delivered to
ようになっている	it has been arranged that things happen in this way
形式 （けいしき）	form
付き合い （つ あ）	association, friends, social group
愛好する （あいこう）	to love, be fond of

主婦の集まり　　　　gathering of housewives

自然食品店　　　　　natural foods store

個人のお客さん　　　individual customers

保育園　　　　　　　a nursery school

非常にさまざまな形　　a great many different forms

Segment 4

家族農業　　　　　　family farming

小規模農業　　　　　small-scale agriculture

消える　　　　　　　to vanish

消えつつある　　　　to be in the process of/ on the verge of vanishing

場合　　　　　　　　in the case of

厳しい状況　　　　　severe/difficult state of affairs

自給自足　　　　　　self-sufficiency (subsistence lifestyle)

中心にする　　　　　to center on, focus on

戦後まもなくまで　　until shortly after the war

工業　　　　　　　　industry, manufacturing

さかんになる　　　　to prosper, thrive

商業　　　　　　　　commerce, business

の影響を受ける　　　to be affected/influenced by

若者 _{わかもの}　　　　　young people

年寄り _{としよ}　　　　　the elderly

やっとやっている　　to be barely making it

後継者 _{こうけいしゃ}　　successor

深刻な _{しんこく}　　　　serious, grave

Supplementary Passage　　The passage is taken from the interview but is not on the DVD. Return to what the farmer says here as you study Lessons 12 and 13.

自然環境 _{しぜんかんきょう}　　natural environment

役立つ _{やくだ}　　　　to be useful, beneficial

溜める _た　　　　　to collect, store

役割を果たす _{やくわり} _は　　to perform a role, function

一時 _{いちじ}　　　　at one time, at once

流れる _{なが}　　　　to flow

洪水調整 _{こうずいちょうせい}　　flood control

張る _は　　　　(the paddy) fills with (water)

生物 _{せいぶつ}　　　living thing, an organism

ミジンコ　　　　*Daphnia* spp.; a small crustacean with the common name "water flea"

ミミズ　　　　earthworm

トンボの幼虫 _{ようちゅう}　　larva of dragonfly; the larva is called ヤゴ

クモ	spider
オタマジャクシ	tadpole
カエル　（蛙）	frog
発生する	to emerge, originate
餌	food, feed
生態系	ecosystem
起こってくる	to come into being, begin to originate
支える	to support
水田	wet-rice paddies
生産	production
健全な	healthy

Related Themes: Contrast the food culture introduced here with the fast-food culture described in Lesson 6, and learn more about traditional agricultural ecosystems, *satoyama* 里山 , in Lessons 12 and 13. Miyata talks about his family in Lesson 1 and his living environment in Lesson 2.

話し合いましょう

１）宮田さんは農業を「一番大切な職業だ」と語っていますが、彼がそう考える理由を述べてください。

| 語る | to tell, relate, narrate |
| 述べる | to tell, state, mention |

2）自分たちが毎日口にする野菜類は、もともとどこで、どのように栽培
されているものでしょうか。また、その栽培方法は自分自身の健康に、さ
らには自然環境にどう影響すると考えられますか。

3）有機農産物の価格はほかの農産物よりも割高になってしまいますが、
それはなぜでしょうか。また、その割高感にもかかわらず消費者が
有機農産物を買い求めるとしたら、それはどのような理由に基づいている
と言えるでしょうか。

価格	price, value 値段
割高である	to be relatively expensive, comparatively high;
	～感　feeling (that it is relatively expensive)
にもかかわらず	in spite of
基づく	to be based on

4）自分が住んでいる地域では、どこで、どのような種類の有機農産物を
買うことができますか。それらの農産物の産地はどこですか。また自分の
庭で野菜を作った経験のある人がいたら、具体的に何を作ったのかを説明
してください。

居住地域	the district in which you live
産地	growing district, place where something is produced

第6課　食べ物と現代のライフスタイル

Cuisine and Contemporary Lifestyles

The evolution of food culture is closely related to the evolution of technology, communications, transportation, architecture, and lifestyle. When I was a child living outside of Tokyo the ice vendor 氷屋さん would bike through my neighborhood during the summer pulling a small wooden cart. He would stop at the homes that contracted his services and saw off a piece of ice for the cooler. Housewives who lacked this convenience, and many who owned an icebox, went shopping every day at one of the small stores near the train station—the fishmonger, the fruit and vegetable shop, the *tōfu-ya*, each run by a family living in back of the store. But from the mid-1960s electrical appliances became widely used, and by the end of the 1970s nearly every home had a refrigerator. The shopping could be done once or twice a week. The kitchen now has become slightly larger, with a plethora of appliances. The family shops around my once suburban train station have been replaced by a Kentucky Fried Chicken franchise, a steak house, a supermarket, a few convenience stores—offering quick meals from sandwiches to *soba*, in plastic wrap or plastic containers—and several bakeries. Just a few stations away is a larger city with fine international restaurants and a number of department stores, in the basement of which one can buy imported foods or a variety of prepared Japanese and international dishes. Food choices abound. Well-equipped kitchens and supermarkets stocked with domestic and imported goods suggest the possibility of creative home-cooking, and yet one characteristic of modern food culture is the serving of prepared or instant foods at home and the eating of food at quick-serve establishments outside. How has our relationship to food changed? What has happened to the home-cooked family meal and what are the social repercussions of its loss?

Katō Masako, our first speaker, is a cooking instructor. She encourages her students to buy local products, reminding them of the expression 一里四方のものを食

べると元気に暮らせ<ruby>暮<rt>く</rt></ruby>る if you eat the food grown locally (literally, within a radius of about 2.5 miles/4 kilometers), you'll lead a healthy life. Products grown locally are suited to the regional climate and soil. They are fresh and flavorful. It is easy to learn how they have been grown and harvested. Katō herself purchases vegetables, rice, and eggs from Miyata, the organic farmer we met in Lesson 5. She can also buy local products at her suburban supermarket, which now features a section for regional farmers. Above the bin with their respective produce is a picture of the farmer and a brief statement about where and how the food is grown. Both urban and suburban residents can join a farmer-consumer alliance, such as Seikatsu Club, an environmentally oriented food-cooperative. Healthy food is available to those who have the interest, income, and time to obtain it.

Katō Masako also encourages her students to eat food in season. In the past people looked forward to seasonal vegetables 旬の野菜 (or fruit, fish, etc.). In the spring one can harvest mountain vegetables 山菜 (or buy the farm-grown varieties), such as bamboo shoots; *seri* (*Oenanthe javanica*, water celery; it looks like celery leaves and tastes a little like parsley); and *fuki* (*Petasites japonicus*, butterbur or sweet coltsfoot). All of these have a slightly bitter taste and are believed to awaken the body after a winter of indoor inactivity. Summer vegetables include tomatoes, cucumbers, and string beans, refreshing in cold salads. Root vegetables are eaten in the late fall and winter. Roasted sweet potatoes and simmered *daikon* warm the body. The widespread use of hothouse technology has made crops like lettuce, tomatoes, and cucumbers available all winter. While it may seem healthy to have these fresh foods year around, winter production of summer produce requires high inputs of energy and agricultural chemicals, and the anticipation and appreciation of seasonal differences are lost.

Not only have we lost touch with nature, says Katō. We are also losing touch with each other. In Japanese cooking there are many terms that refer to adjusting the flavor: 塩加減 salt to taste, 水加減 add water as necessary, 火加減 adjust the heat appropriately. *Kagen* is written with the characters 加える to add to, to increase, and 減

らす to decrease. As one tastes the food being prepared, one adjusts the flavor, or strength, or length of cooking time to suit those who will be eating the meal. This is not just a matter of the palate, explains Katō; it is a matter of the heart. We prepare a meal with love, adjusting the flavor and texture to suit the health or age or special preferences of those we will serve. その加減が人間関係を良い加減にするのです, food prepared thoughtfully improves human relations. For the eater, meals are also a matter of adjusting, of give-and-take. One eats something made a little too soft because grandfather has trouble chewing. Sometimes we get our favorite food; on other days we put up with another's preference. But this type of adjustment or thoughtfulness is not cultivated by contemporary food culture. In Segment 1 Katō speaks further about the effect of our busy lifestyles on food culture and social relations.

In Segment 2, Satō Mayumi, a graduate student in the natural sciences, adds to the discussion, focusing on the repercussion of the fast-food culture on public health and the socialization of children. She is not denouncing fast foods per se—these have existed at least since the eighteenth century, when Edo abounded with street stalls selling *soba*, *sushi*, and *tempura*. It is, rather, the quality of some of this food and our abandonment of children to the fast-food industry that give her concern. What similarities do you find in your own culture?

Segment 1　お料理教室の先生の話

Segment 1.1   TIME CODE 0:33:21

Ｑ　忙しい現代では皆さんはどのような食事をしているのでしょうか。

今の日本は忙しくて、「忙しい」という言葉を一日一回は聞くような気がするぐらい「忙しい、忙しい」ということをよく聞きます。で、特に子供さんは、あのぅ、学校が終わりますと、塾とか、それからピアノのレッスン、追い立てるように忙しい子供たちも増えています。それから主婦の方は、あのぅ、家庭の仕事よりはむしろパートタイマーで、ええ、する仕事の方を選ぶ人が多いですね。それからご主人は、会社の残業で遅くなって帰りも遅いです。ですから一緒に家族が食事をするということがむしろ大変珍しい現象のように思います。

Segment 1.2　（続き）   TIME CODE 0:34:19

ですから家族が、「同じ釜の飯を食べる」という言い方が昔はあるんですけれども、むしろ「同じ釜の飯」ということがなかなか出来にくくなってますとともに、そういう忙しい家族が食事をする仕方というのは、どうしても子供さんは塾の時間に合わせて食事をします。そして、ご主人は遅く帰ってきますから当然遅く、ややもすれば、子供が寝た時間に食事をするということがあります。そうなりますと、主婦もパートで忙しいわけですから、家庭でご飯を作らなくなりますね。そうしますと、だれが作

ったか分からないお総菜を買ってきて、それを食べさせるんですけれども、ばらばらに食べる時には「私がきらい」なものは無理して食べようという気にはなりませんね、一人、ぁのぅ、一人で食べる食事では。ですから、どうしても偏食ということも起こりうると思います。

Segment 1.3   TIME CODE 0:35:22

Q ばらばらに食べるのは寂しいでしょうね。でも、そのほかにもいろいろな問題が生じるのではないかと思います。

そうですね。ぁのぅ、もちろん「個食」には問題がありますね。個食で食べるということは、ぁのぅ、寂しいだけではなくて、家族との一緒に食べる食事と違うのはコミュニケーションができないということです。家族が一緒に食べることによって家族のいろいろな話、それから（でん）文化とか伝統を受け継ぐことであると思います。ですから、そういうものがすべて断ち切れてしまう。また、日本の、ぁの文化的な調理方法や何かも、手伝いも忙しくて、子供さんが親の手伝いをしなくなりますから、当然全部、ぁのぅ、切れた状態になりますから、文化は伝わっていかないと思います。

Segment 1.4   TIME CODE 0:36:12

Q 食べ物に期待することは？

動物は決して、うちの犬も含めて、「今日は、ぁのぅ、うちの犬の夕食時に知り合いの犬を呼んで向かい合って食事をする」ということはありません。で、ぁのぅ、だだ、お腹を空けば空腹を満たすためにドッグフードをむさぼり食べて、それからお水を飲んでという状態を繰り返します。人間は決してそういうことではなく、時には友人を呼んだり、そして毎日家族と顔を合わせて食事をとるということが大変重要なことだと思います。その重要な、その家族の食卓の基本っていうのは、やはり家庭料理にあるかなと思います。今見ていきますと、買ってきたもの、顔の見えないその食卓の風景、そういうものがやはり家族の崩壊（につか）、家族のコミュニケーションの断絶ということ（が）と関わりあってきてるのだと思います。ですから食卓というのは人と人をつなぐ大変重要な場所であると思います。

Segment 1.5 （続き）　　　　　　　　　TIME CODE　0:37:26

ぁのぅ、フランスの、ぁのぅ、思想家の中にブリア＝サヴァランという人がいます。「あなたはなにを食べたか、言ってごらんなさい。私があなたをどんな人だか当ててみましょう」という言い方があります。有名な言葉です。その言葉の中には食べ物というのは大変その人格をも形成し、また心を育てるものであるということも象徴されていると思います。

Segment 2 エコロジーを専攻している大学院生の話

Segment 2.1 TIME CODE 0:37:56

Q 現代の食文化についてお話しくださいますか。

そうですね。ええと、日本人の、まぁ、日本の食文化っていうのが、昔から、あのぅ、ご飯、お味噌汁、それには、お漬物とちょっと魚を食べる、あるいは野菜を食べるっていうのは、伝統的な食文化というのがあったと思うんですけれども、最近はその食文化の欧米化っていうことで、ええ、ものすごく、あのぅ、批判をされているところがありまして、あのぅ、そうですね、ハンバーガーとかそういうコレステロールが高い食物というのが入ってきまして、それが、まぁ、ガン、ガンを余計引き起こすんじゃないか、そういう心臓病の原因になっているのではないかと、そういうのが批判もされていますけれども、単純に日本の食文化だけを、こぅ日本食を食べていれば健康といった時代もまた終わってしまったと思うんですね。それっていうのは、例えば、コンビニエンスストアとか行くと、日本食は、あのぅ、体にいいから日本食を選びましょうと、日本食を選んだところで、もう一番シンプルなおにぎりですら、ものすごく添加物が、もう、すごい長いリストで入っている状態ですし、うどんのような簡単なシンプルな食べ物でも、ものすごいリストなんですね。{ええ。} 人工、なんですね、保存料、人工甘味料、人工の香料、まぁ、そういった（てん）食品添加

物がものすごく入っているんで、ええ、もう人々が、こぅより手軽な食べ物を求めようとしている今では、もうその（欧米化とか）欧米型の食事、あるいは、日本、伝統的な日本の食事、そういうのを関係なく、もうものすごく、こぅ添加物が入ってきてる状態だと思うんで、ええ、もうそうですね、そういった手軽な食物を求めるのではなくて、家庭でどういった、昔から家庭でどういった食べ物を食べていたのか、そういうなんか原点に返って見てみる必要があるんではないのかなって思います。

Segment 2.2   TIME CODE 0:39:52

Q 現代の食文化や食べ方は子供たちにどんな影響を与えているのでしょうか。

子供の犯罪が今どんどん増えているっていうふうに言われていますけれども、こぅ学校の、小学校、中学校の教育だけの問題だけではなくて、やはり、基本というのは家庭になくてはいけないと思うんですね、その一番最初に子供が社会性を学べるのが家庭の中なんで、その家庭の中でのコミュニケーションが消えてしまったら子供の、こぅ情緒が発達っていうのはありえないと思うんですね。その子供が、じゃ、親とどういうところでコミュニケーションがとれるのかといったら、やっぱり食事っていうのはその中心になっている気がするんで、ええ、その中で子供の成長段階で子供がコンビニエンスストアに行って買ってきて一人で食べて、ええ、皆

で食事について話さないような状 況っていうのが非常に、こぅ、子供の
情緒面で影 響を与えると私は思いますね。

Segment 3   回転すし   TIME CODE 0:40:39

いらっしゃいませ！

単語と文法ノート

Title

現代   the present day; modern times; today

Segment 1

The more formal speech style and content of Segment 1 reflect the speaker's role as a professional teacher of cooking. She speaks to you, the audience, as much as to the interviewer. In addition to teaching how to prepare meals from various cultures, the speaker gives lectures on food culture, food issues, etiquette, and presentation. Lessons are held in a one-room outbuilding, consisting of a kitchen with a large central table. The cooking class has become an important social network for a group of women, ranging from their mid-twenties to mid-sixties, who live within a two-hour drive of the speaker's home. Some members have been attending for twenty years.

料理教室   cooking classroom, cooking school

Segment 1.1

忙しい現代   nowadays when everyone is so busy

Verb (plain form)ような気がする   to feel; it seems like/as though (preceding

                   clause)

塾   cram school

とか   and the like

それから	(You may hear this as そいから、because the speaker's れ is very soft.)
追い立てる	to hustle someone along, hurry someone up; to drive away
追い立てられるように	as if being hustled/driven (from place to place) The speaker intended to use this form of the verb.
ように	as if, like
増える	to increase
主婦	housewife
家庭	home, family, household
パートタイマー	part-time worker
選ぶ	to select
残業	overtime work
遅い	late
家族	family
珍しい	unusual, strange
現象	a phenomenon

Segment 1.2

同じ釜の飯を食べる	literally, to eat from the same pot (meaning, to live like a family)
とともに	together with, along with

仕方
しかた
                          manner, way

〜に合わせる
     あ
                    adjust to, synchronize with

当然
とうぜん
                         naturally, as a matter of course

ややもすれば…する   to be apt/prone to do …

寝る
ね
                            to sleep

ご飯
  はん
                          meal

Verb (1st base)なくなる it has reached the point where the action no longer takes

                          place

総菜
そうざい
                         an everyday (household) dish

ばらばらに   separately

無理して…する   to do against one's will
む り

（しようという）気にならない   do not feel like (voluntarily doing)
                    き

偏食
へんしょく
                          an unbalanced diet

Verb (2nd base)うる　得る（うる、える）is a potential suffix: 起こりうる

                          can arise

Segment 1.3

寂しい
さび
                          lonely

生じる
しょう
                          arise, result (from)

個食
こしょく
                          eating alone

文化
ぶんか
                          culture

伝統	tradition
受け継ぐ	to inherit
断ち切れる	to become cut off, severed
調理方法	way of cooking/preparing
手伝い	help, assistance
切れた状態	a state of being cut off/severed/disconnected
伝わっていく	to continue to go down to (the next generation)
	(伝えられていく、to continue to be conveyed/transmitted)

Segment 1.4

期待する	to expect, count on, hope for
決して…ない	definitely not, not at all
含めて	including
向かい合う	to face each other
お腹が空く	one's stomach becomes empty (to become hungry)
空腹	hunger (an empty stomach); 〜を満たす to fill one's stomach
むさぼり食べる	（むさぼり食う）to eat without any manners, 無作法に食べる

状態
じょうたい

condition

繰り返す
く　かえ

to repeat

時に
とき

時々
ときどき

顔を合わせる
かお　あ

to get together

重要な
じゅうよう

important

食卓
しょくたく

dining table

基本
きほん

basis, foundation

家庭料理
かていりょうり

home cooking

風景
ふうけい

scene

崩壊
ほうかい

collapse, breakdown, disruption

断絶
だんぜつ

end, breaking off, breakdown

関わり合う
かか　　あ

to be involved with, have something to do with

Segment 1.5

思想家
しそうか

a philosopher, a (social) thinker

ブリア＝サヴァラン   Jean Anthelme Brillat-Savarin (1755-1826), French

gourmet, lawyer, and politician. Author of *Physiologie*

du Goût (The physiology of taste), in which he said, "Tell

me what you eat, and I will tell you what you are."

当ててみる
あ

to try to guess at

言葉
ことば

words

形成する	to shape, form
心を育てる	to cultivate one's heart/spirit
象徴する	to symbolize; される is the passive form

Segment 2

This conversation is being filmed at the Lake Biwa Museum. In the background we hear announcements, explanations, and sound effects related to the exhibits. Here you have the opportunity to learn to focus on one person's speech against background noise. How many conversations take place in a near silent environment?

専攻する	to major/specialize in
食文化	food culture

Segment 2.1

ご飯	cooked rice
味噌汁	*miso* soup
漬物	pickles
魚	fish
野菜	vegetables
伝統的な	traditional
最近は	in recent days
欧米化	Westernization
批判をされる	to be criticized (Cf. 批判する、批判をする to criticize)

批判されているところがある　(traditional food culture) is in part criticized

for . . . ;　there are elements that are criticized

食物　foods

ガン　cancer

余計　all the more

引き起こす　to cause, bring about

心臓病　heart disease

原因　cause

単純に　simply

食べていれば　conditional form of 食べている

If one habitually eats . . .

健康　health

おにぎり　a rice ball

・・・ですら　even　（さえ）

添加物　an additive

うどん　(wheat) noodles

簡単な　simple

人工保存料　artificial preservatives

人工甘味料　artificial sweeteners

人工香料　artificial flavoring

食品添加物　food additives

欧米型　　　　　　　　　　Western type

手軽な　　　　　　　　　　simple, easy, cheap

求める　　　　　　　　　　to seek

どういった　　　　　　　　どのような

原点　　　　　　　　　　　starting point

に返って見てみる　　　　　to try to go back (to the original point) and look at (what

　　　　　　　　　　　　　sort of food we were eating)

Segment 2.2

影響を与える　　　　　　　to influence

犯罪　　　　　　　　　　　a crime

教育　　　　　　　　　　　education

社会性　　　　　　　　　　sociability; social nature

学ぶ　　　　　　　　　　　to learn; 学べる　potential form

消える　　　　　　　　　　to vanish　消えてしまう ＋ たら (if)

情緒　　　　　　　　　　　emotions, feelings; also pronounced じょうしょ

発達する　　　　　　　　　to develop, grow

ありえない　　　　　　　　not be possible （Verb 2nd base ＋ える）

気がする　　　　　　　　　to have the feeling that

成長段階　　　　　　　　　(at their) stage of growth

しょくじ
食事に着く   to sit down/be seated for a meal

じょうきょう
状 況   state of affairs

めん
面   aspect, side (from the perspective of, in terms of)

Segment 3

かいてん
回転すし   （回転ずし）"rotary sushi"— part of the low-cost, fast-food

movement, *kaiten-zushi* gained wide popularity in the late

1990s. Plates of sushi (and at times desserts) are placed on

a conveyor belt that rotates around a counter. Customers

select what they want, and the final price is tallied

according to the number and color of the plates selected.

The quality varies widely. At the best restaurants, a chef

will prepare the sushi, while at the worst, frozen sushi may

be ordered from abroad (Bestor, 161-163).

話し合いましょう

１）「個食」にはどのような問題がありますか。また「個食」の傾向は、

自分の国でも注目されていますか。

けいこう
傾向   tendency; trend; inclination

ちゅうもく
注目される   to attract attention, be widely noticed

２）自分たちは子供の時、普段から家族揃って夕食を食べていましたか。また、自分の家族の食文化は、自分の人格形成にどのような影響を及ぼしたでしょうか。

普段	usually, ordinarily
家族揃って	the whole family (all members present)
人格形成	character formation

３）自分の食習慣は、自分自身の性格やライフスタイルをどのように反映していますか。また、その食生活が健康状態に与える影響について、自分自身はどのように評価していますか。

食習慣	eating habits
反映する	to reflect
健康状態	state of health
評価する	to evaluate

４）一般的に言って、個々人が何を食べるかによって、家族、社会、自然環境のあり方はどのように変化すると言えるでしょうか。

個々人	an individual

5）第3課の話し手は、家の構造が家族のコミュニケーションのあり方に影響を与えるという話題にふれていました。これを食事、あるいは食卓という問題と結び付けて考えた時、それらは家族のコミュニケーションに対してどのように関わってくると言えるでしょうか。

構造	structure
にふれる	to mention
結びつける	to link
に/に対して関わる	to affect, concern, be involved in

第7課　三人の女性が語る結婚観

Young Women on Marriage

Does marriage still have a place in a young person's dreams? What are the reasons for the rising age of newlyweds? How do young people regard their parents' marriage, and, if they hope to marry themselves, what do they look for in marriage and in a spouse? We address these questions to Endō Rie, Imai Haruka, and Hashimoto Midori, whom we met in Lesson 1. All three are in their late twenties to early thirties. They are college educated, employed full-time, and living at home with their parents. To set their conversation in a broader context, we provide a summary of related statistics and media reports, as well as commentary by two older participants in our DVD.

At the beginning of the twenty-first century single households made up approximately one quarter of all households in Japan, reflecting a variety of lifestyle choices, including a desire to live alone, acceptance of one's homosexuality, living together outside of marriage, and single motherhood (Sugimoto 177). The marriage rate has held steady since 1993, but age at marriage has risen. According to the Bureau of Statistics, in 2004 the average age at which men and women first married rose to 29.6 and 27.8, respectively.

Japan's long economic stagnation contributes to the rising marriage age. In 2004, of the Japanese living at the poverty level, 16.6 percent were young adults from eighteen to twenty-five years of age (Tachibanaki, 49). While we might expect marriage prospects to be low for the unemployed or for those who move from one temporary job to another, even men with full-time jobs find themselves in a difficult position. Corporate culture makes it almost impossible for men to spend time at home. They are pressured to work overtime without pay, and they are discouraged from taking their full vacation time, let alone childcare leave. Men are concerned about holding onto a job as corporate structure changes in an insecure economic climate.

Many Japanese women may choose to remain single or marry later in order to pursue higher education, to establish a career, or to enjoy economic and social freedom.

These are opportunities a woman may not wish to forego in order to assume full responsibility for house and children, to live with a man who is a slave to his workplace, and perhaps to care for her husband's elderly parents as well. If a woman has children she is unlikely to be able to continue working because of inadequate childcare. After the children are older she is likely to find only part-time or non-permanent jobs without benefits.

In the past raising a family was a major reason for marriage. Matsuda Motoko, our second speaker in the following lesson, elaborates on reasons why couples today have fewer or no children. "There are many complex issues underlying the decline of the birthrate, but the one most frequently mentioned is the fact that there is insufficient social support for working parents with children. Related to this is the fact that regional communities have weakened, and we have lost that natural atmosphere in which it was not only the parents, but the community, and society in general, who raised children. In the past, for example, if an adult saw a child doing something bad, she would scold him, so the burden did not fall on the parents alone. Today most parents assume the total burden of childcare, and some say, 'One is quite enough,' while others choose to have no children at all, because child rearing seems overwhelming.

"It could also be that selfish people, those concerned only about themselves, are increasing. There is a tendency to live by 'calculating the balance of profits and losses'
そんとくかんじょう
損 得 勘 定. Of course, this is not a movement in only one direction. There are many women who would love to have a child. Now past their child-bearing years, they regret that they did not have the opportunity to marry or raise a family. They had many dreams and were overwhelmed with work responsibilities. The more responsible they were to the workplace, the more likely they were to let those child-bearing years pass by.

"There are also women who decide to have children outside of marriage. Japanese society does not give sufficient support to these children. But some women of independent economic means have the self-confidence to bear children and raise them as single parents. Society does not think quite so badly of such women and their children as it once did."

The young women who speak in this lesson cite the difficulty of meeting a potential spouse as a problem in delaying or preventing marriage. Matsuda mentions an increasingly popular solution: "There are a number of companies offering go-between services, with programs for both the young and the middle-aged. Recently a male colleague of mine got married after going through a number of *miai* with one of these companies. Some of the old customs have been retained in new, interesting ways."

Katō Masako (Lessons 2, 6) reflects upon her generation: "Several decades ago it was common for people to find partners at work. When the Japanese economy was still strong, prior to the burst of the growth 'bubble' around 1990, companies would hold overnight retreats at a hot spring, or hold a picnic, at which employees from different sections could get together to learn more about the work of their colleagues in a relaxing setting, or simply meet other employees and enjoy free time. Companies might also sponsor 'circles' or clubs for the pursuit of an art form or sport. When budgets became tighter, these activities were reduced, making it more difficult for employees to socialize or meet prospective spouses. Longer working hours cut into leisure time."

Against the backdrop of these social realities we hear the hopes, ideals, and concerns of three young women.

Segment 1   TIME CODE 0:42:51

Q 現在、日本では、女性が結婚する年齢が上がっている、あるいは結婚を望まない女性が増えていると聞きましたが、その理由は何だと思いますか。

（遠藤さん）　ええと、今は女性も結婚したら仕事を辞めるっていう考えから、まぁ、仕事を続けながら家族をもっていくっていうふうな考えに変わってきた人も多くなってきたからじゃないかと思います。

（今井さん）　そうですね。ぁのぅ、男女が出会う、その出会いの場が少ないからだと思います。昔は、ぁのぅ、恋愛をする、男女が、ぁのぅ、職場や、ぁのぅ、サークルなどで出会う機会が多かったと思うんですけれども、それでなくても、ぁのぅ、近所の小父さんや小母さんが男女を結びつけるキューピッドの役割をしてくれたかと思いますが、現在ではそういうことは少なくなってきていると思います。

（橋本さん）　私も同じようなことなんですけど、やはり出会いがないということが問題ではないかと思います。で、日本ではパーティーとかそういったことがありませんので、もう男女の出会いというのは、こぅ、そういったところにあるのではないかなと思うんですけど、日本では、こぅ、大学とかのパーティーみたいなのがないので出会いがないのではないかと思います。

Segment 2   TIME CODE 0:44:23

[Q] ご両親はどんなご縁で結婚なさったのですか。

（遠藤さん）　ええと、お互いの友達を通して知り合ったんですけれども、ま、あの、今の時代とは違って、お見合いに近い形で知り合ったのではないかと思います。

（今井さん）　両親はいわゆる見合いという、ぁのぅ、出会いで結婚しました。と、母が通っていた稽古事の先生と、ええと、父親の方の母親、私にとっては祖母ですけれども、祖母が知り合いでそこの出会いがありました。母親の父親が、私にとって祖父ですけれども、ぁのぅ、そのおじいさんが古い考え方の人で、あまり母を外に出してくれなかったので、自然と（男）、ぁのぅ、男の人と出会う機会が少なかったので、父と見合いをしたのだと思います。

（橋本さん）　ええと、私の母が喫茶店を経営していまして、そこに、お友達たちが集まるような感じのお店だったんですが、そこで父がお客さんとしてきて、そこで二人でお友達たちと、こぅ、仲良くしているうちに、こぅ、二人の気が合ったのか、結婚をすることになったんだと思います。

Segment 3　　　　　　　　　　　　　　TIME CODE　0:45:45

Q 自分の両親の関係は自分にとって理想的だと思いますか。自分もそのような夫婦になりたいですか。

（遠藤さん）　そうですね。あまり深く考えたことなかったんですけれども、ぁのぅ信頼関係、長い間の信頼関係というのがあるのではないかなと思いますので、そういった部分では、そういう信頼関係をもった関係が

できる夫婦でいたいとは思います。ただ、ぁのぅ感情的な面でお互い、こぅ表現するっていうことが本当に少ないので、そういった面では、自分は変えていきたいなと思っています。

（今井さん）　そうですね。難しい質問ですけれども、今の私の年齢から見れば、二人の関係は理想的ではあまりありません。と、二人で築いてきた年月が、ぁのぅ、二人の考え方を似たものにしたのかもしれませんけれども、育ってきた環境や家族構成がそれぞれ違っていましたので、（お互い）ぁのぅ、父と母でかなり考え方がずれているなっていうふうに感じることがあるんですけれども、私にとっては、価値観や考え方の、ぁのぅ、同じ人が理想なのではないのかと思います。

（橋本さん）　私の場合は、父と母が理想なんですけれども、ええと、まぁ、喧嘩をしたりとか、まぁ、仲のいい時は一緒にいたりとかで、ええと、必ず二人で意見が一緒なので、その点ではすごくいいんではないかと思います。

Segment 4　　　　　　　　　　　　　　TIME CODE　0:47:24

[Q] 結婚生活になにを求めていますか。

（遠藤さん）　今やっぱり、あのぅ、女性も男性も、あのぅ、忙しく働いているっていうのが現状かと思いますので、そういった中でやっぱりお互いが、あのぅ、精神的にリラックスできるような、あの、関係ができる家庭というのを作りたいと思いますので、そういう関係を目指しますね。はい。

（今井さん）　経済的な面よりは、むしろ精神的な安定だと思います。好きな人と一緒に生活をして、二人の子供を育てて、お互いに成長していけるっていうことが一番の私にとっては、結婚に対する理想ですので、それ（が）を今の時点では求めています。

（橋本さん）　私の場合は、そうですね、結婚して、こぅ、何っていうんですか、同じ方向を向くというか、価値観が同じ方で、こぅ、父と母のような、こぅ、喧嘩をしてもすぐ仲直りができるような家庭とかを作れるような結婚をしたいと思います。

Segment 5   TIME CODE 0:48:50

Q どんな男性が理想的ですか。

（遠藤さん）　やはり、まぁ、いろんな問題が出てくると思いますので、そういった中で二人で相談して、あのぅ、一人では考えつかないようないいアイディアを出しながら、あのぅ、決めていけられるような、そういう話し合いができる相手を理想とします。

（今井さん）　価値観が同じで、（いっしょ）同じ方向、一つのものを二人で違う方向からでも見ていけるような人と、こぅ、考え方（や）がその時に違ったとしても、すり合わせていけるような人と家庭を築きたいと思います。

（橋本さん）　そうですね、私も同じなんですけど、やはり、こぅ、いつも暖かい気持ちで一緒にいられるような人がいいです。で、こぅ、いつも、こぅ、何ていうんですか、こぅ、冷静でいられる人が理想です。

単語と文法ノート

Title

結婚観 (けっこんかん) views of marriage

語る (かた) to talk; to tell; to relate; to narrate; to chant; to recite

Segment 1

年齢 (ねんれい) age

望む (のぞ) to desire, aspire to

増える (ふ) to increase

辞める (や) to quit

家族 (かぞく) family

出会う (で あ) to meet

出会い (で あ) an encounter; 〜の場 (ば) a place/situation in which one might meet or become acquainted with someone

恋愛 (れんあい) love. Cf. 恋愛結婚 (れんあいけっこん) a love match/marriage

職場 (しょくば) workplace

サークル a (reading, painting etc.) circle or club; a group activity

機会 (きかい) opportunity

小父さん (お じ) a man (not related to you); often an endearing appellation; children and young people use this term as a direct address or to refer to a man older than they in the neighborhood.

小母さん	a woman (not related to you); a counterpart to 小父さん
結びつける	to bring together
キューピッドの役割	the role of Cupid

Segment 2

両親	both parents
縁	chance, karma, fate; connection
〜を通して	through
知り合う	to become mutually acquainted
見合い	a meeting with a view to marriage; 〜結婚 an arranged marriage
通う	to commute; to attend
稽古事	an art or skill one acquires by taking lessons (such as piano, tea ceremony, *kendō*)
祖母	my grandmother
祖父	my grandfather
自然と	naturally
喫茶店	coffee shop
経営する	to manage
仲良くする	to get along well; to make good friends with

二人の気が合ったのか perhaps because the two found that they were

compatible

Segment 3

関係 relationship

理想的な ideal

夫婦 husband and wife, married couple

深い deep

(Verb た)ことがない not have the experience of (doing the verb)

信頼 trust, reliance

信頼関係 a relationship of mutual trust

そういった部分では in that regard

感情 emotion(s), feeling(s)

面 aspect, side

お互い mutual, reciprocal

表現する to express (Seldom does either express any feeling for the

other.)

変える to change

変えていきたい from 変えていく。The auxiliary verb いく indicates that

an action or state continues from the time of mention into

the future. Cf.（Verb て）くる、below.

な、なあ expresses a wish or hope (after a verb of desire or hope)

難しい   difficult

質問   question

築く   to build; to establish

築いてきた   from 築いてくる. The auxiliary verb くる indicates that

an action continues from the past into the present, or from

elsewhere in the direction of the speaker. It may also

indicate the beginning of a process.

年月   years and months; time

似る   to resemble, be alike

育つ   to grow; to be brought up

育ってきた環境   the environment in which one has been brought up

家族構成   family structure

それぞれ   each; respectively

ずれる   to be out of step (tune)

感じる   to feel

価値観   sense of values

喧嘩する   to quarrel

Verb たり Verb たり （する） to do things like verb (1) and verb (2)

とか・・・とか   conjunctions listing two or more items or actions as

examples of a number of possibilities

必ず   always; invariably; certainly

意見 opinion

一緒 together

その点では in that regard

すごくいいんではないかと思います

> のではないか makes the opinion less direct and hence more polite

Segment 4

結婚生活 married life

求める to wish for, desire; to look for

現状 present situation; status quo

そういった中で within that context, framework

やっぱり as I said/thought; after all; too, likewise; still, all the same

精神的に mentally, emotionally, spiritually

家庭 home

目指す to aim at

経済的な economic

安定 stability

育てる to rear (a child)

成長する to grow; 成長していく → 成長していける

～に対する with regard to, concerning

時点 （じてん）	a point in time
方向 （ほうこう）	direction
向く （む）	to face
仲直り （なかなお）	reconciliation
X と仲直りする （なかなお）	to make it up with/ become reconciled with X

Segment 5

相談する （そうだん）	to consult with, discuss
考え付く （かんが）（つ）	to hit on a plan; to think out; to come up with
決める （き）	to decide, agree on; 決めていく → 決めていける → 決めていけられる。 In conversation one is more likely to hear 決めていける or 決めていくことができる(two potential forms). However, some speakers may use 決めていけられる for additional emphasis.
話し合い （はな）（あ）	negotiation, consultation
相手 （あいて）	partner
すり合わせる （あ）	to rub together, adjust to each other, bring into alignment (The speaker is saying that they will discuss issues that come up, clarify differences of opinion, and then find an approach that both of them can accept.)
暖かい気持ち （あたた）（き）（も）	warm feelings

いる   いられる   potential form of verb

冷静   calm, cool, and collected
れいせい

話し合いましょう

１）自分の両親の関係は理想的なものだと思いますか。
りょうしん　　かんけい　　りそうてき

２）（未婚の方に質問します）結婚したいですか。もしそうだとしたら、
　　　　みこん　かた　しつもん　　　　　　けっこん

結婚生活に何を求めますか。
けっこんせいかつ　なに　もと

　　未婚   single, unmarried
　　みこん

３）自分の結婚感は、自分の出身地の社会的・文化的な価値観に影響され
けっこんかん　　　　　しゅっしんち　しゃかいてき　ぶんかてき　かちかん　えいきょう

ていると思いますか。
おも

４）自分の出身地では、ある人物の社会的な評価が結婚しているかどうか
しゅっしんち　　　　じんぶつ　しゃかいてき　ひょうか

によって影響されるということはありますか。また、それは男性と女性
えいきょう　　　　　　　　　　　　　　　　　　　　　だんせい　じょせい

との間で違いますか。
あいだ

　　出身地   one's hometown (city/village/birthplace)
　　しゅっしんち

　　人物   person
　　じんぶつ

　　評価   evaluation
　　ひょうか

　　影響する   to influence
　　えいきょう

　　　じょせい かた しょくぎょうかん
女性の語る職業観

Women and Work

　　　Kada Yukiko is a professor of environmental sociology and also works as a curator at the Shiga Prefectural Lake Biwa Museum, the location of this interview. She did graduate work at the University of Wisconsin, where she conducted research on economic growth and social change in developing countries, and she earned her Ph.D. from the University of Kyoto. As an undergraduate she began conducting fieldwork in Africa. One of her ongoing projects is a study of the relationship of residents of the Mangochi district in Malawi to Lake Malawi.

　　　Kada devotes most of her time, however, to studying the relationship of lakeside communities to Lake Biwa, in the past and in the present. In 1981 she joined the Lake Biwa Research Institute, where she gathered environmental information covering 3,000 lakeside neighborhood organizations and 120 water systems. Keenly aware of the value of local knowledge and amateur science, Kada helped shape the Lake Biwa Museum into a facility that invites the public to conduct research with the museum staff.

　　　On the DVD Kada tells us about her work, comments on major problems confronting women who aspire to professional careers, and provides specific examples from her own work of ways in which women can offer different perspectives. An advocate of regional and local autonomy, Kada has not been reluctant to share informed opinions with politicians. She says that since she is a woman, she is an outsider from the beginning, so she is less threatening to the establishment than if she were a man.

　　　As this book goes to press, Kada has achieved her greatest victory and now faces her greatest challenges. On July 2, 2006, Kada won the Shiga gubernatorial election on an environmental platform without the support of the major political parties. She is the fifth woman to serve as a prefectural governor in Japan.

　　　Our second speaker, Matsuda Motoko, is a highly respected freelance editor. As an editor she not only reviews text, but determines the format in which the book will be published. Her work includes children's books; books of poetry, art, and photography; and books related to the natural environment. In a coincidental link to Kada Yukiko, in 2006 Matsuda edited a book by Lake Biwa photographer Imamori Mitsuhiko, titled 『お じいちゃんは水のにおいがした』 (Grandpa smelled like water), which follows one year in the life of an elderly subsistence fisherman living on the western shore of Lake Biwa. His lifestyle provides a rare example of the ability to live in balance with nature. These topics are closely related to Matsuda's childhood. Matsuda grew up in a rural area close to both mountains and sea, and in grade school she published a collection of her own stories, 『どんぐりのぼうけん』 (The adventures of an acorn). She recalls something an established writer told her at the time: 見ることは考えることだ To see is to think. "Even one stone," Matsuda says, "can tell an amazing story if you look at it closely. It makes you think of endless questions, and each answer is a discovery, a new chapter."

On the DVD Matsuda tells us about her work and about new paths women have forged in the business world. When I asked if she had encountered discrimination early in her career while working for a large publishing company, Matsuda replied: "Yes, but not so much in terms of salary. It was more related to the job position I was assigned. I accepted this as a challenge and tried to get difficult assignments to prove that I could handle them." Her creativity and ability to turn anything negative into positive energy are keys to her success. Once, to clear her mind, Matsuda spent hours in a field near her house photographing the opening of one flower bud. "After watching each petal slowly unfold, I found myself clapping at the end of the performance. I was smiling again."

Addressing women's eagerness to try out new ideas and roles, Matsuda said: "Certainly if we look at the general trend, women are more energetic and positive, willing and eager to take on new challenges. Perhaps men are more susceptible to outside criticism and evaluation. To some extent the family and society are responsible for implanting in them the gloomy and coercing idea that they must 'become someone' 何者かにならなければならない, forcing them to be more conservative, sometimes to the point of atrophying as individuals. To the extent that women have the leeway to fall into either camp—traditional or progressive—their dreams of trying out something new are more powerful. After all, their status cannot fall any lower, so they have nothing to lose.

"In terms of the job market, because the majority of consumers are women, and because companies want to seize this consumer base, positions needing a woman's sensibilities are increasing. The number of women starting their own business is also on the rise. At present, the economic wave is moving in the direction of promoting women in the workplace."

Media reports on women in the workplace are not so encouraging. Neither the Equal Opportunity Law 男女雇用機会均等法 passed in 1986, nor its 1999 revisions, have the clout to enforce substantial change in hiring, retention, and promotion practices. Japan continues to maintain its unique M-shaped curve for the female labor force. Women work until they are married, drop out of the labor force while they raise a family, and return to work when the children are older. As one commentator notes, working wives today are not necessarily a sign of social change. Today married women are expected to keep house, raise the children, and help support the family financially through part-time work. Depending on one's viewpoint, this could be labeled exploitation, rather than progress (Brasor). If internal change is generated only slowly, perhaps it will be the more dynamic forces of economic globalization that will spur workforce diversity and greater gender equality throughout society. However, as is evident with our two speakers, some women in Japan are not waiting for change; they are driving it.

Segment 1　　　　　　　　　　　　　　TIME CODE　0:50:04

[Q] 嘉田先生は、環境社会学者としてどんなお仕事をなさっていますか。

はい。主に四つございます。一つは研究ですね。で、環境社会学の中でも、特に人と水の関わりを生活環境史という立場からです。で、二つ目は、博物館での企画であるとか、ええ、一種の社会的広報ですね。それから三つ目は大学で今教えております、環境社会学を。それから最近多いのが地域活動です。｛そうですか。｝で、特に日本がここ三十年ほど急速に変化してますから、ちょっと昔の暮らしぶりとか、ちょっと昔の人と環境の関わりということ、今の若い人、子供たち、まったく知らないわけですね。で、それを伝えるために、ぁのぅ、地域で、お年寄りと子供たちと一緒に川を歩いたり、あるいは、ぁのぅ、そこでワークショップをしたりというようなことの地域活動ですね。その四つです。

Segment 2   TIME CODE 0:51:07

Q 今日の日本の職場で、女性が直面する困難な問題は何でしょうか。

ええと、これ、どこと比較するかですけれど、アメリカ、ヨーロッパと比較

するとやはり日本の場合に、専門職につく、あるいは仕事する上で

大変難しいと思います。三点あると思うんですけれども、一つは、ぁのぅ、

家族をもって仕事をすることが大変難しい。どういうことかというと、

結婚するまではいいんですけれども、子供が生まれたときに、子供たちを

育てる社会的サポート、まぁ、保育園であるとか、あるいは保育園に入っ

ていてもいざという時になかなか病気になったらどうするとか、というよ

うな社会的サポートの仕組みがまだ弱いんですね。それが一つです。それ

から二つ目はですね、同じ資格を持っていても、社会の側がやはり女性の

方は能力低いんじゃないのかということをも強く信じていますから、そ

このところの社会的認識がまだまだ弱い。それから三つ目は女性自身の問

題でしょうね。ぁのぅ、なかなかある志を持ち続けることができなくて、

まぁ、妥協するとか、あるいは自分でいわば自己納得のエクスキューズ、

言い訳をしてしまうというようなこともあって、そういうさまざまな要因

が関わってなかなか家族を持ちながら仕事を続ける、それ専門職以外もで

すけれども、が難しい状況ですね。

Segment 3 　　　　　　　　　　　　　TIME CODE　0:52:34

Q　今なさっている仕事について話してくださいますか。

ええと、私は、ええ、フリーで編集者をやってます。で、最初の十一年間は会社に勤めて編集者をやってました。そのあとにフリーランスになって、もうフリーランスになってからの方が長いですね。で、もう２５年もこの仕事をしてますからたくさん作ってきましたけれども、ええ、ジャンルは絵本、それから童話、まぁ、子供たちに向かって作っているケースが多いです。…ええ、それからもう一つは、ぁのぅ、一番新しく作った本で、これは、ぁのぅ、詩人が書いた、ぁのぅ、詩と、それからこの人自身が、詩だけではなくて絵を描いていまして、その絵を合わせた、いわゆる、ぁの、画集のようなものです。…この人はまど・みちおさん、で日本の子供たちだったら誰でも知っている歌を作ってます。ええ、ちょっと歌いましょうか。｛はい。｝

ぞうさん

ぞうさん

おはなが

ながいのね

そうよ

かあさんも

ながいのよ

これは「ぞうさん」という歌^{うた}なんですけど、これは日本の国の子供たちだ^{にほん くに こども}ったら誰でも知っている歌です。…この人は今年９４歳になる人で、私^{だれ し うた ひと ことし さい ひと わたし}はとても尊敬していまして、で、絵もすごいのですけども、ぁのぅ、詩が、^{そんけい え し}世界のいろいろなつながりを、ぁのぅ、謳っている詩がたくさんありまして、^{せかい うた}で、だからこそ今のような時代に作りたいと思って、心を込めて作りま^{いま じだい つく おも こころ こ つく}した。

Segment 4   TIME CODE 0:54:15

Q 今、多くの女性が会社に所属せずに、フリーの仕事を選んでいると聞^{しょぞく えら}きましたが、それはなぜでしょうか。

ぁのぅ、もちろん男性でも、そういう人たちはたくさんいるんですけれども、たしかに、ぁのぅ、女性たちが昔よりも、ぁのぅ、なにかに属するというよ^{むかし ぞく}りは自分で自分の足で歩く独立心が、ぁのぅ、強くなってきたと思います。^{じぶん じぶん あし ある どくりっしん つよ}で、フリーランスでやるだけではなくて、自分が会社を興すとか、企業を^{かいしゃ おこ きぎょう}

興すとか、そういう女性たちもとても増えてますね。で、それは、ぁのぅ、理由はいくつもあると思いますけれども、ぁのぅ、以前よりは、女性たちの仕事が女性だからと言って差別されることが昔よりは減った、まだ少しありますけれども、昔よりは減ったこと。あともう一つは、むしろ女性たちは、昔は働かないで、家の中で、ぁのぅ、お料理を作ったり、そういうことをするのが当たり前だと思われていただけに、逆に女性たちは自由なんですね。で、何をしたっていい。それからもう一つは、ぁのぅ、女性の、ぁのぅ、特徴の一つだと思いますけれども、大きな差ではなくて、少しの差に敏感ですね、女性は。で、少しだけ違うっていうことにとても敏感だから今の時代で、ぁのぅ、大きな違いではなくて少しの差っていうところ（で）が、人に共感を与えることっていうのはとても増えてきてると思うんですね。だから、女性たちが、ぁのぅ、考えるものというのが、世の中に受け入れられやすくなってる。で、結局企業もそういう女性の感性を求めてるところが昔より多くなったと思いますね。

Segment 5　　　We return to our first speaker.　　　　　TIME CODE　0:56:01

Q　専門職につく女性にどのようなアドバイスをしたいと思いますか。

そうですね、ぁのぅ、私は男性と女性とかなり本質的に違う場面と同じ場面があると思うんですけれども、例えば、私自身が研究をしてきた、ある

いは琵琶湖博物館の提案をしてっていうところで何か発想が違うんですね。

さまざまな研究のパースペクティヴであるとか、あるいはいろいろ運営

をする上でも、例えば琵琶湖博物館などでも、ぁの、女性というか私自身

が特に子供を育ててきた経験から子育てのお母さんは何に興味を持つだろ

うとか、子供たちはどういうふうにここで過ごすだろうという、いわば

来館者の立場とか、社会の立場というのをいつも（頭に来る）、こぅ思い

浮かぶわけすね。でそのことを、ですね、遠慮せずにどんどん公的なとこ

ろで主張していく、それも強く主張するのではなくて、確実にデータを

持って冷静に主張することが大事だと思います。…例えば、具体的な話、

この琵琶湖博物館を作る時に、女性のトイレの数の問題、私女性の方がト

イレの数たくさん必要だと主張したんです。その時に、まぁ、女性がトイ

レするのに何分かかるか計ったんです。一分三十秒でした。男性は三十

秒です。一対三ですね、同じ人数だったとしても。そういうふうにデータ

をもとに、だから女性のトイレがたくさん必要ですよということを冷静に

公式な社会で提案をしていくというようなことが大事ではないでしょうか

ね。{それは大事ですよね。}はい、それぞれの立場から見えることがあ

るわけで、それを遠慮せずに確実に主張していく、そうすると社会が少

しずつ変わっていきます。

単語と文法ノート

Title

職業観	views of one's occupation; views on work

Segment 1

環境社会学	environmental sociology
関わり	connection, relationship
生活環境史	environmental history of daily life/livelihoods
博物館	museum
企画	planning; project
一種の	one kind of
社会広報	public relations
地域活動	community activities, regional activities
急速に	rapidly
変化する	change
暮らしぶり	way of living. ぶり is a suffix indicating appearance or way of doing, based on ふり personal appearance; pretense.
伝える	to convey
お年寄り	an elder, an older person

Segment 2

職場	workplace
直面する	to face
困難な	difficult
比較する	to compare
専門職につく	to get/have a professional job
育てる	to bring up, raise
保育園	a nursery school
いざという時に	in an emergency
なかなか（病気になったら）	In this case なかなか means "quite."
	かなりの程度であるさま、ずいぶん、相当に。
仕組み	structure, mechanism; arrangement
弱い	weak
資格	qualification(s)
能力	ability
低い	low
をも	も may replace case particles は、が、を。When following を、も adds special emphasis.
信じる	to believe
認識	consciousness

なかなか（〜ない）　not easily, not readily; 簡単には、すぐには + negative.

志　　　　　　　　ambition, aspiration, resolve

妥協する　　　　　to compromise

言わば　　　　　　so to speak; as it were

自己納得のエクスキューズ self-convincing excuse

言い訳する　　　　to make an excuse; to make up a pretext

要因　　　　　　　a primary factor; a main cause

関わる　　　　　　to be involved in, have a hand in; to affect, concern

Segment 3　　*Zōsan* lyrics courtesy of Mado Michio and Shinchōsha.

まど・みちお　『まど・みちお画集、とおいところ』新潮社、2003.

編集者　　　　　　editor

勤める　　　　　　to be employed

ジャンル　　　　　genre

絵本　　　　　　　picture books

童話　　　　　　　children's tales, stories

詩人　　　　　　　poet

描く　　　　　　　draw, paint; えがく paint, draw, sketch

合わせる　　　　　to match up with, join together

画集　　　　　　　book of paintings/drawings

まど・みちお　本名 (actual name)、石田道夫. 1909 年生まれ.

尊敬する	to respect
つながり	connections
心を込めて	with all one's heart; wholeheartedly

Segment 4

所属する	to belong to
せずに	しないで
属する	to belong to; to be affiliated with
独立心	spirit of independence
会社を興す	to set up a company
企業	a business enterprise; a company
増える	to increase
差別	discrimination
減る	to decrease
逆に	conversely
特色	distinctive feature; distinguishing characteristic/quality
差	a difference
敏感	sensitivity; sensibility
共感を与える	to express/show sympathy

受^うけ入^いれる	to receive; 受け入れられる potential form + suffix やすい 、 easy to do the verb: 受け入れられやすい
感性^{かんせい}	sensitivity; sensibility
求^{もと}める	to look for

Segment 5

提案^{ていあん}	a proposal; a suggestion
発想^{はっそう}	a way of thinking; an approach
運営^{うんえい}	management; operation; administration
経験^{けいけん}	experience
子育^{こそだ}て	child rearing
興味^{きょうみ}	interest
過^すごす	to spend (time)
来観者^{らいかんしゃ}	a visitor
思^{おも}い浮^うかぶ	to come to mind. Before she used this phrase, the speaker said 頭^{あたま}に来^くる、 which I have placed in parentheses. 頭に来る may be used synonymously with 思い浮かぶ to mean 思い出す、 to recall, to come to mind. In colloquial Japanese, however, 頭に来る means 怒^{おこ}る、 to be

offended at/by; to get angry.   Perhaps she wanted to avoid

any confusion.

<ruby>遠慮<rt>えんりょ</rt></ruby>せずに　　　　　　　　without reservation

<ruby>公的<rt>こうてき</rt></ruby>な　　　　　　　　　　public; official

<ruby>主張<rt>しゅちょう</rt></ruby>する　　　　　　　　　to assert; to make a case (that/for)

<ruby>確実<rt>かくじつ</rt></ruby>に　　　　　　　　　　with certainty

<ruby>冷静<rt>れいせい</rt></ruby>に　　　　　　　　　　calmly; staying cool; with presence of mind

<ruby>具体的<rt>ぐたいてき</rt></ruby>な　　　　　　　　　a concrete, an actual (story, case, example, etc.)

<ruby>計<rt>はか</rt></ruby>る　　　　　　　　　　　to measure

<ruby>秒<rt>びょう</rt></ruby>　　　　　　　　　　　　second

<ruby>公式<rt>こうしき</rt></ruby>な　　　　　　　　　　formal, official

(That is, a professional woman should express her opinion

in a public place or context in a calm, cool way with

supporting data.)

話し合いましょう

１）Segment 4 の話し手である<ruby>編集者<rt>へんしゅうしゃ</rt></ruby>は、<ruby>女性<rt>じょせい</rt></ruby>は「<ruby>少<rt>すこ</rt></ruby>しの<ruby>差<rt>さ</rt></ruby>に<ruby>敏感<rt>びんかん</rt></ruby>」で、その「<ruby>少<rt>すこ</rt></ruby>しの<ruby>差<rt>さ</rt></ruby>というところが<ruby>人<rt>ひと</rt></ruby>に<ruby>共感<rt>きょうかん</rt></ruby>をあたえる」と<ruby>言<rt>い</rt></ruby>っています。これに対して Segment 5 の話し手である<ruby>社会学者<rt>しゃかいがくしゃ</rt></ruby>は<ruby>自<rt>みずか</rt></ruby>らの<ruby>経験<rt>けいけん</rt></ruby>に<ruby>基<rt>もと</rt></ruby>づいた<ruby>事例<rt>じれい</rt></ruby>をあげていますが、それは何でしょうか。

自_{みずか}らの　　　　　　　　one's own; (one's) personal

事_{じれい}例　　　　　　　　　an example

2）自分の国では、専門職_{せんもんしょく}に就_つく女性_{じょせい}はどのような困難_{こんなん}に直面_{ちょくめん}していますか。その具体例_{ぐたいれい}をあげて説明_{せつめい}してください。

困難_{こんなん}　　　　　　　difficulties, troubles

3）（男子学生を含_{ふく}めて）自分、あるいは、自分自身の両親_{りょうしん}は、どんな仕事をしていますか。クラスメイトに話し合ってみましょう。

第9課　　小学校、高校での体験
だい　か　　しょうがっこう　こうこう　　たいけん

School Days

Japan is a highly literate society. In recent years, however, Japanese educators have identified and discussed the growing prevalence of a range of problems that Japan shares with many other developed countries. These include a lowering of academic standards, intolerance of difference, increasing violence in the schools, the growing dropout rate, the inability of high school or college graduates to find suitable jobs, and a widening gap between those who can afford to supplement their children's education or send them to private schools and those who must rely on public schools. A discussion of the school system tends to elicit strong feelings. After introducing the three segments on the DVD, we provide a spectrum of commentary from the participants. These remarks are likely to generate much class discussion!

In Segment 1 we observe an apparently ideal school environment—but one which cannot be sustained within the current framework of economic priorities. Sachi Yoshio, a dedicated and creative schoolteacher, recently retired, tells us about a small elementary school at which he taught for his last six years. Rapport among students, between students and teachers, and between faculty and community is excellent. This school is the center of local culture. The community participates in school events and follows the children's activities and progress. Owing to budget constraints, however, the government plans to close the school and bus children to the next largest town.

Sachi relates on the DVD those values he feels most important to nurture in students, and he laments the fact that children today have so little time to play and often no place to play and no one to play with. Off-camera, he offers a few reasons: Because children are sent to various lessons and to cram school, they have little free time. Or, even if they do not go to *juku*, because most of their peers do, there is no one available to play with. Both Sachi and his wife have worked for decades in the public school system. They are proof that some teachers are deeply committed to the children who have filled their lives.

Kusuoka Yasushi, a museum curator with a doctorate in biology, speaks about his difficulties in adjusting to the Japanese school system when his family returned from Canada. Kusuoka lived in Ottawa from ages five to ten. He and his siblings spoke English even at home. Though his parents tried to teach him *kanji*, he was not interested. His most memorable classroom in Ottawa was the wild natural environment. Unlike Kusuoka, Japanese children living in foreign countries generally attend a Japanese school in their area or attend Japanese-language school after regular school or on Saturdays to make it easier to reenter the school system when they return home. Social and academic reintegration can be challenging, and the government has assigned special teachers to some schools to assist the transition of repatriated students.

Taniguchi Yōko, our third speaker, describes club activities 部活^{ぶかつ}, which she believes are the most distinctive feature of Japanese high schools. Off-camera she relates that this was one of the most enjoyable aspects of school. This experience, more than anything else, she says, cultivated a sense of cooperation and team spirit. Not all the participants share her enthusiasm. *Bukatsu* can also be a place where younger students 後輩^{こうはい} are abused by their seniors 先輩^{せんぱい}, says another participant.

Bukatsu are often divided between sports 体育^{たいいく}クラブ、and other activities, ranging from the study of *manga* to sewing and chorus, all grouped as "culture clubs," 文化^{ぶんか}クラブ. Taniguchi belonged to the basketball club. She explains: "At my school, students were not required to participate in a club. It was a personal choice. Those who chose not to participate were designated the 'returning-home club' 帰宅部^{きたくぶ}." Taniguchi participated in a one-year high-school exchange program in Australia, where she was interested to find that students leave school right after class, and all sports and other youth activities take place off campus.

Younger participants in the DVD project and parents with children in school were especially interested in educational issues. The most critical response came from a participant who attended public schools through high school (and wished to remain anonymous): "The principal characteristic of K-12 education in Japan is the system of 'brainless memorization' バカ暗記. You memorize exactly what the teacher writes on the board or exactly what is written in your textbook. In this type of system it is not possible for the student to consider the process that goes into formulating a response and to think about the implied or unexpressed factors that may lead to a certain conclusion.

"Students preparing for exams learn only facts and techniques for remembering these facts. For example, there are endless mnemonic devices, such as ナクヨ 鶯 、 平安京 [Listen to] the warbler sing! —[for the founding of the] Heian capital. (ナク ヨ suggests both 七九四 and 鳴くよ.) Every day I chanted year periods and other historical dates, as if I were chanting the *nembutsu* 念仏 (invoking the name of the Buddha). But I failed to attain enlightenment. I found nothing enjoyable in an educational system in which I was deprived of the pleasure of thinking.

"Based on my experiences in elementary through high school, I perceive the following major problems in the Japanese school system: (1) Because of the emphasis on rote memorization, there is no time or context—including class discussion—for the development of critical thinking; and (2) because a person's excellence is judged within very narrow and unified parameters, students do not learn to recognize and appreciate the diverse abilities and individual qualities of others. This is a root cause of *ijime*, bullying.

"Another issue is the decline of the educational function of the home. Many parents outsource all of their children's education, and yet at the same time they are critical of the school system. News articles are increasing about parental indifference and, in the worst cases, violence toward children. When the parents cannot provide an example of cooperation within the family or with their children's teachers, how are students to acquire models to interact cooperatively at school? Neither parents nor teachers encourage children to think, speak, and behave in an independent way. They do not give children a sense of reality of the world outside. Children retreat into fantasy worlds of *manga* and computer games, losing their will to interact with the real world."

Taniguchi Yōko attended a public elementary school and then went to a private junior high and high school. She notes that one good thing about public schools is that each receives equal funding, and so the facilities are about the same wherever you go. The curriculum is standardized, and teachers rotate to other schools after a number of years. The aim is to give each student an equal opportunity, although the danger is that each is molded for a standard outcome.

Taniguchi attended *juku* before taking the entrance exams for junior high and for college. She mentions some differences between cram school and regular school: "Without attending *juku* I would not have known the information called for on the tests, or even how to take an entrance exam. *Juku* teachers have more freedom than those in regular school, and they have to be very good to keep their jobs. I enjoyed my world history teacher when preparing for college exams. Not only was he an inspiring lecturer, but to capture student attention he came to class dressed in the style of a 1980s rock star.

"I am not against memorizing facts. You have to build a foundation before you can develop your own thoughts or creations. In all Japanese traditional arts you learn the basic forms, and only after you have mastered these are you permitted to display your own creativity. However, rather than memorizing facts just to pass entrance exams, it is necessary to learn how to apply these facts to actual life in society. To achieve this, one thing I would like to see from the elementary level on up is a class on critical thinking in which an issue is introduced and students have the opportunity to discuss and develop an opinion about it."

A participant with a child currently in sixth grade provides another view of *juku*: "All my daughter's friends attend *juku*, and she would feel left out if she did not join them. The teachers in her public school do their best, but they have to teach to the middle or lower levels so that they don't lose some of the less able students. Then they don't have time to teach all of the required materials. Nowadays, *juku* are a regular part of school life for most city children."

A parent with a college-age daughter says: "In response to popular demand for 'education that gives children room to grow' (ゆとり 教 育), in April 2002, the academic program in public schools was simplified and the hours reduced. Then parents became uneasy, and those who could afford to do so sent their children to *juku* or to private schools. Often children are told to attend cram school in order to prepare for such-and-such a school at the next level. The goal is to enter a particular faculty of a particular university, graduation from which will result in a particular type of job. These decisions are generally made by parents. They may think they are doing their best, but they tend to deprive their children of autonomy 自主性 ." The need to cultivate independence and promote the exercise of personal initiative are addressed by our first speaker, Sachi Yoshio.

Segment 1   ある山の中の小学校   TIME CODE 0:57:58

Segment 1.1

Q　この学校の紹介をしていただけますか。

ええ、現在、ええ、子供は全校で十七名います。それから教職員、先生たちは十二名、本当に、こう、小規模な学校です。ええ、周りは山に囲まれていて、そして学校のそばには清滝川という川が流れていて、自然がいっぱいの美しいところにある学校です。

Segment 1.2   TIME CODE 0:58:35

Q　子供たちにどんなことを伝えるのが一番大事だとお思いになりますか。

まあ、日頃思っていることは、もっとも大事なことは、人に対する思いやりの心、友達を大切にする心という、もうこれがもっとも大きなことで

す。次に自分自身の子供たちの問題として、自分で考え、自分で判断し、自分から行動するという、いわゆる自主自立の気持ち、それが次に大事なことだと思ってます。

Segment 1.3   TIME CODE 0:59:16

Q　アメリカでは、子供はテレビやコンピューターゲームの影響で外で遊ばなくなり、想像力も衰えているということが話題になっています。日本の場合はいかがでしょうか。

日本もまったくアメリカと同じような事情があります。ええ、テレビ、それから、ええ、テレビゲーム、そういうことに対してものすごく一日の時間を費やすということで、ええ、想像力、それから創造力、そういうものが失われています。まぁ、とにかく、そのぅ、今子供たちにおかれている現状としては、まず、こぅ、そういう子供たちと接する、友達と接する時間がないということが一つ。その次に、その時間はあるけれども接したい友達がいない、仲間がいない。それからもう一つは、そういう友達と遊んだり生活するような、その空間が少なくなってきている、いわゆる時間の「間」、仲間の「間」、それから空間の「間」、こぅ、三つの「間」が、今、昔と比べて、薄くなった、少なくなったということが子供たちのそ

ういう想像力、あるいは自主性、自立性を、こぅ、失わせている大きな原因だと思います。

Segment 2　音楽の時間　　　　　　　　　　　　TIME CODE　1:00:40

「スマイルアゲン」(We hear only the refrain.)

Smile again smile again　うつむかないで

Smile again smile again　笑ってみせて

Smile again smile again　どんなあなたも　みんな好きだから　(repeat)

Segment 3　　　　　　　　　　　　　　　　　TIME CODE　1:01:53

男子生徒

Q　学校でなにが一番楽しいですか。

　　　友達と遊ぶことです。

Q　で、この学校のよさは何でしょうか。

　　　自然に溢れてること。

Q　どんな遊びが好きですか。

　　　野球です。

女子生徒

Q　学校でなにが一番楽しいですか。

　　　遊ぶことです。

Q　この学校のよさ、いいところ、はなんでしょうか。

　　　フレンドリー班でいろいろな活動をすることです。

Q 何を勉強するのが好きですか。

　　体育と音楽です。

　　「鯉のぼり」　文部省唱歌　　　　　(We hear the last two lines.)

　　甍の波と　雲の波

　　重なる波の　中空を

　　橘かおる　朝風に

　　高く泳ぐや　鯉のぼり

Segment 4　　　　　　　　　　　　　　　　TIME CODE 1:02:57

Q 楠岡さんは、子供のころ、カナダに長期滞在されていますが、帰国後

日本の学校に慣れるのは難しかったですか。

そうですね。あのぅ、私の父と母が、まぁ、あまりこぅうるさい両親じゃ

なかったんで、あのぅ、家の中でも兄弟でも、あの、日本語はほとんど喋

らずに、英語で喋ってたんで、あの、日本の小学校に戻ってきまして、

それでやっぱり国語が、まぁ、非常に苦手でして。で、例えば日本語です

と、あのぅ、数詞って言いまして、あの、数を数える時に、例えば鉛筆です

と一本、二本、で本だったら一冊、二冊っていうのがありますけれど、そ

れが分からなくて、それで、あのぅ、数える時にすべて「個」で数えたんで

すね。だから車が一個、二個とかっていうふうに数えたらば、ぁの、

同級生に笑われたりしまして、そのへんが苦労しました。

{高校に入ってもまだ何か問題がありましたか。}

そうですね。で、僕は基本的に、あまり、まぁ、勉強が好きじゃないとい

うか、なんで、まぁ、ぁのぅ、あまり国語の勉強、今でも苦手でして、それ

でやっぱり高校に入っても漢字があまり、ぁのぅ、よく分からなかったんで、

ぁのぅ、成績も非常に悪くて、それで国語の先生がこの子は間違って高校に

入ってきたんじゃないかとか思ったりして、それで、ぁのぅ、僕の入学試験

の答案を調べたらしいんですけれど、その時には一応、まぁ、１００

点満点中５０点は取っていたと、で、まぁ、ぎりぎりで通ったんですけど、

まぁ、その時、その学年ではやっぱり一番最低線で通ってたみたいです。

Segment 5   TIME CODE 1:04:32

Q 日本の高校生の生活について少しお話しくださいますか。

ええと、私が考える、ぁのぅ、日本の高校生の、まぁ、生活で、こう、特殊なの

は、部活っていうのがあるところだと思います。部活っていうのは、ぁの、

まぁ、別名クラブ活動ともいうんですけれども、バスケットボールとか

陸上部とか、あとブラスバンド部とかいろんな手芸部とか、いろんなクラ

ブがあって、で、授業が全部終わった放課後と、あとは朝練と言って、授業が始まる前に集まって、で、みんなで、あのぅ、部室とか体育館で集まって、あのぅ、何ていうか、まぁ、友達たちと、まぁ、一緒に活動をします。で、それは非常に特殊かなというふうに思います。で、その部活は、まぁ、忍耐力をつけるとか、協調性を培うとかいったような教育的な側面もあるんですけれども、あとは、あのぅ、友達を作るというふうな、仲間を作るという意味で非常に、あのぅ、ま、日本の高校生の生活にとっては、非常に重要な要素だと思います。で、私も、あのぅ、そのころにできた友達とは今でも付き合っています。

単語と文法ノート

Title

体験　　　　　　　(personal) experience

Segment 1.1　In order to appreciate the special attention these children receive, compare the student/teacher ratio at this elementary school with that at the small school in the interviewer's hometown. In her rural Alaskan community there are three teachers for the twenty-six students, in kindergarten through twelfth grade.

現在　　　　　　　at present

全校　　　　　　　the entire school

〜名　　　　　　　a counter for people

教職員 <small>きょうしょくいん</small>	the teaching staff of a school
小規模な <small>しょうきぼ</small>	small scale
周り <small>まわ</small>	surroundings, environs
囲む <small>かこ</small>	to surround;
	X に囲まれる <small>かこ</small> (passive): to be surrounded by X
流れる <small>なが</small>	to flow
自然 <small>しぜん</small>	nature
いっぱい	to be full (of); here: to be bountiful
美しい <small>うつく</small>	beautiful

Segment 1.2

伝える <small>つた</small>	to convey
日頃 <small>ひごろ</small>	always; customarily
もっとも	the most
思いやりの心 <small>おも　　　こころ</small>	thoughtfulness; sense of compassion
大切にする <small>たいせつ</small>	to value, take good care of
自分自身の <small>じぶんじしん</small>	of one's own
判断する <small>はんだん</small>	to make a decision
行動する <small>こうどう</small>	to take a course of action
自主自立 <small>じしゅじりつ</small>	independence and self-reliance

Segment 1.3

影響　　　　　　　　　　influence
(えいきょう)

想像力　　　　　　　　　imagination; imaginative power
(そうぞうりょく)

衰える　　　　　　　　　to become weak, be enfeebled
(おとろ)

話題になる　　　　　　　to become a topic of conversation, be in the news
(わだい)

事情　　　　　　　　　　the situation; the state of things/affairs
(じじょう)

費やす　　　　　　　　　to spend, waste, squander
(つい)

創造力　　　　　　　　　creative power; creativity
(そうぞうりょく)

失う　　　　　　　　　　to lose;　失われる　passive form of the verb: to be lost
(うしな)　　　　　　　　　　　(うしな)

　　　　　　　　　　　　X が 失われている　X are lost (literally, were lost and

　　　　　　　　　　　　remain lost)

子供たちにおかれている現状　　　"the present situation that is placed/imposed

　　　　　　　　　　　　upon children."　Generally one would find the particle の

　　　　　　　　　　　　used here, rather than に。　今子供たちのおかれている

　　　　　　　　　　　　現状 would mean "the present situation in which children

　　　　　　　　　　　　are placed." In this case が is interchangeable with の。

現状　　　　　　　　　　the present (existing) state (situation, circumstances)
(げんじょう)

接する　　　　　　　　　to come in contact with
(せっ)

仲間　　　　　　　　　　companion, mate; group of friends
(なかま)

空間　　　　　　　　　　space
(くうかん)

昔　　　　　　　　　　　the past
(むかし)

比べる   to compare

薄い   thin; weak; little; 薄くなる ＝ 少なくなる

自主性   independence

自立性   self-reliance

失う   X を 失わせる   causative form of the verb:

                        to cause to lose X

Segment 2

音楽   music

うつむく   to hold one's head down

笑う   to smile, to laugh; 笑ってみせる to put on a smile

Segment 3

溢れる   to brim over with, be full of

班   a squad or group. Children in an elementary-school class

                        are divided into groups. Members of each group are

                        expected to look out for each other and are often held

                        responsible for each other in terms of finishing homework

                        or doing a project.

活動   activity (e.g., student activity)

体育   physical education

鯉のぼり   carp streamers (put up to celebrate Children's Day)

文部省 （もんぶしょう）	Ministry of Education; now, Ministry of Education, Culture, Sports, Science and Technology (MEXT), 文部科学省（もんぶかがくしょう）
唱歌 （しょうか）	1) singing. In the old school system this was a subject in elementary schools. In 1941 the subject name changed to 音楽（おんがく）. 2) songs created for school classes between the beginning of the Meiji period and the end of World War II. (See the introduction to Lesson 15.)
甍 （いらか）	ridge tile (tile on the ridge of a tiled roof); roof tiles
波 （なみ）	wave; undulating rows
雲 （くも）	cloud The undulating rows of roof tiles and the undulating clouds are like overlapping waves.
重なる （かさ）	to overlap; to lie on top of each other
中空を （なかぞら）	through midair
橘 （たちばな）	mandarin orange
かおる	to smell sweet, be fragrant
朝風に （あさかぜ）	in the morning breeze
を泳ぐ （およ）	to swim through (midair, carried high in the morning breeze fragrant with the scent of orange blossoms)

Segment 4

<ruby>長期滞在<rt>ちょうきたいざい</rt></ruby>	a long-term stay
<ruby>帰国後<rt>きこくご</rt></ruby>	after returning to one's native country
<ruby>慣れる<rt>な</rt></ruby>	to become accustomed to
うるさい	nagging; annoying; fussy; annoyingly noisy
<ruby>喋る<rt>しゃべ</rt></ruby>	to talk, chat, chatter (less formal than 話す)
<ruby>国語<rt>こくご</rt></ruby>	Japanese language (a class subject)
<ruby>苦手<rt>にがて</rt></ruby>	a weak point
<ruby>数詞<rt>すうし</rt></ruby>	numeral; counter (here, the speaker refers to "counters" for different objects)
<ruby>数<rt>かず</rt></ruby>を<ruby>数える<rt>かぞ</rt></ruby>	counting numbers (of things)
<ruby>同級生<rt>どうきゅうせい</rt></ruby>	classmates
<ruby>笑う<rt>わら</rt></ruby>	to laugh; <ruby>笑<rt>わら</rt></ruby>われる passive: to be laughed at
<ruby>苦労する<rt>くろう</rt></ruby>	to suffer, have trouble
<ruby>成績<rt>せいせき</rt></ruby>	(academic) record; (exam) results; grades
<ruby>答案<rt>とうあん</rt></ruby>	answers (on an exam); <ruby>答案<rt>とうあん</rt></ruby>を<ruby>調<rt>しら</rt></ruby>べる to grade examination papers, but here the speaker says his teacher looked into or investigated his exam results.
<ruby>調べる<rt>しら</rt></ruby>	to investigate; look (inquire) into
<ruby>一応<rt>いちおう</rt></ruby>	roughly; tentatively

１００点満点中５０点とる to get a score of 50 out of a possible 100 points

Also expressed as: １００点満点で５０点をとる

ぎりぎりで通る   to just barely pass

最低線   the lowest line (here, the minimum score)

Verb (2nd base)みたい seems like ... (equivalent to ようです and very common

in colloquial speech)

Segment 5

特殊な   special, particular, unique

部活   クラブ活動   club activities

別名   another name

陸上部   athletic club, field and track club

手芸部   handicraft club

放課後   after school

朝連   club practice sessions that take place before morning

classes begin

忍耐力   perseverance; endurance

協調性   cooperation; spirit of harmony

培う   to cultivate; to foster

側面   side

重要な (じゅうよう)   important

要素 (ようそ)   an (essential) element; an (important) factor

付き合う (つきあう)   to socialize with, hang out with

話し合いましょう

１）左地先生 (さち) によると、今の日本では、子供たちが遊ぶ時間や空間、また仲間 (なかま) が少なくなってきていると言われています。この三つの「間 (かん)」が少なくなっている理由 (りゆう) について考え、クラスメイトと話し合いましょう。（第３課と第６課の話も参照 (さんしょう)。）

　　　　参照する (さんしょう)   to refer to

２）（子供の時に何年か外国滞在 (がいこくたいざい) の経験 (けいけん) があるクラスメイトに質問 (しつもん) します）帰国後 (きこくご)、新しい環境 (かんきょう) のなかで、学校やそれ以外 (いがい) の日常生活 (にちじょうせいかつ) のなかで困った (こま) こと、あるいは慣れる (な) のに大変 (たいへん) だったことはありましたか。

３）日本の高校 (こうこう) での部活 (ぶかつ) の役割 (やくわり) は、自分の高校 (こうこう) でのスポーツおよび音楽 (おんがく) のプログラムとどう違う (ちが) と思い (おも) ますか。部活 (ぶかつ) については、留学生 (りゅうがくせい) たちにも聞いてみましょう。

４）日本の教育制度 (きょういくせいど) と自分の国の教育システムの違い (ちが) について話し合いましょう。

第１０課　三人の大学経験

Three Views of University Life

Although compulsory education in Japan extends only through the ninth grade, over 97 percent of youth complete high school. In April 2004, moreover, 45.3 percent of students proceeded to universities, junior colleges, or technical colleges (MEXT). Our three interviewees, Matsumoto Kentarō, Satō Mayumi, and MORI Sōya (his preferred Romanization), all have graduate degrees.

Matsumoto, who was a graduate student at the time of filming, tells us about his student lifestyle. Next, Satō, who did her undergraduate work in Japan and the United States, received her master's degree in England, and is currently a Ph.D. candidate in ecology in Japan, relates her views of undergraduate education in Japan and the United States. Like Satō, Matsumoto was disappointed with his initial undergraduate experience. He made the somewhat unusual decision to transfer to another school in his junior year, where he was pleased with the quality of the professors and their willingness to communicate with students. He also benefited from a more flexible curriculum and the opportunity to develop an independent major. As in any country, the quality of the faculty may differ from one discipline to another and from one university to another.

Our final speaker, MORI Sōya, talks to us through an interpreter about learning American Sign Language (ASL) while conducting graduate work in economics at the University of Rochester in New York. You may find parallels with your own language-learning experience. MORI can communicate in seven languages. As a child he learned Japanese Sign Language and Japanese. In junior high he began learning English. In college he studied German, followed by ASL. And to assist him with his work, he has added Filipino Sign Language and International Sign Language.

Off-camera, one participant addresses the social value of college: "Most students who are not averse to study and whose parents can afford the tuition and living expenses attend a university or junior college. Parents often say, 'Attending a university is not just for desk study. It's also necessary in order to provide you with the variety of

experiences you need before you can become a full-fledged member of society.' (大学は
机^{きじょう}上の勉強のためにだけ必要^{ひつよう}なのではなく、実際^{じっさい}に「社会人」になる前にいろ

いろな経験^{けいけん}を積^つむために必要なんだ。)   As a result, there are students who spend

most of their time doing part-time jobs or participating in club activities. Those really

interested in a particular field of study go on to graduate school, where the motivation

level is very high."

　　　"This level of freedom in the undergraduate experience is not necessarily a bad

thing," comments MORI. "I established a Japanese Sign Language Club at Waseda

University, and many hearing students attended to learn JSL and become acquainted with

Deaf culture. Some of them helped me in classes by taking notes and interpreting. If

they had been too busy with their own academic life to take part in the club, they would

not have been able to support me. This is another aspect of using one's time to explore

new things and contribute to society while attending college."

Segment 1　　学生^{がくせい}としての生活^{せいかつ}　　　　　　TIME CODE 1:05:41

Q 京都^{きょうと}での学生生活^{がくせいせいかつ}について話^{はな}してくださいますか。

Segment 1.1

ええと、ですね、あのう、僕は今、その京都の郊外に、その、一部屋を借りて住んでいます。あのう、ワンルームマンションというふうに言ったりするんですけれども、あのう、大体、まぁ、ここは僕今住んでいる部屋なんですけれども、まぁ、大体、まぁ、大きさとして一般的には6畳から9畳ぐらいの部屋を、まぁ、値段的には京都だと五万円以下ぐらいで借りて、で生活しています、多くの学生さんたちは。で、まぁ、部屋の中にはですね、一部屋、そのほかに（その台所）キッチンがついていて、で、あのう、トイレと風呂が一つになったユニットバスという形状のその部屋がついています。

Segment 1.2　　　　　　　　　　　　　TIME CODE　1:06:33

Q 学生の目から見た京都についてもう少しお話しください。

あのう、まぁ、京都は夏すごく暑くて、冬寒い。まぁ、盆地なんで。で、まぁ、すごく蒸し暑かったり、夏とかはするんですけれども、あのう、広さとしては、結構、まぁ、狭い盆地なので、まぁ、自転車に乗ってどこでも行けてしまうという、そういう手軽さが、まぁ、僕としては気に入ってます。ええと、（都市）町の中心に出るに大体十分ぐらい自転車でかかるんですけれども、まぁ、歩いて数分のところにもう山があったりということで、まぁ、そ

の山も、自然も、その町の中のいろいろなその都市文化も両方楽しめる、

そういう環境になっています。で、その観光客がその京都にはたくさん、

あのう、まあ、来るんですけれども、まあ、その観光都市、京都のイメージって

いうのは、やっぱり、その、古いお寺がたくさんあったりですとか、その

歴史があったり、まあ、そういう部分を思い浮かべられる方が多いんじゃ

ないかっていうふうに思うんですけれども、あのう、実際中に住んでみると

ですね、学生の人口、大学の数が、まあ、非常に多いということで、結構そ

の若者文化の発信地としての役割を果たしてると思います。

Segment 1.3   TIME CODE 1:07:47

Q 普段はどんな食事をしていますか。

まあ、学生の中でたくさん、あのう、アルバイトをする人もいますし、そう

じゃない人もいると思うんですけれども、まあ、あのう、僕の場合には、

結構、その経済的にも厳しいところがあったりするので、その自分のその

部屋の台所で食事を作ることが多いです。自炊っていうふうにいうんで

すけれども。はい。｛はい。｝で、まあ、作る料理としては、まあ、日本人

だから、その和食ばっかりかというと必ずしもそんなこともなくて、あのう、

まあ、スパゲッティであるとか、まあ、洋食をその中心に食べることは多い

ですね。で、この、（そのアパート）、あのう、ワンルームマンションの下

が、あのぅ、スーパーマーケットになっているので、そこで買い物ができる

ので、すごく便利です、ここは。

Segment 1.4   TIME CODE 1:08:31

Ⓠ 外食の場合は、どんなところが好きですか。

あのぅ、京都には結構安くおいしく食べられる店が多くて、まぁ、僕がよく、

その、回るのはラーメン屋なんですけれども、あのぅ、京都のラーメン屋は、

非常にレベルが高くて、で、あのぅ、ラーメンというといろいろなその種類

があって、例えば九州、あのぅ、九州の方の豚骨ラーメンとか、あるいは、

その北海道ラーメンとか、まあ、色々地域性と相当結びついている部分が

あるんですね。

Segment 1.5   TIME CODE 1:08:58

Ⓠ 日本の大学生はいろんなアルバイトをしていますね。例えば、どんな

アルバイトをしていますか。

それこそいろいろだと思うんですけれども、肉体労働からもっとその知的

なアルバイトまで、例えば、あのぅ、ま、僕が今まで経験したことから言い

ますと、その、まぁ、工場で働いたりとか、あるいは、その警備員みたいな

こともやってましたし、あるいは、そういうことをやっている人も多いで

す、実際に。で、あのう、ある程度、その自分が今まで経験してきた、そのう、

まぁ受験勉強を生かして、高校生、あるいは、中学生、さらには小学生

に、その、勉強を教える家庭教師であるとか、その予備校の、その先生のよ

うなことをしている人も多いです。

Segment 1.6   TIME CODE 1:09:41

Q 家庭教師の場合は、一時間どのぐらいもらえますか。

ちなみにですね、あのう、この京都の町は、あのう、住民に対してその学生の

数が非常に多いということで、あのう、まぁ、家庭教師のアルバイトをしよ

うとしても学生、教える側が余っちゃうんですよね、うん、ということは、

あのう、非常に、まぁ、そのアルバイト代も安くなってしまう。大体、まぁ、

聞いた話で、まぁ、一般的なことは言えないんですけれども、あのう、

東京大学、東京にある東京大学で、その（の）学生で、その家庭教師を

やろうとした人たち、やろうとした人の話なんですけれども、一時間教え

ると五千円もらっていた。ただ、京都だと二千円とか三千円にしかならな

いっていう、｛そうですか。そんな差があるのですか。｝そういう差もあ

るみたいですね。｛はい｝はい。

Segment 2 日本とアメリカの大学の比較

Segment 2.1   TIME CODE 1:10:30

私は最初日本の大学へ行きまして、ぇぇ、それで、ぁのぅ、日本の大学って

いうのは、こぅ入る時に難しくて、出るのは簡単とよく批判されるんです

けれども、それで、まぁ、大学生が大学の中の勉強をしないと、そういっ

た批判から最近の日本の大学では、ぁのぅ、こぅ入学試験といっても、

入学試験を難しくして、こぅ入ってから勉強しないという体制を少しでも

直そうと、入学試験そのものがいけないんじゃないかと言われてきてるよ

うですけれど、今、こぅ大学生が勉強しないっていう状況を改善するの

に、単純に、こぅ入学試験だけを易しくしても、例えば、ぇぇ、今は、こぅ

入学試験も簡単、入るのも簡単、中に入って勉強もしないで、要するに出

るのも簡単と、前よりも、こぅ非常に、前よりも悪くなっている気がする

んで。で、そうですね、私は、こぅ大学に入った時に確かに、まぁ、

入学試験で疲れていて、もう少し遊びたいという気持ちもあるんですけれども、まぁ、同時に大学の勉強っていうものにものすごく期待をしていたんですが、実際に入ってみたら、授業がとても簡単なんでね、ええ、宿題はないし、一年に一回の最後のテストにちょっと勉強すればパスできると、そのような状況では、とてもやる気っていうものが出てこなくなってしまうんで、ええ、先生自体の、こう熱心さってのも感じられない、ええ、その中で、こう勉強しなくてもそのコースを通ってしまえるんだったら、なぜ勉強する必要があるのかっていう、やる気が、こうどんどん失せていくっていう状態でしたんで、ええ、そうですね。

Segment 2.2　（続き）　　　　　　　　　　TIME CODE　1:12:06

アメリカの、今度、大学へ行ってみて、先生がまずものすごく熱心で、アメリカの学生は勉強するってのはもちろんものすごく感じたんですけれども、それ以前に先生がものすごく熱心なんで、勉強しないと付いていけない状態ですよね、先生の方も。日本の場合は、もう、まず先生がやる気がない、でもその先生からの、もしかしたら、意見とすれば学生がやる気がないから自分たちもやる気がなくなると。まぁ、入学試験（が）をどうするかっていう問題もあると思うんですけれども、もうそれだけでは日本の大学の根本的な問題が直らないと思うんで、え、まずは、こう授業の質

を上げて学生が勉強をしなければいけないし、したいと思うようなね、

環境を作っていかなければいけないと思いますね。

Segment 3　　留学生として新しい言語を学ぶ　TIME CODE　1:12:55

Q　森さんはニューヨークのロチェスター大学に留学した時、アメリカ

の手話法を習うのは難しいと思いましたか。

手話というのはきちんとした言語ですよね。本当に自分の言いたいことを

きちんと話す、また議論をするという場合には身振りではできません。そ

してアメリカ手話を勉強してたくさんの聾者に会って、そうですね、二

ヶ月ではまだ無理でしたね。まあまあ相手の言っていることを分かるよう

になるためには六ヶ月以降、やっぱり六ヶ月以上必要で、また自分が言い

たいことを話せるようになるにはさらに一年以上がかかりました。毎日

聾者と接していても簡単に身につくものではないと思います。

単語と文法ノート

Title

経験　　　　　　　　　　an experience

Segment 1.1

郊外　　　　　　　　　　suburbs

借<ruby>り<rt>か</rt></ruby>る   to rent; to borrow

〜たりする   a single たり often denotes generalization; the double たり

                   pattern suggests that one does things like verb 1 and verb 2,

                   or, among a group, that some will do the first verb, while

                   others do the second. This speaker makes frequent use of

                   the single たり pattern as part of his conversational style.

一般的に   generally

〜<ruby>畳<rt>じょう</rt></ruby>   a counter for *tatami* mats; rooms are generally measured in

                   terms of the number of mats they would contain, even if

                   they are carpeted or have flooring. One mat is

                   approximately 3 feet by 6 feet.

<ruby>値段的<rt>ねだんてき</rt></ruby>に   in terms of price

<ruby>以下<rt>い か</rt></ruby>   equal to or less than; not exceeding

<ruby>形状<rt>けいじょう</rt></ruby>   shape; form; configuration

Segment 1.2

<ruby>盆地<rt>ぼん ち</rt></ruby>   a basin

<ruby>蒸<rt>む</rt></ruby>し<ruby>暑<rt>あつ</rt></ruby>い   hot and humid

<ruby>結構<rt>けっこう</rt></ruby>   かなり

<ruby>狭<rt>せま</rt></ruby>い   narrow, small

<ruby>行<rt>い</rt></ruby>ける   potential form of 行く

〜てしまう	The auxiliary verb しまう is often used in conversation for emphasis.　It may also indicate 1) completion of an action; or 2) something done unfortunately or inadvertently.
手軽さ	simplicity
Xが気に入る	X appeals to (the subject)
自然	nature
都市文化	city culture
両方	both
楽しむ	to enjoy; 楽しめる、 potential form
環境	environment
観光客	tourist(s)
観光都市	tourist city
歴史	history
部分	aspect(s); part, portion
思い浮かべる	to call to mind; to recall
人口	population
数	number(s)
非常に	extremely
若者文化	youth culture
発信地	point of take-off

| 役割を果たす | to play a role |

Segment 1.3

普段	usually
場合	case
経済的に	economically
厳しい	severe; harsh
自炊	to do one's own cooking
和食	Japanese cuisine
必ずしも・・・ない	not always, not necessarily
洋食	Western cuisine
中心	the core, the focus; the main part

Segment 1.4

外食	eating out; 〜する to eat out
種類	categories, types
豚骨	Kagoshima-style cooking based on stock made of pork with the bones attached (literally: "pig bone")
地域性	regional characteristics
と/に結びつく	to be linked to, be related to

Segment 1.5

肉体労働 （にくたいろうどう）	manual labor
知的な （ちてき）	intellectual; mental
経験する （けいけん）	to experience
工場 （こうじょう）	factory
警備員 （けいびいん）	a guard
Noun みたい	like (the noun); colloquial equivalent of Noun のようです
実際に （じっさい）	actually
ある程度 （ていど）	to some extent, to a certain extent
受験勉強 （じゅけんべんきょう）	studies for entrance examinations
生かす （い）	to bring to life; to make the best use of
さらに	further
家庭教師 （かていきょうし）	a private tutor; a home tutor
予備校 （よびこう）	大学（だいがく）などの入学試験（にゅうがくしけん）のための教育（きょういく）をする各種学校（かくしゅがっこう）。 (university) exam cram schools. 予備、preparation. 各種学校、a school that falls in the "miscellaneous" category.

Segment 1.6

ちなみに	by the way; in this connection
住民 （じゅうみん）	residents

側（がわ）   side

余（あま）る   to be in excess; to be too many

あまっちゃう   あまってしまう

差（さ）   difference

Verb(3rd base)みたい it seems, appears that. Colloquial equivalent of

Verb (3rd base)ようです。

Segment 2   This is one of several segments filmed in a museum. Again you have the
opportunity to learn how to focus on one voice amidst other sounds.

比較（ひかく）   comparison

Segment 2.1

批判（ひはん）する   to criticize;

批判（ひはん）される passive form: to be criticized

入学試験（にゅうがくしけん） entrance exam

体制（たいせい）   system; organization

直（なお）す   to fix; to reform; to set to rights;

直そうと volitional form

状況（じょうきょう）   state of affairs; circumstances; situation

改善（かいぜん）する   to improve; to make better

単純（たんじゅん）に   simply

要（よう）するに   in short, to sum up

気<ruby>き</ruby>がする	to have the feeling that . . .
確<ruby>たし</ruby>かに	certainly
疲<ruby>つか</ruby>れる	to be tired
同時<ruby>どうじ</ruby>に	at the same time
期待<ruby>きたい</ruby>をする	to hope for; to look forward to; to anticipate
授業<ruby>じゅぎょう</ruby>	a class; instruction
やる気<ruby>き</ruby>	feel like doing; motivation
自体<ruby>じたい</ruby>	itself; themselves
熱心<ruby>ねっしん</ruby>さ	eagerness; enthusiasm; zeal
感<ruby>かん</ruby>じる	to sense, feel
通<ruby>とお</ruby>る	to pass
必要<ruby>ひつよう</ruby>	necessary
失<ruby>う</ruby>せる	to disappear; to vanish

Segment 2.2

以前<ruby>いぜん</ruby>に	before
付<ruby>つ</ruby>いて行<ruby>い</ruby>く	to keep up with, keep pace with
もしかしたら	perhaps; by some chance
意見<ruby>いけん</ruby>	opinion
根本的<ruby>こんぽんてき</ruby>な	basic, fundamental

質   quality

Segment 3

手話   sign language;   〜を使う   to use (talk in) sign language

きちんとした   exact; precise; regular; proper

言語   language

議論する   to discuss, debate

身振り   gestures

聾者   a deaf person, 耳の聞こえない人

無理   impossible

相手   the person one is speaking to

以降   以後   after, from (six months); (the interpreter rephrased

                           this clause, using 以上)

以上   more than, over

接する   to come in contact with, meet

身に付く   知識・学問・技術などが自分のものになる

                           (knowledge, skills) are acquired, learned. (Intransitive)

                           The transitive equivalent is X を身に付ける。

話し合いましょう

1）日本に留学し、現地の学生に自分の国での学生生活を説明するとし
たら、どんな話をしますか。大学のある町、住居、食事、アルバイト、
余暇の使い方などについて話してみましょう。

　　　　余暇　　　　　　　　free time; 自分の自由に使える、あまった時間;
　　　　　　　　　　　　　　ひま

2）日本の留学生から大学の入試制度や授業内容、あるいは師弟関係な
どについて質問し、その結果をクラスメートに発表しましょう。

　　　　入試制度　　　　　　entrance exam system

　　　　授業内容　　　　　　content of lectures/classes

　　　　師弟関係　　　　　　teacher-student relations

3）未知の言語を学んでいく時、相手の言葉を理解することが最初にでき
はじめ、自分の言いたいことを話せるようになるのはやはりもう少し時間
がかかります。子供の頃に母国語を学んだ過程を思い出し、それについて
話し合ってみましょう。

　　　　未知の　　　　　　　unknown

　　　　母国語　　　　　　　one's native language

　　　　過程　　　　　　　　process

第１１課　アニメと漫画について語る

Communicating through Anime and Manga

Japan is the world's largest producer of both *manga* (cartoons and comics) and *anime* (animated films). Japan's media industry has gained worldwide attention and market share through products such as Miyazaki Hayao's multiple-award-winning *anime* *Spirited Away*『千と千尋の神隠し』(2001) and *Princess Mononoke*『もののけ姫』(1997); Pokemon video game software; and the English-language *manga Shōnen Jump*. For many young English speakers, these products are a gateway to Japanese culture. Our first speaker, Matsuda Motoko, a freelance book editor, discusses the medium of animation in the context of the work of Miyazaki Hayao. Our second speaker, Matsumoto Kentarō, a recent Ph.D. with a special interest in media theory, discusses the ways in which *manga* are received and read and the extent to which this genre has permeated contemporary Japanese society.

Manga make up nearly 40 percent of printed matter published in Japan today, and English-language *manga* represent one of the fastest growing categories in American bookstores. Often *anime* originate in *manga*. A classic example is Miyazaki Hayao's *anime Nausicaä of the Valley of Wind*『風の谷のナウシカ』(1984), production of which was made possible by the popularity of his *manga* of the same name, begun two years earlier. Thirteen years in the writing, *Nausicaä* won the Japan *Manga* Artists' Association Award in 1994; it has sold more than ten million copies in Japan alone.

Manga are not a new genre in the Japanese literary tradition. *Manga* may be considered an outgrowth of Edo-period (1600-1868) *ehon*, picture books, in which the blank space around woodblock-print illustrations is filled with text and dialogue (Tanaka). A nation-wide forum for the study of *manga*, 日本マンガ学界 (Japan Society for Studies in Cartoons and Comics) was first convened in 2001, and a number of universities have departments dedicated to *manga* studies. *Manga* are considered not only a form of entertainment, but a form of communication with a unique style that has been able to penetrate a wide spectrum of society. Specific topics in *manga* studies include the influence of this genre on the thought and behavior of young people, the question of whether *manga* depicting violence should be censored, the role of *manga* in academics, its use in advertising, and its use in community promotion projects.

Segments 1~3　　　宮崎駿のアニメについて

Segment 1

Ｑ 宮崎さんの作品はどうして実写ではなくてアニメの形でなければなりませんか。

Segment 1.1　　　　　　　　　　　　TIME CODE 1:13:32

あのう、表現するものをどういうものに載せていくかというのはとても重要な問題だと思うんですね。私も編集者をやっていますから一つの話をどういう大きさの本にし、どういう紙の上に印刷するかっていうことは、そういうテクスチャーを選ぶっていうことは、とても大事なことだと思います。で、宮崎さんの場合は、宮崎さん自身がずっと若いころからアニメーターだったという彼自身の歴史がまず一つありますね。それから、あのう、アニメーションというのは、とても年齢の広い人たちに向かってものを届けるのにとても優れたメディアだと思います。私がやってる絵本

もそうですけれども。で、そういう意味で、ぁのぅ、もう一つは、ありえな
い世界を出現させることができますね。

Segment 1.2　（続き）　　　　　　　　　　TIME CODE　1:14:31

それと、もう一つは日本人の、ぁのぅ、ええ、得意なこと、こう細かいこと
をやるのが日本人はとても得意ですから、ええ、ぁのぅ、実写ですごくお金
をかけて作るよりも、自分たちの手作りで細かいことをやるのは得意なん
ですね。ですからそういう意味で、ぁのぅ、宮崎さんの、ええ、メッセージ、
彼のアニメーションはただ動きが面白いとかそういうことではなくて、そ
の中にメッセージが入っている。だからそのメッセージを伝えたい、その
メッセージは大人だけに伝わったんではだめだ、子供たちから伝わらなけ
ればいけない、そういうメッセージですから。で、しかも大人にも伝わっ
てほしい。で、そういう時に、ぁのぅ、そのアニメーションというメディア
を使い、そして物語という形にそのメッセージを載せて伝えていくこと
はとても的確な選択だったと思いますね、ええ。

Segment 2

Ｑ　宮崎さんのテーマは現代社会におけるさまざまな問題をどう反映して
いると思いますか。

Segment 2.1   TIME CODE 1:15:29

もう、それはそれだけでたくさん喋れるくらいあると思いますけど、ええ、

宮崎さんの作品を見ていると、善と悪で分かれてないんですね。で、それ

は、あのぅ、日本、まぁ、私は日本人ですから、日本にいれば自然に感じて

ることなんですけれども、例えば、神様という考え方、それもあのぅ、まぁ、

キリスト教であればイエスとか、そういう、あのぅ、象徴的な人がいま

すけれども、日本人の場合は、仏教もありますが、もともとそこにある、

あのぅ、木や石ころや、いろいろなものたちにみんな神様がいるっていう

考え方があります。で、それはアニミズム。で、その中には、あのぅ、一

つのものの中にさまざまな、あのぅ、価値観がたくさんあるという、あの、え

え、考え方が、アニミズムっていうのは、あのぅ、アメリカの方に分かって

もらえるかどうか分かりませんが、そういうものがあると思うんですね。

Segment 2.2   （続き）   TIME CODE 1:16:29

で、宮崎さんは今のこの世界の状況を考えた時に、あのぅ、共に生きる

とはいったいどういうことなのか、それをいつもすごく考えている人だ

と思うんですね。で、それは自分と違うものを叩き潰すことではなくて、

お互いの差を見つけて認め合って、そして一緒に生きていくこと、で、差

を認め合うっていうことはとても勇気がいることですね。

Segment 2.3　（続き）   TIME CODE　1:17:03

ですから、『もののけ姫』でも、あのぅ、お互いが違う、違うことを求めて
いる時に戦いが起こりましたね。だから一時期戦いが起こる時もある。
だけれども、最後には、違いを認め合って、そして共にアシタカとものの
け姫は別々に生きていくことを選びますね。で、そういうメッセージ、あ
と『ナウシカ』の話なんかは、一見腐ってしまった海、あのぅ、森、その中
にただ腐っているのではない、それを叩き潰せば世の中がきれいになるわ
けじゃない、その腐っているものが実はものごとを清めている、きれいに
している作用も同時に持っているんだよということを、あのぅ、物語の中
に入れていますね。

Segment 2.4　（続き）   TIME CODE　1:17:52

ですからこう力で押しつぶして押さえつけて、あのぅ、作り上げる世界で
はなくて、力では辿り着けない世界があるんだと、で、それを世界中の
人たちに伝えたいっていう、そこは今の、あのぅ、ような時代になったら
余計にそのメッセージは深いものがあると思いますね。

Segment 3   TIME CODE　1:18:15

Q　女性の主人公が多いのはなぜでしょうか。

それはおそらく宮崎さん自身が男の人ですから、そういう意味で女性に対する憧れもあるんでしょうね（笑）。それはあるでしょうけど、あとは、もう一つは、やはり、まぁ、私自身が女性ですけれども、ぁのぅ、女性が持っている、何ていうんでしょう、力、ぁのぅ、理屈ではなくて、ぁのぅ、こぅ共感していく、理屈でものごとを理解するのではなくて、直感でものごとに共感していく、そういう力というものの象徴として女性を出しているんじゃないかなと思います。

Segments 4~5　　　　　漫画について

Segment 4

Q 漫画はもちろん娯楽という目的で読まれていますが、人気の理由はそのほかにもありますか。

Segment 4.1　　　　　　　　　　　　TIME CODE　1:18:57

ぁのぅ、まぁ、人生のモデルというか、生き方を学ぶための、あるいは、その社会における振る舞い方を学ぶための、そういう、まぁ、モデルが詰まったそういう媒体として、その漫画を読むっていうケースも結構あるんじゃないかなと思います。{そうですか。} はい。ぁのぅ、中では、まぁ、すごく人気があるその漫画家がその、まぁ、非常に若いその世代に影響を持ってい

て、まぁ、一種のそのオピニオン・リーダー的な役割を果たしていること

というのもあったりすると思いますね。

Segment 4.2　　（続き）　　　　　　　　　TIME CODE 1:19:35

ただ、あのう、まぁ、日本の漫画の中にはそのかなり、その過激なその

暴力描写とか性描写を含むものとかも入ってたりするので、（まぁ、そ

の）その漫画のその登場人物の例えば行動パターンであるとか人格とか

を内面化するっていうことは、まぁ、時として非常に大きな問題をはらん

でいるっていうこともあるんじゃないかなというふうには考えています。

Segment 5　　　　　　　　　　　　　　TIME CODE 1:20:02

Q 漫画の受容はどういうふうに変わってきたと思いますか。

あのう、まぁ、以前、漫画を読むっていうことは、まぁ、僕の感覚、僕自身の

感覚としては、けっこう後ろめたい行為だったような気がするんですよね。

あのう、勉強しないで漫画ばっかり読んでいると親に叱られるっていうこ

ともけっこうありましたし、まぁ、どちらかって言ったら、まぁ、その怠慢的

なっていうような目で見られがちな、まぁ、行為であり、まぁ、そういう

行為と結びついたその媒体だったと思うんですけれども、まぁ、今は、もう、

社会のいろんな所でその漫画の地位が上がっているというか、あのう、読ま

れる場自体も相当いろんな所に広がっているような気がします。例えば、

この京都にもですね、漫画喫茶っていう、ええ、漫画を読みながら、ぁのぅ、例えばコーヒーやソフトドリンクを飲める、そういう店っていうのがすごく増えていますし、漫画定食屋みたいなのもけっこうあったりするんですね。それだけではなくてですね、例えばこの京都にもその漫画を研究するためのその専門的な学科を設けた大学っていうのもありますし、{そうですか} あるんです。それとか、ぁのぅ、漫画学会というのもあるんですね。

単語と文法ノート

Segments 1~3   宮崎駿のアニメについて

Segment 1

実写 (じっしゃ)	actual representation (here: use of real scenery and actors in film)

Segment 1.1

表現する (ひょうげん)	to express
載せる (の)	to place (something on something else); to load, carry
重要な (じゅうよう)	important, crucial
編集者 (へんしゅうしゃ)	editor
印刷する (いんさつ)	to print

選ぶ   to select

自信   confidence

届ける   to convey, deliver

優れる   to surpass, be superior; to be excellent

ありえない世界   an impossible world, a world that cannot exist

出現させる   to cause to appear/emerge

Segment 1.2

得意だ   to be skillful at, good at

細かい   detailed

手作り   by hand; ～の handcrafted

伝える   to convey, transmit (transitive)

伝わる   to pass (from author to audience); to go down to (posterity);

                              to be conveyed; to be transmitted (intransitive).

X だけに伝わったんではだめだ   it won't do for it to be conveyed only to X

                              (It's not good enough for the message to be conveyed only

                              to adults.)

伝わらなければならない   it must be conveyed (It must be conveyed first from

                              the level of children.)

伝わってほしい   (he) wants it to be conveyed (to adults as well)

伝えていく   to continue to convey

的確な選択   exactly/precisely the right choice

Segment 2

<ruby>反<rt>はん</rt></ruby><ruby>映<rt>えい</rt></ruby>する	to reflect

Segment 2.1　Cf. Lesson 18, Segment 2.

<ruby>喋<rt>しゃべ</rt></ruby>る	to talk; 喋れる to be able to talk (potential form)
	Note: 喋る is less formal than 話す.
<ruby>善<rt>ぜん</rt></ruby>と<ruby>悪<rt>あく</rt></ruby>	good and evil
<ruby>自<rt>し</rt></ruby><ruby>然<rt>ぜん</rt></ruby>に	naturally, without conscious effort
<ruby>感<rt>かん</rt></ruby>じる	to feel
<ruby>象<rt>しょう</rt></ruby><ruby>徴<rt>ちょう</rt></ruby><ruby>的<rt>てき</rt></ruby>な	symbolic
<ruby>場<rt>ば</rt></ruby><ruby>合<rt>あい</rt></ruby>	case
<ruby>仏<rt>ぶっ</rt></ruby><ruby>教<rt>きょう</rt></ruby>	Buddhism
<ruby>神<rt>かみ</rt></ruby><ruby>様<rt>さま</rt></ruby>	a god, a spirit
アニミズム	animism
<ruby>価<rt>か</rt></ruby><ruby>値<rt>ち</rt></ruby><ruby>観<rt>かん</rt></ruby>	values, sense of values

Segment 2.2　Cf. Lesson 9, Segment 1.2; Lesson 18, Segment 3.

<ruby>状<rt>じょう</rt></ruby><ruby>況<rt>きょう</rt></ruby>	state of affairs; conditions
<ruby>共<rt>とも</rt></ruby>に<ruby>生<rt>い</rt></ruby>きる	to live together (compatibly)
<ruby>叩<rt>たた</rt></ruby>き<ruby>潰<rt>つぶ</rt></ruby>す	to shatter; to smash; to knock to pieces
お<ruby>互<rt>たが</rt></ruby>いの<ruby>差<rt>さ</rt></ruby>	each other's differences

見つける   to find

認め合う   to mutually recognize, acknowledge;

                                   to approve (in the other)

勇気   courage

X がいる   （X が要る） X is necessary;

                                   勇気がいる it takes courage

Segment 2.3

『もののけ姫』   *Princess Mononoke* (Miyazaki Hayao, 1997)

もののけ   もの (1) matters, things; (2) something that bears the form

                                   or substance of a thing or the idea thereof, け （気、怪） .

                                   気   spirit; hint; semblance

                                   怪   something unusual/supernatural and threatening

                                   もののけ the spirit/apparition of some unknown thing that

                                   may haunt or distress (often in the sense of exacting

                                   revenge)

一時期   a period of time

戦いが起こる   a battle/encounter takes place

ナウシカ   『風の谷のナウシカ』、 *Nausicaä of the Valley of Wind*

                                   (Miyazaki Hayao, 1984)

一見   at a glance

腐る   to rot, decay

Verb (3rd base)　わけじゃない it doesn't mean that . . .

ものごと	things, matter, everything
清^{きよ}める	to purify
作用^{さよう}	function
同時^{どうじ}に	at the same time

Segment 2.4

押^おしつぶす	to crush, smash
押^おさえつける	to suppress, bring under control
作^{つく}り上^あげる	to create; to bring to completion
辿^{たど}り着^つく	to arrive at, reach, make one's way to
	辿り着けない　(negative potential)
余計^{よけい}に深^{ふか}い	all the deeper

Segment 3

主人公^{しゅじんこう}	protagonist, lead character
理屈^{りくつ}	reason, logic
共感^{きょうかん}	empathy
理解^{りかい}する	to understand
直感^{ちょっかん}	intuition
象徴^{しょうちょう}	symbol, emblem

Segments 4~5   漫画について

Segment 4

娯楽   amusement, recreation

人気   popularity

Segment 4.1

人生   life

社会における振る舞い方   social behavior, way to conduct oneself in society

詰まる   to be full of, packed with

媒体   a medium; media; vehicle (of)

若い世代   younger generations

影響を持つ   to hold/have an influence

一種の   one kind of

オピニオンリーダー   opinion leader

役割を果たす   to perform a role

Segment 4.2

過激な   radical, extreme, violent

暴力描写   descriptions/depictions of violence

性描写   descriptions/depictions of sex

含む   to include

登場人物 _{とうじょうじんぶつ}

the characters (in a book or play)

行動パターン _{こうどう}

behavioral pattern

人格 _{じんかく}

character; personality

内面化する _{ないめんか}

to internalize

時として _{とき}

時には、たまに at times

はらむ

to be contained within, be pregnant with

Segment 5

受容 _{じゅよう}

acceptance, reception

以前 _{いぜん}

before; once; formerly; on an earlier occasion

感覚 _{かんかく}

feeling, sense

後ろめたい _{うし}

guilty, shady

行為 _{こうい}

behavior

気がする _き

to have the feeling that

叱られる _{しか}

to be scolded (passive)

怠慢的な _{たいまんてき}

怠慢な negligent, idle, lazy

見られがちな _み

見られる to be looked upon; + suffix がち to tend to,

to be prone to (be/do something undesirable)

結びつく _{むす}

to be related to, linked to/with

地位 _{ち い}

position, rank, social standing

読まれる場自体	the places themselves where they are read (自体 itself)
相当	かなり
広がる	to spread out, extend
増える	to increase
定食	a set meal (lunch, dinner); a fixed menu
Noun みたいな	like, resembling
あったりするんですね	there are things like; it's typical to find things like
専門的な	professional
学科	a course of study; a department (in a university)
設ける	to establish, set up
学会	a learned society

話し合いましょう

1）話し手によると、宮崎監督の作品に含まれる「共に生きる」というメッセージは「自分と違うものを叩き潰すことではなくて、お互いの差を見つけて認め合って、そして一緒に生きていくこと」だと説明されています。現在、数々の闘争が地球上で起こっていますが、その解決方法として宮崎さんのメッセージを生かすことはできるでしょうか。また、宮崎監督の「共生」のメッセージにどのような意見を持ちますか。

闘争（とうそう）   conflict; fight

地球上（ちきゅうじょう）   all over the world

解決方法（かいけつほうほう）   means of solving

生かす（い）   to bring to life (by applying it to this situation)

2）自分の一番好きなアニメ、またはアニメ監督（かんとく）について話しましょう。

3）各自（かくじ）の国の漫画（まんが）の読み方（よ・かた）と受容（じゅよう）のされ方は日本人のそれらとは違うでしょうか。もしそうでしたら、どういうふうに違（ちが）いますか。読み方（よ・かた）と受容（じゅよう）のされ方については、日本人の留学生（りゅうがくせい）たちにも聞きましょう。

各自の（かくじ）   your; each, respective

受容する（じゅよう）   to accept, be receptive to; 受容（じゅよう）のされ方（かた）

                                  the way they are accepted or received.

ら   a pluralizing suffix on nouns and demonstrative

                                  pronouns.

                                  日本のそれらとは違（ちが）うでしょうか。Do they

                                  differ from those of Japan? [in the way they are

                                  read and the way they are received].

                                  Other uses of ら：ら may be used as a humbling

                                  suffix, as in わたしら、うちら、おいら　(the

                                  likes of me).

第１２課　　自然環 境をどう見るか

Perceptions of Nature

Katō Sadamichi, a professor of environmental and nature literature, describes a
cultural tendency to value nature close at hand, particularly the nature of *satoyama* 里山
landscapes. *Satoyama* refers to traditional agricultural and subsistence ecosystems that
have evolved and been maintained over centuries through diversified, cyclical
agricultural practices, uniting villages 里, paddies and fields, ponds and streams, and the
wooded hills 山 around them. Though the diverse agricultural landscape of old has
largely fallen to neglect or development projects, *satoyama* is still viewed by many as an
archetypal idyllic landscape ふるさとの自然, the characteristic scenic Japanese
countryside.

　　Careful management of coppice woodland by local people concerned for the
health of their community and living environment has demonstrated the sustainability of
satoyama productivity. Inputs to the *satoyama* system are rain, sunlight, and local labor.
Outputs have for centuries been the basic necessities of Japanese country life—clean
water, rice, fruits and vegetables, meat, wood and other fibers, and fuel. Leaves and
understory plants from woodlands are composted and used to fertilize fields and paddies.
Branches are used directly for fuel or made into charcoal. Trees are harvested at a
desired size and their stumps allowed to sprout, thereby regenerating the forest. The
woodland is managed to maintain an open canopy, allowing in ample sunlight, which, in
turn, maximizes understory diversity. Further, the tended *satoyama* mosaic is rich in
edge habitats, or ecotones, and hence supports a diversity of native wildlife that need
mixed habitats—for example, water and grasslands for dragonflies, or wetlands,
grasslands, and woodlands for birds of prey.

　　The managed *satoyama* landscape prevents flooding and soil erosion by slowing
the passage of rainwater from steep mountains to the sea. Passing through wooded

hillsides, terraced rice paddies, vegetable fields, grasslands, and then lower paddy lands, the tempered runoff nurtures wildlife, provides for human use, replenishes underground reservoirs, and partially evaporates before gently entering local streams and rivers. The relatively intact Japanese countryside stands in marked contrast to the deforested, eroded, ravaged landscapes of countries like Haiti and Honduras, where the devastation and misery of such natural events as storms and earthquakes are multiplied.

However, the future of *satoyama* fell into doubt in the 1960s when fossil fuels abruptly replaced wood and charcoal, and chemical fertilizers replaced compost. At the same time, rural residents began abandoning the rigors of country life for the amenities and opportunities of the expanding cities. Those who remained in rural areas have been less willing or able to tend the woodlands and the more difficult terraced fields that had sustained their ancestors. When *satoyama* woodlands and terraces cease to be managed, their products go unused and natural succession leads to the development of more uniform, dark, closed-canopy forests with reduced biological diversity. Worse yet, as suburban towns develop, hills are leveled and valleys are filled for homes and golf courses. *Satoyama* landscapes today still compose about 20 percent of Japan's land area, but their loss to abandonment, development, and natural succession is a growing concern (Takeuchi 武内 *et al.*).

While *satoyama* forests (today mainly in private ownership) often contain a mosaic of forest types, including mixed forests of oak and pine, most of Japan's national forests are plantations of *sugi* and *hinoki* (both in the cypress family) and *karamatsu* (a pine) (Boufford *et. al.*). Not only do these forests lack diversity, but they, too, have fallen into decline because of high labor costs. Instead of managing its own forests, Japan has turned in recent decades to cheaper forest sources abroad, a practice that many observers characterize as exploitive. The environmental impact on old growth forests in Southeast Asia has been particularly severe (Dauvergne).

Of late there has been interest among both rural and urban residents in restoring and maintaining *satoyama* where possible. In their view, the ecological and environmental services provided are essential to the long-term health of the Japanese landscape and people. Further, they see *satoyama* as central to Japanese culture.

Professor Katō takes his literature students on field trips to *satoyama* locations to appreciate and learn from these resources.

Katō mentions one further example of nature close at hand even in urban areas: the woods belonging to local shrines or temples, *chinju no mori* 鎮守の森. Katō's interest is informed by his research on Minakata Kumagusu 南方熊楠 (1867-1941), naturalist, folklorist, and philosopher. Kumagusu (he is referred to by his given name) fought the Meiji government's plan to amalgamate villages and towns, in the process of which many local shrines would be abolished. Lost too would be the woods that had been protected for centuries, often containing rare species of endemic plants. Kumagusu wrote passionately about the need to preserve both the biological and cultural integrity of these sacred places.

In contrast to landscapes associated with human communities, Japan has wilderness areas of sufficient size to host, for example, a brown bear population, in subarctic Shiretoko, Hokkaidō, and an endemic species of wildcat 山猫 (やまねこ), in subtropical Iriomote in Okinawa. Our second speaker, Odajima Mamoru, is a naturalist, retired nature videographer, and advocate of wilderness protection. He describes the rapid changes that took place in postwar Japan, bringing, simultaneously, severe pollution incidents, such as the mercury poisoning of marine waters by factory effluent, and widespread environmental degradation caused by the poorly planned and needless building of dams, flood control projects, and coastal erosion controls. In the view of many observers, the collusion between the ruling Liberal Democratic Party and the construction industry has destroyed natural systems throughout Japan.

Our final speaker, Kada Yukiko, professor and museum curator, introduces us to a new approach in environmental sociology, 生活環境主義 (せいかつかんきょうしゅぎ) "the principles of one's living environment." This refers to a new kind of environmentalism—one not based on technological fixes or conservation of nature in parks, but built on the principles that allow a human community to live in balance with the local natural environment. Often we find ourselves speaking in the past tense, looking at a time when such a balance existed. We seek out the principles upon which this balance was achieved and see if we

can restore them—perhaps with the help of public policy—in our current living
environment. 生活環境主義 is a doctrine based on the "closeness" of water and other
elements of nature to our daily lives. The speaker works with communities to find ways
to restore this sense of closeness. These principles are locally or regionally based and
may be particular to a profession or group. Kada will provide specific examples in
Lesson 13, Segments 2 and 3.

Segment 1　　　　　　　　　　　　　　　　　TIME CODE　1:21:17

Segment 1.1

Q　日本の伝統的な自然観の典型とはどういうものでしょうか。

日本の自然観は、身近な自然を大事にするっていう自然観、まぁ簡単にい

うとそうだと思います。その身近な自然っていうのは、例えば、里山って

いうのがありますけども、ぁぁすぐ人の住んでいる近くに田んぼがあった

り畑があったり、その畑のすぐそばに森があったり、で、その森にはい

ろんな動物が住んでいるし、その森の木を切って家を建てるのに使ったり、

竹をとってきていろんな道具を作ったりしますね。それから、ぁぁ木の葉

を集めて肥料にしたりしますし、その山から流れてくる川の水を使って田

んぼを作りますけども、その田んぼには、ぁぁ何ですか、いろんな生き物、

ぁのぅ泥鰌とかそういうものが生きているし、川には魚もいるしという、

そういうふうに人間がこの田んぼを作ったり、畑を作ったり、そのぁの

生活のために自然を使うんだけれども、ぅーん何て言いますか、そういう

住んでるところと、他のいろんな木とか生き物とが、こぅ分かれていない

っていうかね、連続してるっていうのが、でそういうのを大事にしようっ

ていうのが日本の身近な自然を大事にする自然観ですね。で、里山のほか

にもう一つ、ぁのぅ鎮守の森って言いますか、ええお寺とか、神社の周りに

必ず森があるんですけれども、それをこぅ何百年間も大事にするっていっ

う、何て言いますかね、昔からの風習と言いますか、そういうのが、

何ですか、典型的な日本の自然の風景ですけども、そういうのが日本の

自然観。

Segment 1.2   TIME CODE 1:23:33

Q 鎮守の森についてもう少しお話くださいますか。

日本の村とか古くからの町ですね、新しい町はそうじゃないかもしれませ

んけれども、その人間の住んでいる村や町に近づいていくと、遠くから見

ても、ええ背の高い木が、その森がね、見えます。それはたいていその

神社かお寺だと思って間違いありません。で、もう百年以上たつと木は

上に成長するのを止めて、こうだんだん丸くなってくるんですね。ですから神社の森とかぁぁお寺の森っていうのは、ぁのぅ上の方が丸まった形の木が立ってるんですね。で、それを鎮守の森っていいまして、それは鎮守の森っていうのは、その村とか町を守ってくれる森なんですね。

Segment 2   TIME CODE 1:24:30

[Q] 日本の自然環境は戦後急に変わりましたが、多くの人たちはその高度成長がもたらした環境問題をどう感じているのでしょうか。

まぁ環境問題っていうのは大きく（言う）分けて二つのことを言っているわけですね。環境破壊というのと、それから環境汚染というのを合わせて環境問題というふうに言ってるわけですね。まぁ自然環境の問題というふうに言ってるわけですね。で、その場合、残念ながら、日本ではその二つ

がですね、同時進行にこのわずか、まぁ第二次世界大戦のあとの五十年、六十年という、まぁその半世紀ぐらいの間にですね、急激に自然は破壊され、同時に自然は汚染されていくという、その二つが同時進行。そして、かつてはそういう問題のヨーロッパ、北ヨーロッパとか、アメリカに比べたら後進国であったのに、今やもう先進国なんですね。まぁ五十年という時間っていうのは人間にとって長いんですね。ですから身の周りが変わっていっても案外気がつかないっていうかね。そのために、日本に住む人たちがその二つの問題の重大さ、深刻さに気づいていないんじゃないか。

Segment 3   TIME CODE 1:25:35

Q 嘉田先生が提案なさった「生活環境主義」という概念を説明していただけますか。

ええと少し難しいかもしれないんですが、環境問題というのは二つの種類があると思ってます。一つはすでに問題が起きたあと、例えば水俣病のような問題が起きた後にその問題分析するという、それを環境問題の社会学と言っているんですけれども、私たちはもう一つ、環境共存の社会学、つまり問題が起きる前に人と自然、人と環境がいかにうまく共に生きていくかという共存の論理を見つけていこうと。で、生活環境主義はその後者の方、つまり人と環境の共存の論理を見つけて

いこうと。それも特に地元で、地域で、生活している人たちの立場、
農業であるとか、漁業であるとか、林業であるとか、あるいは子供た
ちであるとか、そういう生活をしている人たちの立場から、人と環境と
いかに折り合いをつけていくかということを生活環境主義ではやっており
ます。

単語と文法ノート

Title

自然環境   natural environment

Segment 1   Segment 1 of this lesson is closely related to Lesson 5 and to Lesson 2, Segment 3. Lesson 12 serves as a preface for Lesson 13.

Segment 1.1

典型   representative model ; 典型的な   typical

伝統的な   traditional

自然観	view of nature
身近な	close by; close to one; familiar
大事にする	to take good care of
簡単に	simply
例えば	for example
里山	a village and surrounding nature (described by the speaker); the emphasis is often on the surrounding woodlands
田んぼ	wet-rice paddy
畑	vegetable field
動物	animals
切る	to cut
道具	tools, implements
葉	leaf, leaves
肥料	fertilizer
生き物	living things
泥鰌	a loach (a kind of fish)
分かれる	to become separate; 分かれている to be separate
連続して（い）る	to be continuous (here: all of these elements of *satoyama* exist as an interrelated system)

鎮守
ちんじゅ

その地を鎮め守る神。また、その社。
ち　　しず　まも　かみ　　　　　　　　やしろ

地　　　place
ち

鎮め守る　　　to pacify and protect
しず　まも

社　　a (Shintō) shrine
やしろ

鎮守の森
ちんじゅ　もり

the grove of a village shrine (or temple); Cf. 鎮守の社
ちんじゅ　やしろ

a village tutelary shrine

寺
てら

(Buddhist) temple

神社
じんじゃ

(Shintō) shrine

必ず
かなら

always

風習
ふうしゅう

manners and customs; practices

風景
ふうけい

scenery

Segment 1.2

背の高い
せ　たか

tall

以上
いじょう

more than

成長する
せいちょう

to grow

止める
や

to stop, cease

丸い
まる

round; 丸くなる to become round
まる

丸まった
まる

round (rounded)

形
かたち

shape

守る	to protect	

Segment 2   We meet Odajima Mamoru in Lesson 2, Segment 2.

戦後	第二次世界大戦の後　after World War II	
急に	rapidly	
変わる	to change	
高度成長	high level/rate of (economic) growth	
	(especially in the 1960s)	
もたらす	to bring about, produce, cause	
環境破壊	environmental destruction;	破壊する to destroy
環境汚染	environmental pollution;	汚染する to pollute
合わせる	to put together, combine, unite	
残念ながら	unfortunately	
同時進行	to progress simultaneously	
わずかな	just; mere; little; trifling	
半世紀	half a century	
急激に	very rapidly	
比べる	to compare	
後進国	an underdeveloped country	
先進国	an advanced/developed nation/country	
身の周り	one's surroundings/ environment	

<ruby>案外<rt>あんがい</rt></ruby>	contrary to what one would expect; surprisingly
<ruby>気<rt>き</rt></ruby>がつく	to notice, be noticed; 気づく to notice, realize, become aware of
<ruby>重大<rt>じゅうだい</rt></ruby>さ	seriousness, gravity, importance（さ is a nominalizing suffix that may be attached to adjectives, dropping the い、or to adjectival nouns, dropping the final な）
<ruby>深刻<rt>しんこく</rt></ruby>さ	seriousness

Segment 3   Kada Yukiko, introduced in Lesson 8, was elected governor of Shiga Prefecture on July 2, 2006. She ran on an environmental platform, opposing the construction of several dams and an unnecessary *Shinkansen* station.

<ruby>提案<rt>ていあん</rt></ruby>する	to propose; to suggest; to advance (a new theory)
<ruby>生活環境主義<rt>せいかつかんきょうしゅぎ</rt></ruby>	"the principles of one's living environment"
<ruby>概念<rt>がいねん</rt></ruby>	a concept
<ruby>種類<rt>しゅるい</rt></ruby>	type, category
<ruby>起<rt>お</rt></ruby>きる	to happen, take place; to occur, break out
<ruby>水俣病<rt>みなまたびょう</rt></ruby>	Minamata disease. In the world's most severe case of industrial pollution, Minamata disease, or organic mercury poisoning, became widespread along the Shiranui Sea coast of western Kyūshū from the 1950s, when methyl mercury was introduced into the marine food chain in the untreated effluent from a large chemical factory in Minamata, Kumamoto-ken. Methyl mercury destroys the central nervous system.

分析する   to analyze; 問題分析 analysis of a problem

社会学   sociology

環境問題   environmental problems/issues

環境共存   environmental coexistence; Cf. 共存する to coexist;

                      to exist together; to live and let live

うまく   well, skillfully

共に生きる   to live/exist together

論理   logic

見付ける   to find, discover; 見つけていこう

                      (volitional form of suffix いく)

後者   the latter

特に   especially

地元   local

地域   community, region

生活する   to live one's daily life, make a living

立場   a position, a standpoint

農業   agriculture

漁業   fishery

林業   forestry

いかに   how? in what way?

と折り合いを付ける to come to terms with, reach an understanding or

agreement with

話し合いましょう (You may wish to return to these questions after listening to

Lesson 13.)

１）里山の簡単な図。何百年にもわたる里山での生活のなかで、人々は

その農業生態系をどのように守ってきたでしょうか。また、この生態系

によって様々な生き物はどのように守られてきたでしょうか。話し合って

みましょう。

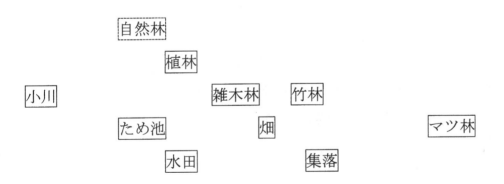

A *satoyama* landscape includes a village and its natural surroundings, from paddy

lowlands up to forested hills. (Some refer to only the forested area as *satoyama*

and designate the general landscape as *satochi* 里地 village lands.) The

configuration of a *satoyama* landscape will vary according to the region. Each

part of the country has its own characteristic trees and shrubs, crops, wildlife, and

domestic animals. The diagram above is but one simplified example. (Those of

you familiar with *anime* will recall that Miyazaki Hayao's *Totoro* takes place in a

satoyama environment.)   See also Lesson 5 and Lesson 13.

しぜんりん
自然林   a natural forest, which may remain toward the wilder, upper region

of the mountain. Conifers are found at higher elevations. Below, in the cool temperate zone, are oak and beech. If mountain forests are protected, they will provide water and nutrients for paddies below. This is believed to be the dwelling place of gods, or *kami*.

しょくりん
植 林   a planted forest—often *sugi* (*Cryptomeria japonica*) and *hinoki*

(*Chamaecyparis obtusa*); the timber is used as a cash crop. As noted in Lesson 4, *hinoki* is also used in many crafts. If the trees are not harvested and thinned, the forest will become crowded and dark and the timber will be worthless. Today it is cheaper to import timber than to manage domestic resources.

ぞうきばやし
雑木林   a mixed woodland—generally used for firewood, charcoal, and

green manure; often consisting of varieties of oak (especially *konara* and *konugi*) or mixed oak and pine. Logs may be used to cultivate *shiitake*. Fallen leaves are added to the compost pile. A natural mixed-slope forest might contain up to 100 species. Sun-loving deciduous species shoot up first and are gradually replaced by the slower-growing shade-tolerant evergreen broadleaf species, creating a dark forest with little understory. The open mixed woodland is maintained by thinning through use.

たけばやし
竹 林   a bamboo forest—used for making poles, construction materials

and farming implements (recall the bamboo grove in Lesson 5). Bamboo is also valued for its edible shoots. If the bamboo growth is not kept under control it will choke all other growth around it. Bamboo shades out the understory, depriving wildlife such as deer and boar of natural food sources.

畑 (はたけ)

vegetable fields. Wild boar raid fields of sweet potatoes, especially if their natural food sources are no longer available. Many other wild animals dwell in adjacent grasslands and thickets, including *tanuki* (raccoon dogs), rabbits, foxes, and birds of prey.

集落 (しゅうらく)

a community (here: engaged in agriculture). Through the 1950s the primary pattern was diversified family farming. Next to a farmhouse might be a chicken coop or pig sty; manure from the chickens and other livestock, as well as from the outhouse, can be used as fertilizer in fields and paddies.

小川 (おがわ)

a stream. This might also be a river, referred to as 里川 (さとがわ)。 Healthy watersheds produce clean, productive streams and rivers.

ため池 (いけ)

an irrigation pond, which may have been used as well to raise fish and edible water plants. Many of these ponds have been maintained for centuries and are important wildlife habitats, particularly for some endangered species such as the giant water bug.

水田 (すいでん)

rice paddy. See the supplementary reading passage in Lesson 5 for the variety of wildlife in organic rice paddies. Near Lake Biwa catfish and carp breed in flooded paddies. Over the centuries several species of tree frog in many locations have become dependent on paddies for their breeding cycle. Today paddies are being enlarged. A faucet is used to introduce water, and there are drainage pipes under the fields. This greatly limits the role of paddies as wildlife habitat. Fish cannot travel from one paddy to another. Certain frogs cannot breed.

マツ<ruby>林<rt>ばやし</rt></ruby>　　　a pine forest. Pine forests grow in the lowlands and are maintained

by heavy use. Fast growing, pines are a favorite for firewood, and

their needles are a good fire-starter. In the soil around them grow

the prized *matsutake* mushroom. In neglected sites in particular,

pines have weakened because of *matsugare*, pine wilt, caused by a

nematode. In Shiga-ken, the *matsutake* has become so hard to find

that one of these tasty mushrooms can fetch up to 10,000 yen.

What are the values in preserving a *satoyama* environment?

２）里山は日本の人々によって管理され、利用される循環農業生態系で

すが、これと同じような仕組みは他の国でも見られますか。その例をあげ

てください。

管理する　　　　　　　to manage, take care of

利用する　　　　　　　to use

循環　　　　　　　　　a cycle

農業生態系　　　　　　agricultural ecosystem

仕組み　　　　　　　　structure, mechanism, arrangement

３）開発の代償として、何か別のものが破壊されることは珍しくありま

せん。政府や企業は、普段から建設と破壊のバランスをどのようにとって

いるでしょうか。話し合ってみましょう。

開発　　　　　　　　　development

代 償   price, compensation

破壊する   to destroy

政府   government

企業   enterprise, corporation

建設   construction

4）生活者の立場から見えてくる「共存の論理」とは、どのようなもの

でしょうか。また、この論理は自分たちが住んでいる地域でも見られます

か。大都市の住民であっても、小村落の住民であっても、ある程度の

環境意識を持ちあわせている人々は、環境と折り合いをつけるためにど

のようなことをしていますか。

小村落   small village

環境意識   environmental consciousness

持ち合わせる   to happen to have

折り合いをつける   to compromise with

Approaches to Environmental Education

The Shiga Prefectural Lake Biwa Museum sits on the shores of one the world's oldest lakes. Lake Biwa ranks among the 250 great lakes on our planet, and today fourteen million people depend on it as the source of their tap water. The lake also serves transportation, commercial-fishing, and recreation needs. Industry and agriculture draw from Lake Biwa, and run-off from developments affects lake water quality. The museum documents the formation and natural history of the lake, as well as the relationship between culture and nature, over the 10,000 or so years humans have inhabited its shores. Many of the exhibits are interactive, and citizens are invited to lead or participate in local research projects and outdoor classrooms. The major goal of the museum is to lead people into the lake environment, "the real museum," that they may understand better their daily connection with the natural world. The lake is not distinct from its human inhabitants; their lives and fate are one. The museum houses research facilities and a large freshwater aquarium, featuring not only the fish of Lake Biwa but those found in major lakes throughout the world. Endangered fish species from Japan are bred in the aquarium's Fish Conservation and Breeding Center.

Two museum curators tell us how the exhibits and activities for which they are responsible lead to a deeper appreciation of and involvement in the lake environment. Our first speaker, Kusuoka Yasushi (Segments 1, 4), introduces museum visitors to lake plankton. He has a strong interest in *satoyama* (introduced in Lesson 12) and he leads a popular outdoor workshop to maintain local *satoyama* sites. This is an ideal activity for families. Participants are able to enjoy certain aspects of the old lifestyle: growing and harvesting sweet potatoes and *soba* (buckwheat); roasting those potatoes, and making noodles from the *soba*; clearing bamboo and making charcoal. They learn the local flora and fauna. As participants come to understand *satoyama*, Kusuoka says, this landscape becomes an entry 入り口 for understanding nature and ecology. However, it would be a mistake, he cautions, to think that by maintaining scenery, we maintain *satoyama*: the cyclic aspect 循環 じゅんかん of resource use is absent. A distinctive feature of the museum is the participation in research projects by local amateur scientists. Kusuoka works with local people to survey the distribution of small shrimp in paddies. Rice paddies provide the ephemeral ponds needed by such shrimp, which, in many other countries have become endangered species.

Next we hear from Kada Yukiko (Segments 2, 3), long-time curator, professor of environmental sociology, and, as of July 2, 2006, governor of Shiga-ken. She too has a great interest in the *satoyama* landscape around Lake Biwa. One of her graduate students, she tells me, is studying *tanada* 棚田 (terraced rice paddy) management. Farmers have provided a number of menus for urban residents who participate in farm life. City folk enjoy learning how to work in the terraced paddies and they buy the final product. It tires local farmers to offer too many services to outsiders, but they are appreciative of outside stimuli and the presence of children in an area abandoned by younger residents. And, while some rural folk welcome newcomers, it is very difficult, explains Kada, to adapt to the long-established social network of a conservative agricultural community. It takes three generations to be considered a local person 三世代過ぎないと地元の人にはなれ さんせだいす じもと ない.

On the DVD Kada discusses exhibits that reflect local lifestyles just before great changes were brought about in the late 1950s and early1960s by the ready availability of electricity, gas, and tap water. Food habits changed. When televisions entered homes and citizens watched American family dramas, they wanted to adopt that lifestyle. Kada's exhibits and activities encourage visitors to think about the impact of their lives on the environment and glean some insight from the social structure of the past, in which conscious and respectful use of natural resources played a greater role in daily life.

Kada's research focuses on the use of water. She explains in her interview the manner in which people used water in different places and at different times to prevent contamination. One way she was able to learn about past practices was to take old photographs, like the ones we see on the DVD, to lakeside villages and to ask older residents to comment on them. Behavior is embedded in environmental context, she explains, but communication about context is difficult to elicit. She found that photographs opened the gate of memory.

A community may think that its way of life is outdated, says Kada. When outsiders emphasize how special certain aspects are, residents may reply, "Oh, but we just take it for granted." This communication makes them rethink the value of local resources. The museum would like to be a coordinator for these inner and outer viewpoints, notes Kada.

Cooperative efforts of the Lake Biwa Museum, Lake Biwa Research Institute, prefectural and local governments, and local citizens' movements have done much to persuade farmers to reduce their use of pesticides, plant managers to control their effluent, and urban residents to think about how they affect their own water supply. As a result, water quality has improved in the lake basin. These groups have also encouraged developers to preserve Lake Biwa's remaining reed beds. Reeds and other aquatic plants purify the water by absorbing nutrients. They provide critical habitat for aquatic insect larvae, spawning fish, and nesting birds. However, the challenge to prevent deterioration of water quality is ongoing.

Segment 1

Segment 1.1　　　　　　　　　　　　　TIME CODE　1:26:38

琵琶湖博物館では、ぁのぅただ展示を見せるだけではなくて、いろいろな

ものをぁのぅお客さんに体験してもらおうということを考えてます。で

すから、例えば、ぁのぅ学校で、まぁ博物館に来られても、体験学習って

いいまして、そういう、まぁ、ぁのぅ例えば、私、専門がプランクトンな

んですけれど、その子供たちと一緒に琵琶湖にプランクトンを取りに行っ

て、それを実験室に持って帰って、顕微鏡で一緒に覗いて名前を調べると

か、そんなことをしてますし、あと、ぁのぅいろんなぁのぅ野外での活動、

例えば、その田んぼですとか、里山に行って、まぁそういう活動をすると

か、そういうこともしてます。

Segment 1.2   TIME CODE 1:27:34

Ｑ　里山と「里山の会」について少しお話し下さいますか。

ええと里山^{さとやま}というのはですね、ぁのぅ昔^{むかし}、まぁ日本^{にほん}の大部分^{だいぶぶん}が、あのう、まぁ、ぁのぅ山^{やま}と、あと、その山^{やま}の麓^{ふもと}にこぅ田^たんぼや畑^{はたけ}があるわけなんですけれど、そのぅ人^{ひと}が住んでいた里^{さと}の周辺^{しゅうへん}の自然^{しぜん}なんです。で、里山の自然っていうのは本来^{ほんらい}ですと、ぁのぅ人^{ひと}が利用^{りよう}してたわけです。例^{たと}えば、ぁのぅ薪^{まき}を取^とるために木^きを切^きるですとか、あと、ぁのぅ木^きを切^きって炭^{すみ}を焼^やく、あと、山菜^{さんさい}を取^とるとか、いろいろ人^{ひと}が利用^{りよう}していたんですけれど、今現在私^{いまげんざいわたし}たちの生活^{せいかつ}の中^{なか}では、ぁのぅ薪^{まき}とか炭^{すみ}ってのは使^{つか}わなくなったわけですね。で、そうしますとその里山^{さとやま}がまぁほとんど利用^{りよう}されなくって、それでどんどん荒^あれ果^はてていってます。で、まぁそれがまぁ日本全国^{にほんぜんこく}で起^おこってるんですけれど、まぁ琵琶湖博物館^{びわこはくぶつかん}では、まぁその里山^{さとやま}を昔^{むかし}の姿^{すがた}に戻^{もど}そうということで、それを再生^{さいせい}するためのプロジェクトを持^もっています。

Segment 1.3　（続き）   TIME CODE 1:28:39

で、あと、里山^{さとやま}の会^{かい}は、例^{たと}えば、その里山^{さとやま}に、ぁのぅそばを植^うえて、それで、ぁのぅそばを育^{そだ}てて、自分^{じぶん}たちで手打^{てう}ちそばを作^{つく}ったりとか、芋^{いも}を植^うえて、それを秋^{あき}にこぅ焼^やき芋^{いも}にして、それで、ぁのぅ里山探検教室^{さとやまたんけんきょうしつ}（の）に参加^{さんか}している子供^{こども}たちと一緒^{いっしょ}に食^たべたりとか、そういうこともしてます。

Segment 2 富江家^{とみえけ}

Segment 2.1 TIME CODE 1:28:58

Ｑ 富江家の展示についてお話しくださいますか。

この富江家というのは、実在の生活をそのまま展示しているんですけれども、昭和３０年代、まあ、１９６０年代ですね、日本は大変大きな変化を、生活様式の変化を、経験いたします。で、それまでは、自然に即した暮らし、例えば川の水も飲めたわけです。琵琶湖の水も直接飲めました、上水道なしで。そういう時代にいかに自分たちの水を汚さない工夫を地元の人たちがしていたかというようなこと、あるいは、目の前の川から魚をとって食べる、あるいは、山からキノコをとって食べる、もちろん、田んぼも、という、その生活様式そのものが大変近い、自然に近い暮らしをしていたんですね。で、そのことを今の子供たちに伝えたい。今の子供たちは水道が入り、下水道も入り、食べ物はスーパーマーケットに行った

らそれもアメリカから、ヨーロッパから、世界中から食べ物が来て、遠い食、水も遠くなってますね、上水道、下水道で、で、その遠い食、遠い暮らしに慣れてしまった子供たちに、近い水、近い食、をそのまま伝えたいというのがこの展示です。

Segment 2.2 （続き）   TIME CODE 1:30:16

ですから、昭和39年、1964年の5月10日午前10時という一断面を実在の家族のそのままの暮らしをリアルに表現をしています。今の子供たちもかなり、「ええ、川でこんなふうに洗い物するの！」とかいうようなことで、体全体で分かってもらえる。それからその時代に私たちが憧れたのがアメリカ的生活様式です。ですから、この富江家の中にはテレビが入ってます。そのテレビにはアメリカのホームドラマを入れました。私自身もそうなんですけど、憧れたんです、アメリカ的生活様式に。そういうふうな一種の時代精神の表現でしょうか。それも展示の中にしたいと思っておりました。

Segment 3   空間と時間の使い分け   TIME CODE 1:31:01

Ｑ　ちょっと昔まで琵琶湖湖畔に住んでいた人たちは、水をどういうふうに使っていたのですか。

Segment 3.1

えeと、例えば、私たちが今見るとほんの５、６メートルの湖辺の、まあ、桟橋という洗い場でも、その５メートルの先の方は飲み水を取るところだから絶対洗い物をしてはいけない。真ん中の方はお茶碗ぐらい洗ってもいい、でもお米をかす、米をとぐというのは、真ん中でしてはいけない。それはもう少し手前の浜の方。というのは、お米をとぐ時のとぎじるは濃度が濃いわけですね、まあ、汚すわけですね、というような形でほんの数メートルでも地元の人たちは一種の生活の合理性の中で使い分けをしていて、また時間も使い分けをしていました。

Segment 3.2　時間の使い分け　　　　　　　TIME CODE　1:31:45

朝早くは飲み水を取る。だから洗い物をしてはいけない。洗濯はお日様が高くなってから、それからおむつのようなもの、まあ、英語で言うダイアパーですね、これは絶対にその台所（の）として使っている洗い場ではしてはいけない、もう少し離れた所、集落から離れた所、船着きであるとか、あるいは田んぼの横であるとか、そういう形でいわば上水、下水の使い分けを地域と、空間、あるいは時間の中でしていた。それは生活の中で水の流れ、生き物の仕組みが見えていたから自分たちで自主管理をしながら工夫をして、それも一人、二人ではなくてとなり近所、

みながそれを守るわけです。みなが守るからそこにお互いの信頼関係ができ

てくるわけですね、約束事ができてくる。

Segment 3.3　昔の暮らしから学べること　　　TIME CODE 1:32:36

で、今の環境問題というのは、私一人ぐらいがやっても、私一人ぐらい

がごみを分別しても、皆が分けなかったら社会はよくならないというよう

なことで、私一人ぐらいということで個人の行動の帰結が自分に戻ってく

るのが見えにくいわけです。最終的には戻ってくるわけですね、

地球環境問題でも。でも、見えにくいわけですね。それが見えた時代は

どうだったか、で、その時代の精神を今に取り戻すとしたら、いかにもの

の仕組み、あるいは人と人とその信頼関係の仕組みを作り出しているかと

いうことは、逆に昔の暮らしから今に学ぶことができるんじゃないのか、

というのが今主に私たちがその博物館、あるいは地域活動でやっている

ことです。

Segment 4　　We return to our first speaker.　　　TIME CODE 1:33:24

Q　琵琶湖の環境問題の中で、何が一番大きい問題となっていますか。

今現在一番大きな問題は、ぁのぅ外来生物の問題でして、それで、ぁのぅ、

北アメリカから、ぁのぅ、オオクチバス、large-mouth bass とそれからブル

ーギルが、ぁのぅ、琵琶湖に入ってきてます。で、ぁのぅ、その外来の魚の

捕食によって、あのぅ、琵琶湖の在来の魚、小さい魚が多かったんですけど、その在来の魚が、あのぅ、急激に減ってきてしまいます。…で、琵琶湖には大体、あのぅ、５０種程度のその固有種と言いまして、世界で琵琶湖にしかいない生物がいるんですけれど、その固有の魚なりなんなりが今、あのぅ、絶滅に瀕しているのは何種も出てきてます。

Supplementary Reading　(This is a written, rather than verbal, commentary.)
Kusuoka Yasushi suggests that nowadays people tend to set their sights on more distant forms of nature, losing their knowledge of and respect for "nature close at hand" as described in Lesson 12. One of the functions of the Lake Biwa Museum is to revive an awareness of nature close to our everyday lives. Unfortunately people have more immediate concerns. What are these?

　　　日本では毎日見慣れた近くの神社の森や田んぼより、遠くの国立公園や湖の自然をありがたがる風潮があります。でも、実際に鎮守の森や田んぼを覗いてみるとそこにはたくさんの不思議や発見があります。

　　　滋賀県立琵琶湖博物館では博物館をフィールドへの入り口として位置づけ、里山など身近な自然について展示をしています。また、住民参加による自然や文化の調査を通じて身近な環境や自然を再確認してもらうきっかけを提供しています。最近、全国的に里山など人が住んでいる地域の自然に対する関心は徐々に深まっています。しかし、まだ、

多くの方が身近な自然より、それぞれの生活に直結するゴミ処理の
有料化など身近な環境問題の方に関心を持っているのも現実です。

単語と文法ノート

Title

環境教育   environmental education

博物館   museum

Segment 1.1   We meet Kusuoka Yasushi in Lesson 9, where he recounts his difficulties in entering the Japanese school system after living abroad, and in Lesson 14, where he describes childhood experiences that were to influence his career.

展示   an exhibit

体験する   to experience

体験学習   learning through personal experience (hands-on learning)

専門   specialty, major

実験室   laboratory

顕微鏡   microscope

覗く   to peer at

調べる   to investigate

〜とか   and the like

野外での   outdoor; out-of-door; in the field

かつどう
活動　　　　　　　　　　activities

た
田んぼ　　　　　　　　　rice paddy

さとやま
里山　　　　　　　　　　See Lesson 12, Segment 1, and this lesson, Segment 1.2.

Segment 1.2

だいぶぶん
大部分　　　　　　　　　the greater part

ふもと
麓　　　　　　　　　　　foot, base (of a hill, mountain)

〜わけだ　　　　　　　　See Lesson 5, Segment 1.1 vocabulary.

さと
里　　　　　　　　　　　a village

しゅうへん
周辺　　　　　　　　　　vicinity

しぜん
自然　　　　　　　　　　nature

ほんらい
本来ですと　　　　　　　originally—if we are talking about how things were;

　　　　　　　　　　　　fundamentally

りよう　　　　　　　　　　　　　　りよう
利用する　　　　　　　　to use; 利用される (passive) to be used

げんざい
現在　　　　　　　　　　at present

たきぎ
薪　　　　　　　　　　　firewood

Verb(3rd base)（です）とか とか may be used between sentences, phrases, or

　　　　　　　　　　　　nouns to enumerate a few examples (often used in

　　　　　　　　　　　　conversation).

すみ　や
炭を焼く　　　　　　　　to burn, make charcoal

さんさい
山菜　　　　　　　　　　edible wild plants

荒れ果てる

to fall into ruin; to run/go wild

日本全国で

throughout Japan

起こる

to take place

姿

form

戻す

to restore (something to its original state)

戻そうと（する）

(volitional form), to try or attempt to restore (it)

再生する

to regenerate

Segment 1.3

そば

buckwheat; buckwheat noodles

植える

to plant

育てる

to raise

手打ちそば

handmade *soba*, or buckwheat noodles

芋

a sweet potato サツマイモ

焼き芋

a roasted sweet potato

里山探検教室

educational field trip(s) to explore *satoyama*

参加する

to participate

〜たり

See Lesson 10, Segment 1.1.

Segment 2　　　富江家^{とみえけ}

This exhibit consists of the Tomie family farmhouse, which was relocated to the museum. It depicts the average lifestyle of a farmer in the late 1950s to mid-1960s, when electrical appliances had just begun to be introduced into daily life. Notice the *kawaya*, an outdoor kitchen located over a stream. Water from the stream was used directly for cooking, washing vegetables, and washing dishes. Carp, raised in a pool, fed on scraps from the dishes. (Note: Outside of the Lake Biwa area, *kawaya* means "outhouse," and the word *kawato* is used for a washing area next to a stream.)

Segment 2.1　　We meet Kada Yukiko for the first time in Lesson 8 and learn more from her in Lesson 12. Kada won the July 2, 2006, gubernatorial election in Shiga-ken on an environmental platform. She is the fifth woman to serve as a governor in Japan.

実在^{じつざい}	real, actual
そのまま	just as it was; just as it is
昭和３０年代^{しょうわ　ねんだい}	the Shōwa 30s (1955-1964)
変化^{へんか}	change
生活様式^{せいかつようしき}	lifestyle
経験^{けいけん}する	to experience
即^{そく}する	to be in line with; to conform to; to be based on, in
暮^くらし	a livelihood
飲^のめる	potential form of 飲^のむ
直接^{ちょくせつ}	directly
上水道^{じょうすいどう}	waterworks (tap water)

なしで   without the means of

いかに   how much, how hard, どれだけ

汚す   to make dirty, contaminate

工夫   a means, a device, a plan

地元   local

あるいは   or

伝える   to convey

水道   waterworks (tap-water system)

下水道   sewer system

慣れる   to become accustomed to

Verb てしまう   emphasis; completely; overtones of regret

Segment 2.2

一断面   one section, a cross-section (here: one moment in time)

実在の家族   a real/ an actual family

表現する   to express

荒い物   laundry

〜とかいうようなこと   things like, things such as

体全体で   with one's entire body

Verb てもらう   to have (someone do the verb);

                          Verb てもらえる   (potential form)

私自身 （わたしじしん）	I myself
憧れる （あこがれる）	to long for, wish for; to be attracted by
そういうふうな	that kind of
一種の （いっしゅ）	a type of
時代精神 （じだいせいしん）	the spirit (mind-set) of the times (of a certain period in time)

Segment 3

空間 （くうかん）	space
使い分け （つかわけ）	different usage according to the situation, occasion
湖畔 （こはん）	lakeside

Segment 3.1　DVD segue photo by Maeno Takashi, courtesy of the Shiga Prefectural Lake Biwa Museum.

湖辺 （こへん）	vicinity of the lake
桟橋 （さんばし）	wharf; jetty; pier
洗い場 （あらいば）	washing place
絶対 （ぜったい）	absolutely
Verb てはいけない	must not do (the verb)
真ん中 （まなか）	in the very center
茶碗 （ちゃわん）	bowls (rice bowls, teacups)

米<ruby>こめ</ruby>をかす	to wash rice, 米をとぐ
手前<ruby>てまえ</ruby>の	on this side of
浜<ruby>はま</ruby>の方<ruby>ほう</ruby>	toward the shore
というのは	that is to say (an explanation of what precedes)
とぎじる	the water in which rice has been washed
濃度<ruby>のうど</ruby>	density; thickness; concentration
濃<ruby>こ</ruby>い	thick, concentrated; strong (tea)
汚<ruby>よご</ruby>す	to make dirty; to pollute
数<ruby>すう</ruby>メートル	a few meters
合理性<ruby>ごうりせい</ruby>	rationality; pragmatism

Segment 3.2   DVD segue photo by Ishiida Kanji, courtesy of the Takashima City Board of Education and the Shiga Prefectural Lake Biwa Museum.

洗濯<ruby>せんたく</ruby>	laundry
お日様<ruby>ひさま</ruby>	the sun (a respectful, somewhat animistic reference) Cf. 太陽<ruby>たいよう</ruby> the sun
おむつ	diaper(s)
もう少し離<ruby>はな</ruby>れた所<ruby>ところ</ruby>	an area a little farther away
集落<ruby>しゅうらく</ruby>	a community; a village
船着<ruby>ふなつ</ruby>き	a harbor, wharf, anchorage

の横〔よこ〕　　　　　　next to, by the side of

X であるとか、Y であるとか　　X, for example, or Y

いわば　　　　　　　　so to speak, in a manner of speaking

地域〔ちいき〕　　　　　region

水の流れ〔みず／なが〕　　the flow of water

生き物〔い／もの〕　　　living things

仕組み〔し／く〕　　　　the structure (here: the structure of life, the web of life)

自主管理〔じしゅかんり〕　self-regulation

工夫をする〔くふう〕　　　to devise (a plan); to contrive (a means); to think out

となり近所〔きんじょ〕　　one's neighbors

守る〔まも〕　　　　　　to protect

お互いの〔たが〕　　　　mutual

信頼関係〔しんらいかんけい〕　a relationship of mutual trust

約束事〔やくそくごと〕　　established commitments, conventions

Segment 3.3

学ぶ〔まな〕　　　　　　to learn; 学べる〔まな〕　(potential form)

環境問題〔かんきょうもんだい〕　environmental problems

分別する〔ぶんべつ〕　　　to separate, segregate into categories

分ける〔わ〕　　　　　　to divide

行動 （こうどう）	behavior, actions
帰結 （きけつ）	conclusion; consequence; result
最終的に （さいしゅうてき）	ultimately
地球 （ちきゅう）	the earth
Verb(2nd base) にくい	difficult to do the verb
精神 （せいしん）	spirit; mind (heart)
取り戻す （と）（もど）	to regain; to recover
Verb (3rd base) としたら	(hypothesis) if we were to . . .
作り出す （つく）（だ）	to produce; to make; to devise (a plan)
逆に （ぎゃく）	conversely
主に （おも）	primarily
地域活動 （ちいきかつどう）	regional or community activities

Segment 4

外来生物 （がいらいせいぶつ）	an introduced/exotic/non-native organism
オオクチバス	largemouth bass (*Micropterus salmoides*)
ブルーギル	bluegill sunfish (*Lepomis macrochirus*)
捕食 （ほしょく）	predation; 〜する to prey on
在来の （ざいらい）	the (species) naturally or commonly found in an area
急激に （きゅうげき）	suddenly; drastically; abruptly

減る	to decrease
種	a species; a kind; a type
固有種	endemic species
Xにしかいない	are found only in X
魚なりなんなり	expressing one among many possibilities (those endemic fish and what have you—among other things)
絶滅に瀕する	to be on the verge of extinction

Supplementary Reading

見慣れる	to become used to seeing; 見慣れた familiar
遠くの	faraway, distant
国立公園	national parks
〜をありがたがる	to show signs of being thankful for, of valuing がる is a verbal suffix that may be added to the stem of adjectives, to the suffix たい, and to adjectival nouns, changing the feeling expressed from objective to subjective. The words to which it is added generally express a psychological or physiological state experienced by someone other than the speaker.
風潮	trend; tendency
実際に	actually
不思議	wonder; marvel; mystery

発見 <ruby>はっけん</ruby>   discovery

滋賀 県立琵琶湖博物館   Shiga Prefectural Lake Biwa Museum

位置づける   to place, situate, position (here, also suggests: intend as)

身近な   close by

展示   exhibition; display; 展示する to put on display

住民参加   resident participation

による   by means of, through the agency of (modifies a noun)

調査   survey

X を通じて   through/via X (modifies a predicate)

認識する   to become aware of; to understand; to take cognizance of

再〜   prefix meaning "again" (here: once again become

                             aware of)

きっかけ   opportunity; start, beginning

提供する   to offer

関心   an interest; a concern

徐々に   gradually; little by little

深まる   to become deeper; to deepen;

                             関心が深まる to get more deeply involved

直結する   to have a direct connection

ゴミ処理   disposal/treatment of garbage

有料化   有料   a charge, a fee   ＋ ～化   a suffix indicating

change; to implement fee-based garbage disposal

現実   reality; actuality

話し合いましょう

1）自分が卒業した高校には「環境教育」に触れる授業や課外活動がありましたか。もしあったとしたら、それはどのような授業または活動でしたか。さらに現在勉強している大学では「環境教育」の分野がありますか。もしあるとすれば、その分野では環境はどのような視点から研究されていますか。

     触れる   to touch upon, address

     課外活動   extracurricular activities

     分野   field (of study)

     視点   perspective

2）自分たちの町に環境教育を目的とする博物館がありますか。あるとすれば、それはどんな所ですか。

3）身近な自然が開発されていく過程で、日常生活に必要な「水」や
「燃料」などの天然資源は私たちから遠のいていきます。自分たちが毎
日使っている水はどこからひかれ、また、どこに流れていくのでしょうか。

開発する	to develop
燃料	fuel
天然資源	natural resource(s)
遠のく	to become distant
流れる	to flow; to be carried away

4）自分の居住地域に外来生物が生息している場合、それらはどのよう
な問題を引き起こすでしょうか。話し合ってみましょう。

外来生物	introduced species; nonnative/exotic organisms
生息する	to inhabit, live
引き起こす	to cause, bring about

第１４課　子供のころの思い出

Childhood Memories

Two speakers, Ishii Kazuko and Kusuoka Yasushi, recall childhood events that shaped the course of their lives.

Segment 1　戦争で学問の機会を失う

Ishii Kazuko was a schoolgirl in Chiba-ken during World War II, shortly after the commencement of hostilities between the United States and Japan. On the DVD she describes how excited she was to have the opportunity to attend a girls' higher school in 1941, and what a disappointment it was to lose her chance at advanced education to the war.

Ishii and her older sister lived with her maternal grandmother in the hills of the Bōsō Peninsula across the bay from Tokyo, while her mother and five other siblings lived with her father in the city. Each day she and her older sister commuted to school by steam train. When it was no longer safe to remain in Tokyo, Ishii's mother and siblings also moved into her grandmother's house.

"It was more like a dilapidated cottage," says Ishii. "Just an L-shaped hut of three rooms, hastily constructed by Grandfather when his home collapsed in the Great Kantō Earthquake of 1923. After Grandfather's death, Grandmother supported herself with a small shop selling candy, *miso*, and *shōyu*. She occupied the six-mat room with the *butsudan*, while Mother and all of the children slept in the eight-mat room. We also had a small room with an *irori*, around which the family sat to eat. Next to this was a lower area with an earthen floor where we cooked. Every day my mother gathered firewood in the hills to heat the evening meal. In front of the house we had a vegetable garden of about 80 *tsubo* (approximately 2,880 square feet; 0.065 acre). This was the source of food for the nine of us. We ate mainly sweet potatoes, but we were lucky to have this much.

"Young people in Japan today do not know the meaning of war. When young women study flower arrangement with me we talk about many things, and I make a point of sharing my memories with them. As the years pass there are fewer and fewer of us left to tell these stories. Our memories help us understand the pain of others experiencing war and poverty today. They help us understand the way in which the state forces its citizens to become a partner in violence.

"I remember the day the war ended. On August 15, 1945, the sky was blue throughout Japan. Our little house, tucked up in the hills, was silent. Mother was reading the newspaper, opened up on the frayed *tatami*. I was sitting next to her, reading over her shoulder. Suddenly a woman who lived nearby came running up to the house, calling out, 'We lost the war.' 'What will we do?' responded my worried mother. But as time passed, it appeared that we could live safely.

"That evening, when my grandmother and siblings returned home and the one naked light bulb came on, Mother looked at her seven children and said quietly, as if embracing us all at once, 'Tonight we'll remove the black cloth shading the bulb. We can live openly now.'"

Sixty years later, on August 14, 2005, the *Tokyo Shimbun* published a two-page series of articles about the war specifically for school-age children. Ishii circled the incidents she remembered most clearly from her childhood. In 1941 the Basic Necessities Control Ordinance was promulgated, placing daily necessities such as rice and clothing under a rationing system. Further, the government decreed that citizens must donate items made of metal to be melted down and recast as weapons of war. These included pots and pans, hardware on gates, mailboxes, park benches, and even temple bells. In the same year, children ceased to be children. Elementary schools were renamed "national schools" 国民学校, and children were labeled "young citizens" 少国民. At school they were indoctrinated to become the future soldiers of Japan. In 1944, when firebombing by American forces became intense, many urban children were separated from their families and evacuated to rural areas where they suffered from loneliness and malnutrition.

Air-raid drills were a routine practice in Ishii's school, as you will see in one of her photographs. The first incendiary air strike on Japanese soil occurred on April 18, 1942. By 1944 American B-29s were dropping firebombs throughout the country in their attempt to force Japan into submission. Japan was unable to defend its airspace, and its citizens were helpless. The death toll and devastation reached their height on March 10, 1945, when more than 300 B-29 aircraft flew over Tokyo, targeting especially the area divided today into Sumida-ku, Taitō-ku, and Kōtō-ku, leaving it a burned wasteland. This single air strike killed more than 100,000 people and rendered one million homeless. All told, 64 cities, including Tokyo, Yokohama, Nagoya, Osaka, and Kobe, were hit, leading to a greater civilian death toll from firebombing than would result from the atomic bombs dropped on Hiroshima and Nagasaki.

During Ishii's childhood there were six years of compulsory elementary education, but students whose families could afford the tuition had the opportunity to continue their studies. About 10 percent of boys might enter a five-year middle school, and a small percentage of these might go on to three years of higher school and then three years of university. Boys in a non-academic track could attend technical school instead of middle school. Girls could attend a four-year or five-year higher school and a very small number might attend a three-year private women's college, perhaps the equivalent of a boys' higher school or today's junior colleges. Ishii tells us how the curriculum at her girls' higher school gradually changed until, in 1943, students were recruited full-time to assist the war effort. Even while students labored in factories, she relates, their parents continued to pay tuition. How could the state justify depriving its children of their youth, its society of an educated citizenry? This was total mobilization for war as Japan's defeat loomed.

Q 日米戦争が始まった時は十代でしたね。

Segment 1.1   TIME CODE 1:34:18

そうでした。あのう、１３で女学校に入って、もうとっても学校って、まあ、楽しい、小学校の時よりも女学校に入った時の方がもっともっと楽しくて、英語のお勉強も入ってますからね。お勉強するのがとても楽しかった。一年の、一年間は無事に過ごしました。二年生になって少し、今度英語の勉強はカット、ね。で、国語とか数学、それからお裁縫、そういう科目は通常の通りやりました。そして今度三年生になりました。三年生になったらもう授業は殆どなし、このソーイングね、裁縫、それから国語、数学、そのくらいでしたね。あとは、畑に行くんです、ええ、畑に学生、クラスメート全部一緒に畑に行って、泥をひっくりかえしてサツマイモを植えたり、それから、あのう、田んぼに行って、田んぼ（の）にその苗を植える、もう、もちろん勉強なしよ、学業なしです。そして、それが終わると家へ帰ります。でも、少しでもね、国語のお勉強、数学のお勉強があるっていうことは楽しいことでした。だから、その泥んこになって働く時間よりも、それは、以上に、その勉強が出来る時間、その方がずっと幸福でしたね。そして四年生になる。四年制の学校でしたからね。四年生になったらもうすべて学業はカット、そして工場へ連れて

行かれた。で学徒動員っていう、その美名のもとにね、工場へ、全員、

学校中全部、ぁ、学校中じゃないわね、私たちの四年生の学年全部が

工場へ行きました。そして飛行機の部品を、その、私たちが、女子の

学生が、飛行機の部品を作るの。毎日毎日工場へ行って、そして工場へ

行く時にはもうもちろん一切の自由がなし、全部規則、規則、軍隊みたい。

…そして、ぁのぅ、四年、四年生の時のその飛行機の部品を作る作業のあと

で、いよいよ空襲が激しくなったんですよね。で、空襲が激しくなっ

た時に、もう、学生だから私たちはまだじゅう、13、14、（15）、

16歳ですよね。だからもし爆撃にあって、もしものことがあると大変だ

からって、全員今度は家へ帰ることになりました。自宅へみんな。それは

嬉しいことでしたね。家へ帰れば母がいる、母がなにかしらご飯作ってく

れる。

Segment 1.2　　（続き）　　　　　　　　　TIME CODE　1:37:30

戦争はね、どういうことであるかっていうことは子供には分からない。た

だ「勝つ、勝つ、日本は勝つ」って、それしかなくて。そして、ぁのぅ、

学生が、映画を時々私たちは見せられて、その中に学生が、ぁのぅ、大勢、

ぁの、男子のね、学生が大勢で兵隊のように隊列を組んで行進するのが出てくるんですね。あの人たちはみんな生きて帰れないっていうことは私たちは聞かされますね。でも、やっぱりまだね、十代の時っていうのは生と死との、この本当に天地ほどの差のある生と死っていう問題は、なかなかぴんと来ないんですね。で、そのころ、その流れた歌が戦後ね、戦争が終わったあとでだんだん大人になってからね、その時の歌がいかに悲しい歌ばっかりだったかっていうことがだんだん分かってきましたね。ですから、ぁの、ただ私たちは夢中で、その工場から自宅へ引き上げてきて、今度自宅から学校へ通って、学校に工場の、その部品を作る道具が全部工場から運ばれてきてるんです。で、それをまた学校でやすりをかけて、そして部品を作る。それは、ぁのぅ、もちろん、勉強なしよ。ですからその時ちょうど四年制の女学校の、その卒業式っていう時期になったんですけれど、卒業式はできない。みなさん、お家で待っててくださいって言われて、自宅で待っている内に終戦になったんですね。

Segment 1.3　（続<small>つづ</small>き）　　　　　　　　　TIME CODE　1:39:22

でも、そのね、学校<small>がっこう</small>へ（行<small>い</small>くって）、行きながら、その、勉強<small>べんきょう</small>をさせられ

なかったっていう、それがね、私<small>わたし</small>はずっといつまでもいつまでも国家<small>こっか</small>っ

てなんだろうっていう思<small>おも</small>いがしますね。それは今平和<small>いまへいわ</small>でね、物<small>もの</small>があって

有難<small>ありがた</small>い、ぁの、明<small>あか</small>るい国<small>くに</small>ですけれどもね、あの十代<small>じゅうだい</small>の多感<small>たかん</small>な時代<small>じだい</small>にね、

勉強<small>べんきょう</small>ができなかったっていう、で終<small>お</small>わった時<small>とき</small>にはもうまったく生活<small>せいかつ</small>が

急変<small>きゅうへん</small>していて、学校<small>がっこう</small>に行<small>い</small>こうと思<small>おも</small>えば行<small>い</small>けますよ、でももうお金<small>かね</small>がない、

学校<small>がっこう</small>へ行<small>い</small>こうとしてもお金<small>かね</small>がないから、もう働<small>はたら</small>きに行<small>い</small>かなくちゃいけな

い。それで、ぁのぅ、私<small>わたし</small>の若<small>わか</small>い人生<small>じんせい</small>をスタートしたんですけれども、許<small>ゆる</small>さ

れたほんの一時期<small>いちじき</small>ね、たった四年間<small>よねんかん</small>っていう学校<small>がっこう</small>へ行<small>い</small>くのが許<small>ゆる</small>されている、

そして親<small>おや</small>が月謝<small>げっしゃ</small>を払<small>はら</small>ってくれる、その期間<small>きかん</small>に勉強<small>べんきょう</small>ができなかったってい

う、私<small>わたし</small>はもし戦争<small>せんそう</small>のね、ぁの、恨<small>うら</small>みつらみ、もし言<small>い</small>うとしたらそれですね。

…で、それと同時<small>どうじ</small>に、後<small>あと</small>になって本当<small>ほんとう</small>に、こぅ年<small>とし</small>をとってくるにしたがっ

て、さまざまなそういう記憶<small>きおく</small>がね、しっかりと根<small>ね</small>を下<small>お</small>ろしてるんですね。

悲<small>かな</small>しかったこと、嬉<small>うれ</small>しかったこと、で悲<small>かな</small>しかったことはその学徒動員<small>がくとどういん</small>で

男子<small>だんし</small>の学生<small>がくせい</small>が全部戦地<small>ぜんぶせんち</small>へ行<small>い</small>きましたね。それをしっかり覚<small>おぼ</small>えてしまったか

ら、８月１５日<small>にち</small>っていうその戦争<small>せんそう</small>に負<small>ま</small>けた日<small>ひ</small>、これは私<small>わたし</small>にとっては

一番悲<small>いちばんかな</small>しい日<small>ひ</small>でね。…それが、まぁ、戦争<small>せんそう</small>における、なんですか、私<small>わたし</small>の大<small>おお</small>

きな大きなあれですね、（残った）気持ちのかすって言いますかね、そん
なもんね。

Segment 2　　もう一つの教室　　　　　　　　TIME CODE 1:41:22

Kusuoka Yasushi, a freshwater biologist, shares childhood experiences that sharpened his
ability to observe nature and instilled a passion for the natural world.　His words echo the
memoirs of our greatest field biologists, such as Edward O. Wilson, who attribute their
interest in the natural sciences to childhood explorations of swamps and woods, or even a
vacant lot, overgrown with "weeds" and home to local fauna.　In Lesson 13 Kusuoka
tells us more about his work, and in Lesson 9 he describes his adjustment to the Japanese
school system after living in Ottawa, Canada, from ages five to ten.

Q　今生物学関係の仕事をなさっていますが、子供のころの経験が現在の
お仕事にどのように結びついたのか、印象的な思い出をお話しください
ますか。

Segment 2.1

ええとですね、まあ、小さいころ、もう物心ついたころから、あのぅ、生き物が
大好きで、で、三歳ぐらいのころから、あのぅ、家に僕がいないと母親は近
くの魚屋さんに僕を探しに行ってて、それで、だいたい朝から晩まで僕は
魚屋さんの店先でじっと魚を見てたらしいんですね。それでもう三歳ぐ
らいで魚屋の魚の名前を全部言えたらしいんです。で、あと、虫取りと
かが大好きで、まあ、蝶々取ってきて家の中で、こぅ、それを飛ばしたりと

か。そんなことをしてました。…｛お母さんが蝶々について何を言った
か、その話も（ああ、はいはい）して下さいませんか。｝はい。ええとです
ね、まぁ、ちっちゃな家だったんですけど、その家の中で、あのう、蝶々を
飛ばしてたんですね。で、蝶々っていうのはもう、光のある方にこう
飛んでって、まぁ、そこで、まぁ、時間がたったら死んでしまうんですけれ
ど、まぁ、部屋の中で蝶々を飛ばしてて、ある日、母親がその窓際の
蝶々を集めて、その塵取りに入れて、僕のところ持ってきて、「これ
全部お前が殺したんだよ」っていうふうに僕に言いました。で、それを見
て、もう、すごくこぅ悲しくなって、で、それ以降大学に入るまではもう
虫取りはしなくなりました。

Segment 2.2　（続き）　　　　　　　　　　　　TIME CODE 1:42:40

で、まぁ、最初住んでたのが東京だったんですけど、それがカナダに行き
まして、それで、まぁ、カナダに周りに自然がいっぱいあったわけで、も
う毎日朝から晩までこぅ暇さえあれば、森の中に遊びに行ってたりとか、
そういうことをしました。でも、そういうことをしたおかげで、今博物館
に勤めてまして、それで博物館ですといろんな質問が来るわけです。それ
で、まぁ、虫の質問、魚の質問とかいろんな質問が来るんですけれど、ぁ
のぅ、他の人が答えられない質問があった場合には、必ず僕のところに回

ってくるんです、最後^{さいご}には。で、僕^{ぼく}の方^{ほう}で何^{なん}とか答^{こた}えられるということで、

あのぅ、まぁ、ちっちゃいころに、そういう、あのぅ、本当^{ほんとう}の学校^{がっこう}の勉強^{べんきょう}とは

違^{ちが}って自分^{じぶん}でいろいろ見^みつけてった発見^{はっけん}というのは忘^{わす}れないもんで、それ

は今^{いま}の仕事^{しごと}でも役^{やく}に立^たっています。

単語と文法ノート

Title

思^{おも}い出^で   memory

Segment 1

戦争^{せんそう}   war

学問^{がくもん}   learning; studies

機会^{きかい}   opportunity

失^{うしな}う   to lose

Segment 1.1

Because the interviewer lived with the speaker as a child and again during college, the speaker's conversational style is very familiar, relaxed, and direct.

日米戦争^{にちべいせんそう}   Japan-United States war, following Japan's assault on the

          U.S. fleet at Pearl Harbor on December 7, 1941

十代^{じゅうだい}   one's teens

義務教育^{ぎむきょういく}   compulsory education

女学校	a girls' (high) school in the prewar educational system
無事に過ごす	to pass by safely; to live through without event
国語	Japanese language
裁縫	sewing
科目	subject
通常の通りやる	to do as usual/as normal
畑	field
泥	mud, dirt
ひっくりかえす	to turn over
サツマイモ	sweet potato
植える	to plant
田んぼ	rice paddy
苗	seedlings
学業	academic work; studies, lessons
泥んこになる	to get muddy
幸福	happiness; happy; lucky; fortunate
四年制	a four-year (school) (制　system);
	Cf.　四年生 fourth grade, fourth year (in school)
工場	factory

連れて行かれる   to be taken (passive form, used in the sense of an action
                        that adversely affects the speaker)

学徒動員   mobilization of students for the war effort: students were
                        sent to work in factories or sent directly to the front or to
                        serve in special attack (*kamikaze* 神風) units.

美名   under the pretext/in the name of

全員   all members

飛行機の部品   airplane parts

一切の自由がなし   there was not a bit of freedom (なし ＝ ない)

規則   rules, regulations

軍隊みたい   like/resembling the army

作業   work

爆撃   bombing

自宅   one's own home

嬉しい   happy, glad

なにかしら   somehow or other; something or other

Segment 1.2

勝つ   to win

兵隊   soldier(s)

隊列を組む   to assemble in rows; to form ranks

行進する	to advance
聞かされる	to be told
天地ほど差のある	as different as heaven and hell (as far apart as heaven and hell)
ぴんと来ない	doesn't make sense readily, isn't readily understood
そのころ流れた歌	songs that were current, that were on the air at that time

By 流れる the speaker refers to radio broadcasting. Later this verb was also used when referring to music played on a record and amplified for people to hear in the streets.

戦後	after the war
いかに	how
悲しい	sad
夢中で	as if in a dream, as if in a daze
自宅へ引き上げる	to return home
道具	tools
運ばれてきてる	運ばれる＋きている had been carried there (and left for us)
やすりをかける	to apply a file; to file or rasp
卒業式	graduation ceremony
時期	time, period
内に	while

終戦　<ruby>しゅうせん</ruby>   end of the war

Segment 1.3

させられなっかった was not allowed to (passive of causative)

国家　<ruby>こっか</ruby>   state

有難い　<ruby>ありがた</ruby>   thankful

多感な　<ruby>たかん</ruby>   impressionable

急変　<ruby>きゅうへん</ruby>   sudden change

ほんの一時期　<ruby>いちじき</ruby>   just one period, only one time

月謝　<ruby>げっしゃ</ruby>   monthly tuition/fee

恨みつらみ　<ruby>うら</ruby>   resentment, bitterness

もし言うとしたら   if I were to say

年をとってくるにしたがって　<ruby>とし</ruby>   as I grew older

記憶　<ruby>きおく</ruby>   memory

根を下ろす　<ruby>ね　お</ruby>   to set down roots

戦地　<ruby>せんち</ruby>   battleground

負ける　<ruby>ま</ruby>   to lose

戦争における　<ruby>せんそう</ruby>   pertaining to the war

残った　<ruby>のこ</ruby>   remaining

気持ちのかす　<ruby>き　も</ruby>   the dregs of my feelings

そんなもんね   That's more or less how I feel about it.

Photographs in the DVD   (Notes on the photos were provided by the speaker and translated by the interviewer/author.)

Opening scene

  ❖   Classmates who shared the same room with me at the factory dorm. Notice the headbands: they say *kamikaze* 神風 and have the *hi no maru* 日の丸 symbol.   Note also that we are still wearing shoes.

Segment 1.1

  ❖   Entrance ceremony at Girls' School, April 1941. Age 13. A happy day. (Text, p. 220.)

  ❖   Second year at Girls' School. July 1942. Note that the uniform is still a skirt.

  ❖   We are sent to work at a factory. Our uniforms are just like those of male factory employees. (Text, p. 222.)

  ❖   Bucket brigade—fire drill for air raids. 1943, at Girls' School.

Segment 1.3

  ❖   With friends. Note the footwear. There were no more shoes to be had—we were told to write home for a pair of *geta*.

  ❖   Group of six: a day off. Note the guard, left rear. My classmates and I were always accompanied by a soldier.

Segment 2

Segment 2.1

生物学関係の   related to biology
（せいぶつがくかんけい）

経験   experience
（けいけん）

現在	at present
結びつく	to result in, be related to
印象的な	impressive, striking, memorable
物心つく	to reach an age at which one begins to take notice of things
魚屋	fish store; fishmonger （人）
探しにいく	to go to look for
店先	store front
じっと	intently; immobile
虫取り	insect collecting
とか	and the like
蝶々	butterflies
飛ばす	to let fly, set loose to fly
ちっちゃな	a diminutive or childlike form of 小さな
窓際	by the window
塵取り	dustpan
殺す	to kill
それ以降	after that (time), from then on; それ以後ずっと

Segment 2.2

自然	nature

博物館　　　　　　　　museum

勤める　　　　　　　　to be employed at

に回ってくる　　　　　to come around to

発見　　　　　　　　　discovery

話し合いましょう

１）もし戦争のせいで高校の教育を受けることができなかったとしたら、自分は今どのようなことをしていると思いますか。教育の機会を失うということは、自分の人生観にどのような影響を与えるでしょうか。

人生観　　　　　　　view of life

２）若いころの経験の中で、学校以外にもいろいろな「教室」があったはずです。自分にとってどんな「教室」が大事でしたか。

<ruby>第<rt>だい</rt></ruby>１５<ruby>課<rt>か</rt></ruby>　　<ruby>日本<rt>にほん</rt></ruby>の<ruby>歌<rt>うた</rt></ruby>――「<ruby>里<rt>さと</rt></ruby>の<ruby>秋<rt>あき</rt></ruby>」と「<ruby>茶摘<rt>ちゃつみ</rt></ruby>」

Japanese Songs and Their Context

Japanese children's songs *dōyō* 童謡 have been likened to haiku in that both the melody and lyrics evoke seasonal scenes and emotions. In this episode we hear an autumn song, *Sato no Aki* 里の秋、calling forth the beauty and loneliness of an autumn evening in a remote village, followed by a summer song, *Chatsumi* 茶摘、with its lively rhythm and bright tone.   Sasaki Yasuko, a professional pianist, and Yamazaki Mayumi, a professional singer, have shared the stage on many occasions, resulting in the comfortable working relationship you see on the DVD. Nowadays, they note, children usually sing only the first and second verses of *Sato no Aki*. The third verse, alluding to Japanese soldiers returning from the South Seas at the end of World War II, has little resonance with those born after the war. Most who sing the song are unaware of its origin.

The lyrics for *Sato no Aki* were written by an elementary school teacher named Saitō Nobuo 斉藤信夫, who was fond of writing poetry in his spare time. The poem on which our song is based was originally called *Hoshizukiyo* 星月夜, "A Starlit Sky"—something many of us cannot readily see with current levels of urban light pollution. But back in Shōwa 16 (1941), when Saitō-sensei penned his poem, the black night sky over his home in Chiba-ken was filled with stars. Saitō-sensei's original poem contained the first two verses you see in Segment 1, but in the third verse, the speaker prays for the success at war of his father at the front, and in the fourth verse, the child says that when he grows up he too will be a soldier and fight to protect his country. Like so many citizens, Saitō-sensei truly believed in this "sacred" war, from which Japan was sure to emerge the victor. After Japan's defeat, however, he looked back at the lives lost and felt he had deceived his students. His self-criticism was so great that he left the teaching profession and idled his days away at home in the midst of postwar unemployment. Then, one day, Saitō received a telegram from Kainuma Minoru 海沼實, a music composer he had met once years before. The telegram said: スグオイデコウ、カイヌマ [Come right away, Kainuma]. Kainuma had been requested by NHK (日本放送協会 にっぽんほうそうきょうかい Japan Broadcasting Association) Radio to compose music for a song to welcome Japanese troops arriving in Uraga Bay, Kanagawa-ken, from the South Seas on December 24, 1945. Given one week to locate a song, Kainuma searched through old magazines. Lingering over Saitō's poem, he decided it would be perfect if Saitō could be persuaded to change the third and fourth verses. Saitō had several days to execute this task before the ship entered port to the welcoming broadcast. Words failed him, however, and it was not until one hour before the ship's arrival that he walked into the studio with new words for the third verse only. The singer had only that one hour to practice the words and music under Kainuma's direction, but the song was a success. From the next day on, the studio was flooded with mail from empathetic listeners. The setting and emotions conveyed in the song represented the common experience of millions.

As you look through children's songbooks, you may notice that some songs are designated *Mombushō shōka* 文部省唱歌, or songs adopted by the Ministry of Education. *Shōka* means simply "singing songs," but this term came to be used specifically to refer to songs endorsed by the government from the early Meiji period (1868-1912) until the end of World War II for use in elementary and higher-school music classes. Often *shōka* lyrics were didactic (moralistic or nationalistic) and were criticized for their inferior artistic quality. As explained by voice teacher Yamazaki Mayumi, this resulted in a cultural movement from the mid-Taishō period (1912-1926) through the beginning of the Shōwa period (1926-1987) instigated by reputable poets and writers to create songs that were more child-centered and of greater quality. This was part of the larger "Taishō democracy" movement. Songs produced by this movement were called *dōyō* 童謡. One medium of expression for these songs, notes Yamazaki, was the children's literary magazine *Akai tori* (Red bird), shown on the DVD. Today the term *dōyō* is used loosely to refer to children's songs in general, incorporating all types.

Segment 1　里の秋　　　(We hear the first and third verses.)

作詞　斉藤信夫、　作曲　海沼 実　　　　　　TIME CODE 1:43:35

一

　　静かな　静かな　里の秋

　　お背戸に木の実の　落ちる夜は

　　ああ母さんと　ただ二人

　　栗の実煮てます　いろりばた

二

　　あかるい　あかるい　星の空

　　鳴き鳴き夜鴨の　わたる夜は

　　ああ父さんの　あの笑顔

　　栗の実たべては　思い出す

三

　　さよなら　さよなら　椰子の島

　　おふねにゆられて　帰られる

　　ああ父さんよ　御無事でと

　　今夜も母さんと　祈ります

Segment 2   TIME CODE 1:45:33

Q 今日はピアノと声楽の先生に童謡を演奏していただけることを大変嬉しく思います。お二人が音楽に興味を持ったきっかけについてお聞きしたいのですが。

（ピアノの先生）　私は、ぁのぅ、父と母がよく、ぁのぅ、二人で一緒に歌っててね、ええと、あと、父、レコード、昔は蓄音機ですけど、こういう手回し蓄音機で、毎日モーツァルトのを聞かせてくれたので、それがとっても、ぁのぅ、そういうことから自然にやっぱり入って、ぁのぅ、歌も大好きになりましたし、そのままずっと、（つづ）（今の）今に続いてるという感じでいますけど、はい。真由美さんはどうだった？

（声楽の先生）　私はね、ぁのぅ、先生と同じように、ぁのぅ、お父さんもバイオリンが大好きで、昔のこのレコードが何十枚もありまして、それ

を蓄音機とかで、ぁのう、聞いた覚えはあります。それと私の場合には、

小学校の時の恩師が、ぁのう、音楽が、その歌が大好きで、朝「おはよ

う」の歌から始まって、お昼のお弁当を食べる時も「いただきます」の歌

もありましたし、それから皆が、ぁのう、さよならって帰る時も「さよなら、

さよなら」って、きれいな歌でもう一日歌に始まり歌に終わった、ぁのう、

子供の時代を学校で過ごしました。で、それが本当に歌のきっかけだと思

います。

Segment 3   TIME CODE 1:46:52

Q　「里の秋」の背景や意味についてお話しいただけますか。そして、こ

の歌と関係したお二人の思い出があれば、それにもふれていただけないで

しょうか。

Segment 3.1

（ピアノの先生）　「里の秋」は、ぁのう、一番と三番とありましたけれど

も、三番は、ぁのう、ちょうど、ぁのう、ええと、太平洋戦争の終わった時、

昭和２０年ぐらいですかね、に作られたんですけれど、やっぱりその時は

まだ自分のお父さん、それから息子、それから恋人とかがやっぱり戦争に

行ってまだ帰ってこない、で、ぁのう、早く帰ってくるようにって祈りを込

めてっていう、そういう面、ぁのう、歌詞なんですけれども、私の父も、

ぁのう、ちょうどそのちょうど椰子の、椰子の島って、三番目の歌詞にあり

ますけど、椰子の生い茂る島に何年間か行ってきたんですけど、本当に無事に帰ってきたので私が生まれましたけれども、その時代は本当にたくさんに、ぁのぅ、そういう子供たちとか、お母さんたちがいたので、ぁのぅ、でも、メロディーはとっても日本の情緒を表してるので、メロディー自体が美しいので、今は一番と二番がよく歌われますね、三番ではなくって。

Segment 3.2   TIME CODE 1:47:59

（ピアノの先生）　どうですか。

（声楽の先生）　　　そう、戦争時代のこと、今の現在の日本の子供たちにはね、実感がないでしょうから、一番と二番がね、多いですね。で、あのぅ、私のことを、ちょっとね、お話しさせていただくと、ぁのぅ、「里の秋」はもちろんね、秋の歌なので、日本では実りの秋の時期なので、お米がもうたくさん取れる時期なんですね。で、私の家も、そう、お米を作っていたので、そのころ父がこぅ稲刈りをして、稲の穂がもうたくさん積みあがってる、ぁのぅ、稲穂を、ぁのぅ、穂を落とすために、こぅ機械にかけるんですね。で、その殻になった稲穂がたくさん積みあがってる上で私はもう飛んだり跳ねたりしまして、で、その、太陽いっぱい浴びたその稲穂の太陽の匂いが今もすごく頭に残っているんですね。で疲れ果てて、

その中でぐっすり夜遅くまで寝てしまって、親に起こされたっていう思い

が、ぁのぅ、秋の歌を歌う時にはすごく思い出されます。

Segment 3.3   TIME CODE 1:48:57

（ピアノの先生）　　ぁのぅ、その藁にちなんでですけど、私は日本でも

一番、ぁのぅ、雪がたくさん降るところで、ぁのぅ、育ちましたので、冬は、

その、ぁのぅ、藁の布団に、ぁのぅ、ずっと小さい時は寝てました。で、春に

なるとだんだんだんだんその藁の布団が最初はこんなに厚いんですけども、

だんだん薄くて、ぺちゃんこで、それこそ（日本語、なんか）おせんべい

みたいになって、そんな感じで、ぁのぅ、寝てたことを思い出します。

　　（声楽の先生）　　　ね、日本ではせんべい布団っていうんがあるんですよ

ね。今名前でね、うん、ありますね。はい。

Segment 4　茶摘   TIME CODE 1:49:36

文部省唱歌　　　　　　編曲　萩原英彦

一

　　　夏もちかづく　八十八夜

　　　野にも山にも　若葉が茂る

　　「あれに見えるは、茶摘みじゃないか。

　　　あかねだすきに　菅の笠。」

二

日和つづきの　今日此の頃を、

心のどかに　摘みつつ歌う。

「摘めよ摘め摘め　摘まねばならぬ。

摘まにゃ日本の　茶にならぬ。」

単語と文法ノート

Title

里の秋	village autumn (autumn in the village)
茶摘	tea-picking (harvesting of tea leaves in early summer)

Generally the song title is written 茶摘, but this compound

also may be written 茶摘み。

Segment 1

作詞	the words or lyrics (for a song); 〜氏作詞 ＝ lyrics by 〜
作曲	musical composition; 〜氏作曲 ＝ music by 〜
静かな	quiet
背戸	裏の入り口。家のうしろ。

The back door or gate, or the back of the house.

実	a fruit; nut; berry
落ちる	to fall

栗 くり	a chestnut; a chestnut tree
煮る に	to boil
いろりばた	（囲炉裏端）next to the *irori* (sunken hearth); いろりのそば いろりば（囲炉裏場）a sunken hearth over which a pot is hung for cooking
星の空 ほし そら	starlit sky
鳴く な	to cry, call out, sing (birds)
笑顔 え が お	smiling face
椰子の島 や し しま	island of coconuts (South Seas island)
ゆれる	to shake, roll, pitch, sway
無事 ぶ じ	safe
祈る いの	to pray

Segment 2

声楽 せいがく	singing; vocal music
童謡 どうよう	a children's song or poem;　童（child/children）の歌 わらべ
演奏 えんそう	a (musical) performance;　〜する to perform
嬉しい うれ	happy
きっかけ	a beginning; a start; an opportunity
蓄音機 ちくおんき	a gramophone; a phonograph

手回し	turned by hand
続く	to continue
覚え	memory
場合	case (In my case . . .)
恩師	one's (former) teacher (to whom one owes a debt of gratitude 恩)
弁当	a packed (box) lunch

Segment 3

背景	background
関係する	to be related, have something to do with
思い出	memory (memories)

Segment 3.1

太平洋戦争　　　the Pacific War. Historians such as Ienaga Saburō define

the Pacific War as the fifteen-year period, 1931-1945, of Japan's military

involvement in China, Southeast Asia and the Pacific Islands. However, many

other people, educated since the end of the war, consider the Pacific War to be the

period 1941-1945 (the third stage of the "Fifteen-Year War"), in which Japan was

fighting the Allied Forces. The term "Pacific War" was instituted by the Supreme

Command for the Allied Powers (SCAP) in December 1945, giving special focus

to the war between Japan and the United States.

昭和20年	1945
息子	son
恋人	lover
歌詞	words of a song; lyrics
生い茂る	to grow thickly; to be thickly covered with
情緒	emotion; atmosphere; mood
表す	to express
自体	itself
美しい	beautiful
歌う	歌われる(passive) are sung

Segment 3.2

実感	feeling of reality; seem real to one
実り	harvest
米	rice
取れる	to be produced
稲刈り	rice harvesting, reaping
穂	(rice) ears
機械にかける	to put through/ run through a machine

殻 <ruby>殻<rt>から</rt></ruby>　　　　　　　husk, hull

<ruby>積<rt>つ</rt></ruby>みあがる　　　　　　to pile up, accumulate

<ruby>跳<rt>と</rt></ruby>ぶ　　　　　　　　　jump, leap, spring

<ruby>跳<rt>は</rt></ruby>ねる　　　　　　　　to jump, leap, spring

<ruby>太陽<rt>たいよう</rt></ruby>　　　　　　　sun

<ruby>浴<rt>あ</rt></ruby>びる　　　　　　　　to soak up, be bathed in (the sunlight)

<ruby>匂<rt>にお</rt></ruby>い　　　　　　　　　smell

<ruby>残<rt>のこ</rt></ruby>る　　　　　　　　　to remain

<ruby>疲<rt>つか</rt></ruby>れる　　　　　　　　to be tired, become tired; 疲れはてる to be worn out, tired

out

Verb(2nd base) <ruby>果<rt>は</rt></ruby>てる to be utterly, totally . . .

ぐっすり<ruby>寝<rt>ね</rt></ruby>る　　　　　to sleep soundly/heavily

<ruby>親<rt>おや</rt></ruby>　　　　　　　　　　parent(s)

<ruby>起<rt>お</rt></ruby>こす　　　　　　　　　to awaken

Segment 3.3

<ruby>藁<rt>わら</rt></ruby>　　　　　　　　　　(rice) straw

X にちなんで　　　　　　in relation to/in connection with X

<ruby>育<rt>そだ</rt></ruby>つ　　　　　　　　　to grow, be raised, be brought up

<ruby>布団<rt>ふとん</rt></ruby>　　　　　　　　bedding; here she refers to the mattress, <ruby>敷布団<rt>しきぶとん</rt></ruby>

薄い	thin
ぺちゃんこ	flat (as a pancake, or as a rice cracker!)
お煎餅	a rice cracker
煎餅布団	thinly stuffed bedding (thin and hard). Futon are stuffed with cotton that is regularly beaten and fluffed up professionally. When there was no money or worker to do this, the futon became flat and thin. *Sembei buton* suggests poverty and may allude to wartime inconveniences.

Segment 4

茶摘	tea-picking; also written, 茶摘み
文部省	Ministry of Education (old name of the ministry)
唱歌	a song (See the introduction to this lesson.)
編曲	an arrangement (arranged by ~)
夏	summer
ちかづく	to approach
八十八夜	the eighty-eighth day from the beginning of spring
野	plain
若葉	young leaves; fresh green
茂る	to grow thick; to be luxuriant
あかねだすき	bright red cord (used to tie up kimono sleeves)
に	and

菅（すげ）　　　　　　　　sedge (family Cyperaceae, resembles grasses but has a

　　　　　　　　　　　　　solid rather than a hollow stem)

笠（かさ）　　　　　　　　a sedge hat; a woven hat (of rushes or bamboo, which have

　　　　　　　　　　　　　hollow stems)

日和（ひより）　　　　　　fine weather

のどかに　　　　　　　　　tranquilly, serenely, calmly, peacefully

〜つつ　　　　　　　　　　〜ながら

摘（つ）め　　　　　　　　plain command form of 摘（つ）む

摘まねばならぬ　　　　　　つまなければならない

摘まにゃ　　　　　　　　　摘まなきゃ　→　摘まなければ

ならぬ　　　　　　　　　　ならない

歌いましょう

季節（きせつ）にふさわしい童謡（どうよう）または唱歌（しょうか）を選（えら）んで、その背景（はいけい）について調（しら）べ、みんなで歌（うた）いましょう。

　　　季節（きせつ）　　　　　season

　　　ふさわしい　　　　appropriate

　　　選（えら）ぶ　　　　　　to select

　　　背景（はいけい）　　　　 background

第１６課　趣味(しゅみ)

Artistic Pursuits in Everyday Life

What is it that attracts each speaker to a particular hobby?　Some of the hobbies derive from an elite culture that became popularized after World War II.　While there is a tendency to look upon the tea ceremony and flower arrangement as polite arts for the prospective bride, it is more meaningful to look at the learner's personal motivation.　Ishii Kazuko, our first speaker, for example, was inspired to study flower arrangement by a childhood memory.　During the war she lived with her grandmother, mother, and seven siblings in a deteriorating cottage in the hills of the Bōsō Peninsula, across the bay from Tokyo.　Each day her mother would go up into the forest to gather firewood to heat the evening meal.　One quiet afternoon when only Ishii was inside, her mother returned with wildflowers, which she set in a tall bronze vase on a rough board along the wall—the closest thing in the house to a *tokonoma*.　Then she stood back and gazed at the flowers in silence.　Ishii feels that this action reflected her mother's refinement—not something born of education, but of character.　Collecting and arranging the wildflowers—even in this simple 投(な)げ入(い)れ "thrown-in" style—allowed her mother, just for a moment, to step beyond the hardships of war.

Kusuoka Yasushi talks about making buckwheat noodles, *soba*.　This is a traditional form of cooking he can share with those who participate in *satoyama* workshops through the Lake Biwa Museum, where he is a curator.　Participants learn how to grow, harvest, and mill buckwheat—and then make it into noodles.

Endō Rie studies tea.　Since she is also skilled in the wearing of kimono, she can enjoy two artistic pursuits at the same time.

Recently hobbies such as Japanese archery, *kyūdō*, and the wearing of kimono have captivated the interest of young adults as they find something new and exotic in the lifestyles of another era.　Imai Haruka explains this revival of traditional interests, followed by Sasaoka Yumiko (instructor) and Shizuka Yaeko (student), who explain how they developed an interest in kimono, and proceed to demonstrate one kimono style.

Segment 1　　　　　　　　　　　　　　　TIME CODE　1:50:54

Segment 1.1　生け花

花を生けている時は、たとえ自分が上手でなくても、うまくいってる時でも、まったくね、ぁのぅ、自分の時間、本当に自分の世界になっちゃう、なんにも考えない。で、自分の家庭の中で少しばかり問題があっても、それから忙しいことがあっても、なぜかね、その間、花（花とめい）、実際に、こぅ、向かっている時っていうのは忘れちゃうのね。それだけ、ぁのぅ、私はある時ね、生け花ってね、ぁのぅ、魅力、魅力的っていうよりも生け花には魔力があるなあ、っていう感じをもったことあるんですよ。｛っていうのは？｝魔の世界っていうか、それはね、あれじゃない、植物のもっている自然のその大地から出てくる力。

Segment 1.2　そば打ち　　　　　　　　TIME CODE　1:52:04

まぁ、気分転換に、ぁのぅ、そば打ちなんかをしてます。で、そばを打つのは、まぁ、なぜいいかって言いますと、こぅそばを打っている時ってのは、もうそれに集中せざるをえない。で、ぁのぅ、それにずっと集中してますと余計なことを考えなくていいから、まぁ、仕事のストレスとか、そう

いうのも忘れることができますし、あと、やはり、自分の打ったそばってのは、やっぱり、お店のそばよりもおいしいと感じるようになってくんですね。ですから、まぁ、自分でそばを打ってそれを食べるっていうのが好きですね。

Segment 1.3　茶道   TIME CODE 1:52:38

一つは、私の趣味でお茶を習ってまして、そこに行って、その時間、静かなところで、ぁのぅ、決まった動作を静かにやっていくっていうのが心がおちついて、その時間がとても好きですね。

Segment 2　　伝統が新鮮に感じられる   TIME CODE 1:52:57

Q　今井さんは弓道をなさっていますが、弓道のような伝統的なものに興味をもつ若い人たちは増えているようですね。その理由はなんでしょうか。

そうですね。逆に古きよき日本の伝統が新鮮に感じられるからだと思います。ぁのぅ、着物を着たりですとか、袴を履いたり、足袋を履いたり、ぁのぅ、畳のところに、畳に正座したり、そういうことが逆に、ぁのぅ、普通の生活でなくなってきていますので、逆に新鮮なんだと思います。

Segment 3　着物の着付け　　　　　TIME CODE 1:53:20

今回は着物の着付けの先生と、着付けを習っている方にお話を伺います。

Segment 3.1

Q　お二人はどういうきっかけで着物の着付けに興味をもったのですか。

（佐々岡さん）　ええと、私は子供の時から母に着せてもらったり、そういうことが多かったので、大人になったらやはり一人で着れるようになりたいなと思って、あのう、興味を持ちました。

（志塚さん）　はい、ええと、私は若いころから、あのう、日本の伝統工芸である織とか染とか、そういう布の世界にとても興味がありまして、そういうものがとても好きでした。で、それを通じて着物を知って、で、今度は自分できちんと着てみたいなと思いまして、着付けを習うことにいたしました。

Q なぜ着付けの教室が必要でしょうか。

（佐々岡さん）　はい、ええと、以前の日本は、ええと、母親から娘へと着付けを習ったり教えたりした文化があったと思うんすが、最近は、ぁの、ぅ母親も、着物を着れる人が少なくなっておりますので、その分、着付け教室に通ってその手順を習ったり、後はそういう着付けをする職業の人に着物を着せてもらったりすることが多くなっていると思います。

Segment 3.2   TIME CODE 1:54:34

Q 日本人として、外国人の着物姿をどう思いますか。

（志塚さん）　ええと、外国の人が、ええ、着物を着てるのを見るのはとってもいいんですが、やはり着物は日本人の体型とか、ぁのぅ、肌の色とかに合ったものにできているのだなっていうのを再確認するような感じがいたします。

Q 着物を着ることで、気持ちの変化がありますか。

（佐々岡さん）　はい、ええと、着付けには、ええと、いろいろな決まり事や手順がありまして、それを、ぁのぅ、堅苦しいかもしれませんが、やってい

くにつれて、ぁのぅ、心も引き締まりますし、ぇぇと、とても、ぁの、普段と
はまた違った生活や自分になれると思います。

（志塚さん）　着物をきちんと着ている人の優雅さっていうか、動きの何
っていうか、高貴な感じを受けたので、自分もなんかそういうふうになれ
たらいいなと常々思っておりまして、着物の着付けをならいました。

Segment 3.3　着物の着方の手順（主なポイント）TIME CODE 1:55:35

Q 着物の着付けは年齢、性別、TPO、季節、職業などを表している
そうですが、着付けの説明の中で、こういうことにふれていただけますか。

イ）着物は直線裁ちになっておりまして、ぇぇと、一枚の大きなものに
なっています。で、それを着付けをすることによって、ぁのぅ、
着物姿に、ぁのぅ、していきます。

ロ）着物は、ぁのぅ、長く仕立ててありますので、ぁのぅ、着る方の身長
に合わせて、ぁのぅ、丈を決めていきます。

ハ）幅も大きくできておりますので、このように、その着る人の幅に
合わせて、ぁのぅ、変えていきます。

ニ) で、腰紐を結びますが、これが一番大切な部分ですので、これを

ゆるくしてしまったりすると、着崩れてしまって落ちてしまいま

すので、しっかり結びます。…きつい？…大丈夫です。

ホ) 左前が、ぁのぅ、基本になります。で、これを逆にしますと、ぁの

ぅ、亡くなった方を意味しますので、気をつけるようにしてくださ

い。

ヘ) 今日はよそ行きの、ぁのぅ、支度をしております。結婚式ですとか、

お呼ばれした席に着ていく、ぁのぅ、よそ行きです。それですので、

重ね襟といって、ぁのぅ、お喜びが重なるようにという、だからぁ

の、お葬式とかには使いません。

ト) 着物は襟の抜き加減によって年齢ですとか、職業などを表しま

す。で、ミスの装いといいまして、ぇぇと、結婚前の方はなるべく

襟を詰めてきます。で、結婚されると、ぁのぅ、ゆったりした

雰囲気を出すために大きめに抜きます。そして、抜きすぎてしま

いますと、ぁのぅ、芸者さんのようになってしまいますので、普通

の方は注意しましょう。

チ) よそ行きの帯結びですので、ぁのぅ、二重太鼓というお太鼓をいた

します。…で、帯が皺にならないように帯板というのをします。

…（大丈夫です？）…（大丈夫です。）…縛ります。…お太鼓を作るために帯枕というのを使います。

リ）はい、これでよそ行きの着付けが終わりました。ありがとうございました。

単語と文法ノート

Title

趣味	a hobby, an interest; ご趣味は何ですか。

Segment 1.1

生け花	(the art of) flower arrangement
花を生ける	to arrange flowers
たとえ	even if/though; supposing that . . .
なっちゃう	なってしまう
家庭	home; family; household
資料	material; data
向かう	to face
忘れちゃう	忘れてしまう、to forget
	Verb てしまう、to do the verb completely; this auxiliary verb often is used for emphasis
魅力的な	charming,; fascinating; attractive
魔力	magical powers; mysterious charm

魔の世界   a realm of mysterious power

植物   plants

自然の   natural

大地   the earth, the vast earth, Nature

Segment 1.2

そば打ち   making buckwheat noodles; nominal form of verb phrase

                                そばを打つ

気分転換に   for a change; for recreation

                                (literally: for a change of mood/atmosphere)

〜なんか   such as; like

集中する   to concentrate

Verb(1st base) ざるをえない have to do; must do; have no choice but to do;

                                cannot help doing. する becomes せ preceding ざる

余計なこと   extraneous things

感じる   to feel

Verb (3rd base)ようになる   to come to be that (change over time)

                                Here we have: Verb ようになってくる

                                For Verb てくる see Lesson 7, p. 108.

Did you note the many contractions that occur in this speaker's words?

For example,   そば<u>って</u>のは → そば<u>という</u>のは

        〜ようになって<u>くん</u>ですね → 〜ようになって<u>くるん</u>ですね

Segment 1.3

茶道	the way of tea; tea ceremony
静かな	quiet
決まった動作	set movements
心が落ちつく	to feel composed

Segment 2

弓道	Japanese archery （弓術）
伝統的な	traditional
増える	to increase
理由	reason
逆に	conversely
古きよき	good old (days). In literary Japanese 古きよき are the noun-modifying forms of 古い (old) and よい (good).
伝統	tradition
新鮮な	fresh, new
着る	to put on, wear
袴	*hakama*; long skirt, split like pants, for formal wear
履く	to wear, put on (footwear, trousers)
正座する	to sit properly in formal Japanese style

普通の生活   ordinary/everyday life

なくなる   to vanish

Segment 3

着物の着付け   the way of wearing/putting on kimono

伺う   to ask, inquire (polite)

Segment 3.1

きっかけ   a beginning; a start; a chance; an opportunity

着せる   to dress; 着せてもらう to have someone dress you

          (here, in kimono)

着る   to wear; 着れる (potential)

伝統工芸   traditional handicrafts

織   weaving

染   dyeing

布   cloth

X を通じて   through/ via X

きちんと   accurately; exactly; precisely

Verb(plain, nonpast) ことにする   to decide to (do the verb); to make a point of

          (doing the verb); （いたす = humble polite form of する）

教室   classroom

以前の   previous; past (Japan of the past)

<ruby>母親<rt>ははおや</rt></ruby>	mother
<ruby>娘<rt>むすめ</rt></ruby>	daughter
その<ruby>分<rt>ぶん</rt></ruby>	to that extent, accordingly
<ruby>通<rt>かよ</rt></ruby>う	to attend; to go to
<ruby>手順<rt>てじゅん</rt></ruby>	a process; an order; a method; a way of doing
<ruby>職業<rt>しょくぎょう</rt></ruby>	profession

Segment 3.2

<ruby>着物姿<rt>きものすがた</rt></ruby>	appearance of someone in a kimono; wearing a kimono
<ruby>体型<rt>たいけい</rt></ruby>	one's figure; the shape of one's body
<ruby>肌<rt>はだ</rt></ruby>	skin
<ruby>色<rt>いろ</rt></ruby>	color
<ruby>合<rt>あ</rt></ruby>う	to be suited to
<ruby>再確認<rt>さいかくにん</rt></ruby>	reconfirmation
<ruby>変化<rt>へんか</rt></ruby>	a change
<ruby>決<rt>き</rt></ruby>まり<ruby>事<rt>ごと</rt></ruby>	rules
<ruby>手順<rt>てじゅん</rt></ruby>	order
<ruby>堅苦<rt>かたくる</rt></ruby>しい	rigid; hard and fast; formal; strict
〜につれて	as . . . ; with . . . ; in proportion to . . .
	やっていくにつれて as you do it

心が引き締まる   one's heart/mind becomes focused

普段   at ordinary times, usually

優雅さ   elegance, refinement

高貴な   high-born; noble

受ける   to receive

常々   always

Segment 3.3

年齢   age

性別   gender

TPO   time, place, occasion

季節   season

職業   occupation

表す   to express

直線裁ち   made (cut) in a straight line

一枚   one piece (of cloth)

仕立てる   to make (clothes); to tailor (to adjust a kimono to

                        someone's height and girth)

身長   height

丈   height; length

決（き）める — to determine, decide

幅（はば） — width, breadth

変（か）える — to change, alter

腰紐（こしひも） — an *obi* cord

結（むす）ぶ — to tie, fasten

ゆるくする — to loosen

着崩（きくず）れる — a kimono becomes loose and disordered

落（お）ちる — to fall

しっかり — firmly

きつい — tight

左前（ひだりまえ） — (wear a kimono) with the right side tucked under the left

（着付（きつ）け）「左前（ひだりまえ）」という時（とき）の左（ひだり）は、本人（ほんにん）ではなく相手側（あいてがわ）から見（み）た左をさす。

基本（きほん） — the foundation, a basis

逆（ぎゃく）にする — to reverse (the order)

亡（な）くなる — to die

Xに気（き）をつける — to watch out for X; to pay attention to X

〜ようにする — to do (the verb) in such a way that

よそ行（ゆ）き — fine clothes for going out; formal clothes

支度（したく） — preparations; get dressed

けっこんしき 結婚式	a wedding ceremony
お呼ばれした席	a place to which you have been invited
かさ えり 重ね襟	layered neckband
よろこ 喜び	joy
かさ 重なる	to be piled up, layered
そうしき 葬式	funeral
えり 襟	edge of the kimono along the nape of the neck
ぬ かげん 抜き加減	adjustment of how far (the collar, neck band) is pulled out
よそお 装い	dress
つ 詰める	to close up the gap (in the collar, neck band)
ゆったりした	loose, relaxed
ふんいき 雰囲気	atmosphere
げいしゃ 芸者	a geisha. "Wearing kimono is one of the things that distinguishes geisha from other women in Japan. Geisha wear their kimono with a flair just not seen in middle-class ladies" (Dalby, 282). For more on geisha and kimono read Liza Dalby's fascinating anthropological study.
ちゅうい 注意する	to watch out for
おびむす 帯結び	tying up/ fastening the *obi* (sash)
にじゅうだいこ 二重太鼓	a "double drum": refers to a style of fastening the *obi*—there is a double fold

| お太鼓<ruby>太<rt>たい</rt></ruby><ruby>鼓<rt>こ</rt></ruby> | refers to a style of fastening the *obi* in which there is one large flat "bow" or fold in the back. If this is doubled, it is called *nijūdaiko* 二重太鼓. |

| <ruby>皺<rt>しわ</rt></ruby> | wrinkle |

| <ruby>帯<rt>おび</rt></ruby><ruby>枕<rt>まくら</rt></ruby> | oval form or pillow inserted in an *obi* to shape it like a Japanese drum |

| <ruby>縛<rt>しば</rt></ruby>る | to bind, fasten |

話し合いましょう

1）自分の趣味について話しましょう。話し手の趣味は、それぞれ心にゆとりを与えるものですが、自分の趣味もそうですか。説明してください。

| ゆとり | time, space, freedom |

2）留学生たちに、着物をどれぐらいの頻度で着るか、どんな機会に着るか、自分で着ることができるかどうか、聞いてみましょう。

| 頻度 | frequency |

3）日本人以外の人々の着物姿についてどう思いますか。

4）服装とアイデンティティの関係について話し合いましょう。

| 服装 | (the style of) dress; clothes |

第17課　武道——剣道の例

Kendō in Contemporary Society

だい か ぶどう けんどう れい

う はんせい う かんしゃ

打って反省しなさい、打たれて感謝しなさい。

Kendō, the way of the sword, may be viewed as a sport, an art, a discipline, or even a way of life. Umezaki Kunitomo, director of the Aioi Kendō Club, describes some of the special features of *kendō*. "*Kendō* is a martial art that we can all practice and enjoy together, regardless of age or gender. It is competitive, like sports, and it is excellent for the health. As we become more involved we become interested in the evolution of *kendō* from swordsmanship on the battlefield to a discipline that trains the mind and heart, and we learn from the life stories of former masters. These stories contribute to our development as human beings. As we continue our practice, we learn proper etiquette *reihō* 礼法, and we cultivate a sense of compassion and consideration for others. Through *kendō* we come to understand the thought and behavior that underlie the way of the warrior, *bushidō* 武士道, and we take pride in Japan's distinctive cultural traditions.

"Before we begin practice one student representative will stand before the group and chant three precepts: '1. あいさつは、大きな声で元気よくします。 We will exchange all greetings in a clear, spirited voice. 2. はきものは、きちんとそろえてぬぎます。 We will neatly arrange our shoes to face outward when removing them. 3. 正しいことは、進んでします。 We will take the initiative to do what is correct.'

"These are points we take for granted in daily life, but we emphasize them here because we would like for our students to acquire proper manners naturally through *kendō* training. We greet and thank people courteously. Proper etiquette and consideration of others are critical elements in a well-functioning society. The second precept reminds us that even after practice is over, even after executing a successful stroke, even after we have taken some course of action, we will remain mindful and alert. The third precept is difficult even for adults. But, through the gradual acquisition of courage, courtesy, a sense of justice and responsibility—core values in the martial arts—we learn to do what is correct of our own initiative. By helping students acquire these values, we hope that through *kendō* we can train our youth to be competent members of society."

In Japanese moral thinking, correct thought results from correct behavior. Speaking correctly, bowing correctly, arranging one's shoes correctly, and so on are all forms of outward behavior that cultivate courtesy, courage, and a sense of justice and responsibility. *Kendō* trains students to perform certain behaviors as a matter of discipline; these specific behaviors lead to the cultivation of a broader discipline that informs a person's actions throughout life.

On the DVD we hear first from Umezaki Kunitomo, club director. The club includes boys and girls, men and women from ages five to seventy-eight. This community of participants allows different age-groups to interact in a way no longer possible where residential community ties are weak. Umezaki explains that this interaction between age-groups is especially important in *kendō*, which teaches that we can learn from each person, whether more or less advanced than we (上手に習い、下手に学ぶ).

We next hear from three of the children and finally from two mothers of participants, one of whom is herself a new student of *kendō*. What does the director hope to convey or make possible? What do the children hope to learn or gain? What motivated them to take up *kendō*? Many parents today encourage their children to study martial arts so that they will learn proper etiquette and develop strength of body and character. How do the parents interviewed here believe their children will benefit from *kendō*? If you have studied a martial art, how do these hopes and expectations correspond with your own?

Segment 1   剣道のお稽古   TIME CODE 1:59:27

Segment 2   剣道クラブの部長の話

Segment 2.1   TIME CODE 2:01:18

Q 剣道とは、どんな特徴をもった武道ですか。

剣道はですね、ええ、江戸時代の末にですね、ええ、島田虎之助というりっ

ぱな先生がおられまして、その先生が、「剣は心なり、心正しからざれ

ば、剣また正しからず。剣を学ばんとすれば、心より学ぶべし」とおっ

しゃった先生がおられます。そういう意味で剣道は武道ですが、

大変精神面の大変強い、あのう、スポーツだと思っております。

Segment 2.2　　　　　　　　　　　　　　TIME CODE　2:01:51

Q　剣道を通して子供たちに何を伝えたいと思いますか。

あのう、最近、子供たちは、ぁのぅ、友達と外で遊ぶことが少なくなって、ぇえ、同級生では付き合いますけども、上下の子とのお付き合いがありませんから、やはり、こういう場を通じてですね、ぇえ、上下の先輩、後輩とのお付き合いを、こぅ、するっていうことですね、剣道を通じてやるっていうことは汗を流す。で、そういうことが、大事でですね、ぇえ、その中でやはり、ぁのぅ、竹刀で叩く時にですね、ぇえ、決められたところ以外に当たる時あるんですね、たくさんですね。ぇえ、その時に相手に対してですね、痛いでしょうと、そういう思い遣りをですね、こう持つということが大変これ重要だと思いますね。それから、ぁのぅ、やはり、朝早く稽古をやる、夜遅くこぅ稽古をやる、そういうものにもですね、寒い時にも暑い時にもですね、一生懸命みんな出かけていきましてですね、稽古に励むという、大変、こぅ、よろしいですね、体に、健康に大変いいような感じがします。

Segment 2.3　　　　　　　　　　　　　　TIME CODE　2:01:51

Q　剣道とスポーツの違いはなんでしょうか。

ええ、まぁ、剣道は武道といわれているんですが、一つは、ぁのぅ、スポーツはやっぱり勝負、勝ち負けにですね、ぇぇ、大変こだわって、ぇぇ、勝った負けたを重視しますが、剣道は、そこも必要なんですけども、ぇぇ、それ以上にですね、自分の心を鍛えるスポーツだと思いますね。だから、例えば、相手をパーンと打った時ですね、一本勝った時ですね、その時もですね、打って反省をしなさい、打たれてですね、相手から打たれて感謝をしなさい、自分の悪いところを打ってくれた。それ、感謝をしてですね、次の、今度勝負、稽古にですね、備えるというその諺がありまして、そういうものがやっぱり特徴じゃないかと思いますね、スポーツと剣道の違いだろうと思います。

Segment 3　　子供たちの話

Segment 3.1　　　　　　　　　　　TIME CODE 2:03:51

Q　どうして剣道を習いたいと思いましたか。

男の子（１）：うんと、見て、面白そうだなって言って、格好よくなるから
と思って、やりました。

女の子：　お兄ちゃんがやってたから、やりたいと思って。

男の子（２）：ぁぁ、（きん）家の近所に知り合いの先生がいて、それで
誘われて入ってみました。

Segment 3.2　　　　　　　　　　　TIME CODE 2:04:19

Q　剣道をやっていてとても良かったということがありますか。

女の子：　体が丈夫になったこと。

男の子（１）：うんと、先生に習うのが良かった。

男の子（２）：試合とかで勝ったりすると嬉しいです。

{あのう、何年やっていらっしゃいますか、剣道？}

ええ、四年間です。{四年間ですか。で、今は何歳ですか。}今、中一
です。

Segment 4　　　二人のお母さんの話

Segment 4.1　　　　　　　　　　　TIME CODE 2:04:45

Q　なぜお子さんに剣道をやらせたのですか。

お母さん（1）

はい。そうですね。ぁのぅ、やはり「ありがとうございました」とか「お願いします」とか礼儀正しく、ぁのぅ、きちんと皆さんに「ありがとう」と言えるようになってほしかったです。

Segment 4.2   TIME CODE 2:04:59

Q 剣道を通してお子さんに何を学んでほしいと思われますか。

お母さん（2）

ええと、集中力とか、あとは、ええと、気持ちを、何ですか、落ちつけるとか、何ていうんですか、浮ついてないで締まる時はぎゅっと締まるっていうか、気持ち的にも体的にも締まってほしいっていうのと、スポーツの楽しさ、剣道もスポーツですからね、スポーツの楽しさと、やりとげること、何でもやりとげることですね。

Segment 4.3   （続き）   TIME CODE 2:05:28

｛で、森さんも剣道を｝ はい、はじめました。｛なさっていますね。｝ はい。

始めは子供の見学で来てたんです、一緒に連れて。で、見ているうちにどうしてもやりたい、ぁのぅ、今までテレビとかで見てはいたんですけど、生に剣道に触れるきっかけっていうのは今までなくって、子供がやりたいっ

て言って始めたので、見にきて、生で見て、その魅力に取り付かれたっていうか、じっとしていられなくなったっていうか。はい。｛で、森さんは剣道のお稽古をなさって、何がとても良かったと思いますか。｝そうですね、ぁのぅ、日常からもう本当に剣道をやっている時にもうそれにもう集中して、パッて世界がその時だけはもうそれにのめり込めるっていうんですか、なんか、めりはりっていうか、体ももちろん、肩こりって分かります？…が取れたり、メンタル的な面と、あとは、体のリラックス、後でそのいい気持ちになれるっていうのと、両方ですね。精神的にすごくなんか、ぁのぅ、後でゆったりできるでしょう、終わったあと、やってる時はすごく集中して、そのめりはりもいいですね。

単語と文法ノート

Introduction

<ruby>礼法<rt>れいほう</rt></ruby>

etiquette: basic etiquette is one of the essential virtues of the samurai and of the civilized person. In the martial arts <ruby>武道<rt>ぶどう</rt></ruby> there is a saying that practice begins with etiquette and ends with etiquette, indicating that the student is always mindful of expressing humility and respect. *Rei* also refers specifically to the bow. At the beginning of practice, one of the higher ranking students will call out: <ruby>正面<rt>しょうめん</rt></ruby>に<ruby>礼<rt>れい</rt></ruby>、<ruby>先生<rt>せんせい</rt></ruby>に<ruby>礼<rt>れい</rt></ruby>   Bow to the front; bow to the teachers (Tokeshi, 109).

Segment 1

<ruby>剣道<rt>けんどう</rt></ruby>

"the way of the sword"; swordsmanship

<ruby>稽古<rt>けいこ</rt></ruby>

lessons, practice ("to consider and learn from the old"— to learn from masters of the past and from established techniques)

Segment 2

<ruby>部長<rt>ぶちょう</rt></ruby>

here: head of a club, the *kendō* club

Segment 2.1

<ruby>特徴<rt>とくちょう</rt></ruby>

special/distinctive feature

<ruby>武道<rt>ぶどう</rt></ruby>

"the way of the warrior"; martial arts

<ruby>江戸時代<rt>えどじだい</rt></ruby>

Edo period (1600-1868)

の末   the end of   Cf. 幕末、 the last days of the Tokugawa shogunate

おる   ＝いる ; おられる ＝   passive, used as honorific form of おる

剣   a sword （刀）

なり   (literary Japanese) なり makes a statement or assertion （である） or acts as a type of copula.

正しい   right, correct, truthful

正しからざれば   In literary (pseudo-classical) Japanese the *mizenkei* 未然形 (negative base) of adjectives may be formed by adding to the adjective stem the suffix から (derived from く＋あら、 itself the *mizenkei* of あり). For example: 正しくあら becomes 正しから. To this we may add ざれ, the *izenkei* 已然形 (conditional form) of negative suffix ざり(ず＋あり). If we then add the conditional particle ば, we have 正しからざれば : if/when it is not (right, correct, truthful). (Colloquial Japanese: 正しくなければ.)

正しからず   it is not (right, correct, truthful)   （正しくない）

学ぶ   学ばんとすれば   if you plan to learn/study

                 ん is a contraction of the literary suffix む.

                 This is a "volitional" suffix, following the first base, or *mizenkei* 未然形. Colloquial Japanese: 学ぼうとすれば

より   from

Verb (3rd base) + suffix べし   ought (to do the verb);   学ぶべし ought to learn

おっしゃる　　　　　honorific form of 言う

そういう意味で　　　in that sense

精神面　　　　　　　spiritual/mental aspect(s)

Segment 2.2

X を通して　　　　　through, by means of X

伝える　　　　　　　to convey

最近　　　　　　　　recently

同級生　　　　　　　classmates

付き合う　　　　　　to associate with, mix with; お付き合い circle of

acquaintances; those with whom you keep company

場　　　　　　　　　place, setting, occasion

X を通じて　　　　　through, via X

先輩　　　　　　　　one's senior (at school, in a club, etc.)

後輩　　　　　　　　one's junior

汗を流す　　　　　　to work hard to accomplish something

(literally: to shed sweat)

竹刀　　　　　　　　a bamboo sword (for *kendō* practice)

叩く　　　　　　　　to hit, strike

決_きめる	to decide; 決められる　passive form: to be decided, set, established
以外_{いがい}に	other than
当_あたる	to hit, strike (on, against)
相手_{あいて}	a companion; a partner; an opponent
痛_{いた}いでしょう	it must hurt
思_{おも}い遣_やり	sympathy; compassion; thoughtfulness
重要_{じゅうよう}な	important
励_{はげ}む	to make efforts (to do); to devote oneself to; to work hard at (one's lessons)
健康_{けんこう}	health
感_{かん}じがする	to feel as if

Segment 2.3

勝負_{しょうぶ}	victory or defeat; a match; a contest
勝_かち負_まけ	winning or losing;（from 勝_かつ、負_まける）
こだわる	be bound to, be particular about
重視_{じゅうし}する	to consider, regard as important; to set great store by
必要_{ひつよう}	necessary
それ以上_{いじょう}に	more than that

鍛える <ruby>鍛<rt>きた</rt></ruby>える   to forge, temper

一本勝つ <ruby>一本<rt>いっぽん</rt></ruby><ruby>勝<rt>か</rt></ruby>つ   to win one point for hitting the target areas or strike zones in a proper manner

打つ <ruby>打<rt>う</rt></ruby>つ   to hit, strike; <ruby>打<rt>う</rt></ruby>たれる passive form: to be hit, struck

反省する <ruby>反省<rt>はんせい</rt></ruby>する   to search one's conscience; to reflect on one's conduct

感謝する <ruby>感謝<rt>かんしゃ</rt></ruby>する   to thank, express one's gratitude

備える <ruby>備<rt>そな</rt></ruby>える   to have in store (as an asset—here, something to look out for at the next match or practice)

諺 <ruby>諺<rt>ことわざ</rt></ruby>   proverb; a saying

Segment 3 The interviewer is meeting the children and parents for the first time.

Segment 3.1

格好 <ruby>格好<rt>かっこう</rt></ruby>   appearance; <ruby>格好<rt>かっこう</rt></ruby>よくなる to improve in appearance, look better

誘う <ruby>誘<rt>さそ</rt></ruby>う   to invite; 誘われる passive form: to be invited

Segment 3.2

丈夫 <ruby>丈夫<rt>じょうぶ</rt></ruby>   healthy; strong, robust

試合 <ruby>試合<rt>しあい</rt></ruby>   a match, game, competition

中一 <ruby>中一<rt>ちゅういち</rt></ruby>   中学校一年 first year of middle school; (The speaker responds with his level in school rather than his age.)

Segment 4

Segment 4.1

やる	to do; やらせる causative form: cause to do, have do
礼儀	courtesy; manners; etiquette
礼儀正しく	politely; with due courtesy
きちんと	accurately, properly
皆さん	everyone
なってほしい	to want (someone) to become (a certain way)
	なる＋ほしい

Segment 4.2

学んでほしい	to want (someone) to learn まなぶ＋ほしい
思われる	passive of 思う used here as an honorific form
集中力	power of concentration; ability to concentrate
うんと	a great deal, a lot
気持ちを落ち着ける	to compose oneself; to calm one's emotions; to compose one's feelings
浮わつく	to be fickle, frivolous; to be unsettled
締まる	to be firm, steady; to pull oneself together
遣り遂げる	to carry through to completion; to see something through; to achieve

Segment 4.3

<ruby>見学<rt>けんがく</rt></ruby>	a visit in order to observe
<ruby>連<rt>つ</rt></ruby>れていく	to take with one
連れてくる	to bring with one
<ruby>生<rt>なま</rt></ruby>	in the raw, first-hand
<ruby>触<rt>ふ</rt></ruby>れる	to experience, touch, feel
きっかけ	opportunity
<ruby>魅力<rt>みりょく</rt></ruby>	charm; appeal; allure
<ruby>取<rt>と</rt></ruby>り<ruby>付<rt>つ</rt></ruby>く	to possess; <ruby>取<rt>と</rt></ruby>り<ruby>付<rt>つ</rt></ruby>かれる passive form: to be possessed by
じっとする	to stay still, sit tight
いられなくなった	いられる（potential form of いる）＋ ない ＋ なる
<ruby>日常<rt>にちじょう</rt></ruby>	everyday world, routine
<ruby>集中<rt>しゅうちゅう</rt></ruby>する	to concentrate, focus on
<ruby>世界<rt>せかい</rt></ruby>	world
のめり込む	to go into (something) heart and soul; to give oneself up to; to be totally absorbed in
めりはり	modulation, variation; 〜をつける to vary the pace, strike a proper balance
<ruby>肩<rt>かた</rt></ruby>こり	stiffness in the shoulders
<ruby>精神的<rt>せいしんてき</rt></ruby>に	spiritually, mentally
ゆったりする	to feel calm, composed, easy; to loosen up

話し合いましょう

1）武道には剣道だけではなく、柔道、合気道、空手など、様々なものが含まれています。自分自身は日本の武道を習ったことはありますか。もしその経験があったとしたら、何を何年間くらい習っていましたか。武道を習おうとした理由や、またそこから受けた印象についても説明してください。

　　　含む　　　　　　　　　to include

　　　印象　　　　　　　　　impression(s)

2）武道の魅力は、現代の日本ではどのように捉えられているでしょうか。留学生たちに聞いてみましょう。（第16課—Segment 2—も参照。）

　　　魅力　　　　　　　　　attraction; charm; appeal

　　　捉える　　　　　　　　to grasp; interpret (an idea, etc.)

日本の武道は、礼に始まり礼に終わります。

第１８課　ある禅寺の住職の話
ぜんでら　じゅうしょく　はなし

Conversations with a Zen Priest

Hori Shūkō is the twenty-second temple head of this 280-year-old Sōtō Zen temple. Although the thatched roof was replaced by tiles twenty years ago, the original wooden pillars have provided continuity through successive generations. As the only priest at this local temple, Hori has many responsibilities.   He is committed to lifelong training through the practice of *zazen*, sitting meditation. He holds memorial services for deceased parishioners, serves as a spiritual counselor for the community, and engages in community volunteer work. It is his duty to spread the teachings of Shakyamuni, the historical Buddha, and to serve as a role model for the community in living ethically, with a sense of joy and gratitude. He is also expected to train a successor, who is likely to be one of his sons. Hori was adopted by the previous head priest, with the expectation that he would inherit his adoptive father's position. In addition to his temple duties, Hori holds a full-time job as head of the career planning and job placement center at a technical college.

When a priest presides over formal events he holds a type of fan called a *chūkei*, whose upper half remains open. A red fan, as we see here, is used for auspicious or congratulatory occasions and a black fan, for Buddhist ceremonies, such as funerals. The fan may accentuate points made in the priest's talk.

Hori's conversation begins with reference to the eclectic nature of Japanese religion. His discussion then turns to the principle of non-dualism and the interrelatedness of all things. He concludes with views on the role of the clergy in contemporary society.

Segment 1   TIME CODE 2:06:42

Ｑ 日本の宗教は神仏混淆とは言いますが、このことを簡単に説明していただけますか。

Segment 1.1

日本の仏教と神道というのは、昔は一つであった。あのう、隔て、分け隔てすることはなっかったんですね。それが政治的に明治の時代に神仏というのを廃仏毀釈、分ける政策、政治的に行いましたので、宗教的には神仏というのは仏教と神道というふうに分かれてますけれども、一般の方々、私どももそうですけども、寺の中に仏様だけでなく、神様も一緒にお祭りをしております。ええ、一般のお宅でも、仏様の仏壇と神様の神棚という場所が二つ一度、あのう、用意しておりますので、ええ、まぁ、神仏が分かれてると、混合してるんじゃなくて分け隔てをしないのが日本の宗教ではないのかなと思います。

Segment 1.2　（続き）　　　　　　　　　　TIME CODE 2:08:03

私たちはかならず繋がりを持っている、なんらかとの繋がりを持ってる。お父さんとお母さんの因縁によって、繋がりによって、私の命はいただいた。私たちは人の命だけでなくこの宇宙全体、この自然界全体と関わりがある。それを日本人は神、偉大なものがあれば力があるものを神と仰ぎ、私たちは仏様も神であり、神様も、まぁ、仏様と同じように、これはこちら、これはこちらと分け隔てることのないのが仏教ではないのかな。

Segment 1.3　（続き）　　　　　　　　　　TIME CODE 2:08:54

ええ、右に偏らず左に偏らずというのが達磨さんのこの座禅のもとが中庸というんですね。真ん中の道と言いますけども、中庸の考え方というのが仏教です、ぁの大事なところですので、ええ、人間だから、ええ、動物だから、植物だから、同じ命を分けて考えないで一つとして考えますから、ものを食べるときにも「いただきます」、命をいただきます、ええ、野菜の命をいただきます、お肉を食べる時は動物の命をいただいて私の命の糧にさせていただきます。それですから、（あり）「いただきます」という、手を合わせていい気持ちでいただきますので、大事なのは、同じ、「同事」と言って、必ず繋がりがあるんだから、それを分け

隔てることのないようにいたしましょうというのが仏教、日本の仏教の考え方ではないのかなと思います。

Segment 2 TIME CODE 2:10:20

Q そうすると、私たちが普段感じる神道と仏教の「違い」というのは表面的なものに過ぎないのでしょうか。

大きな違いというのは、ぁの、形、儀礼で違いはあります。けれども精神的には、考え方には、ぁの、一般的に、一般の方々は、考えはそんなに違いはないと思います。ええ、神社の中でもいろいろなもの、石を神様に喩えたり、ええ、大きな木を神様に喩えたり、ええ、神木と言います。いろいろなものを神様と見ます。これは太陽（の）、太陽が神であったり、この大地が神であったり、仏教というのはこの大自然全体を一つの繋が

りでまとめてますから、その繋がりという中では、神道、神・道（しん・どう）ですね、神様の道、仏道（ぶつ・どう）、仏様の道というのは分け隔てること、本来はなくていいと思います。

Segment 3　　　　　　　　　　　　　　TIME CODE 2:11:48

[Q] 僧侶の立場の人は、現代社会においてどんな役割を果たすべきだとお思いになりますか。

明るく元気に自分のいただいた寿命を生きられるのは、これが一番の幸せなんではないのかな。そうすると、ぅーん、どこにいても誰にでも平等にこの明るく元気に（素直）、ぁのぅ、楽しく生きるというのは大事な、これは条件ではないのかな。ええ、それを現実にすることが一番大切なことではないのかなと。ええ、いろいろな社会の問題があります。ええ、地球、同じ地球上にいながら、どうして差別があって、テロが起きて、宗教戦争があるのだろうか。ええ、仏教というのはそういう隔たりを分け隔てなく考えるのが私どもの仏教ではないのかなと。…人を敬う心、親を敬う心、自然を大切にする心、この心ということを大切にこれからしていく、それも地球全体でそういうことができるということが一番これからの大事なことではないのかなと思いますし、それを実践して

いかなくちゃならないのが僧侶、私ども宗教家の大事なことではないの

かなと思います。

Segment 4   TIME CODE 2:13:30

雨音をバックに般若心経を読経する。

同事　　　　　　ともに生きよう、分け隔てなく

私たちは必ず何かと繋がりをもっていて、それは人であったり、自然で

あったりします。だからこそ、人を敬う心と自然を大切にする心を忘

れたとき、むやみに人と争ったり、自分の都合だけで自然を傷つけるこ

とが起こるのです。

曹洞宗

単語と文法ノート

Title

住職   the head priest (of a Buddhist temple)

Segment 1

The eclectic nature of Japanese religion may be traced to the adaptation of Buddhism in Heian Japan (794-1185). In this period we see a process in which native *kami* 神 and the transplanted images of Buddhism, such as Amida 阿弥陀, Buddha of the Pure Land, and Jizō 地蔵, guardian of travelers and children, became relatively interchangeable in the mind of the people. Political attitudes toward religion have varied. Hori mentions the anti-Buddhist movement, *haibutsu-kishaku* 廃仏毀釈, which developed in the Meiji period (1868-1912) as the new government sought to weaken the position of the Buddhist clergy and promote the emperor cult by developing a politically controlled State Shintō.

Segment 1.1

神仏混交
（しんぶつこんこう）   Shintō-Buddhist syncretism, also known as 神仏習合（しんぶつしゅうごう）

隔てる
（へだてる）   to separate; to set apart

分け隔てる
（わけへだてる）   divide and separate

廃仏毀釈
（はいぶつきしゃく）   throw out Buddha and overthrow Shakyamuni

政策
（せいさく）   a policy

行う
（おこなう）   to carry out, put into practice

仏様
（ほとけさま）   the Buddha; Shakyamuni; a Buddhist image; the deceased

神様
（かみさま）   a god or goddess; a Shintō deity. From before the Nara

                       period (710-794) *kami* 神 has referred to anything awe-

                       inspiring: spirits of nature, spirits of ancestors, and so on.

(*Sama* 様 came into use as a respectful suffix in the Muromachi period, 1392-1573.) The priest points to a wooden image of Hotei 布袋 , one of the Seven Lucky Gods 七福神 (しちふくじん). Thought to be modeled on an eccentric Chinese Zen beggar priest, Hotei carries a cloth bag, ever full of provisions for the poor.

祭る (まつる) — to deify; to enshrine; to worship

仏壇 (ぶつだん) — a (family) Buddhist altar (Cf. Lesson 2, Segment 1.3)

神棚 (かみだな) — a household Shintō altar (Cf. Lesson 2, Segment 1.2)

用意する (ようい) — to arrange

混合 (こんごう) — mixture

ではないのかなと思います (sometimes shortened to ではないのかなと or ではないのかな) serves as a softening device, making his opinions more humble and less direct. "I wonder if it isn't the case that . . ."

Segment 1.2

繋がり (つな) — connection; link; relationship

因縁 (いんねん) — karmic causes; karma; fate; destiny. In Buddhism *in'nen/in'en* 因縁 refers to the direct, internal causes *in* 因 and the indirect, external causes *en* 縁 that give rise to some result *ka* 果 (結果) (けっか). Everything we perceive is 果、 the result of the interaction of 因 and 縁 .

命 (いのち) — life

宇宙   the universe; the cosmos

自然界   the natural world

関わり   relation; connection

偉大な   great; grand

仰ぐ   to respect; to look up to; to revere

Segment 1.3

に偏る   to lean toward (in a biased way)

達磨   Daruma; Bodhidharma. An Indian monk of the fifth or

                             sixth century who is credited with introducing Zen

                             (Chinese: Chan) thought to China. Making his way from

                             southern to northern China, he is said to have sat in *zazen*

                             for nine years, facing the walls of a cave. The painting of

                             Bodhidharma by Sesshū 雪舟 (1420-1506?) shown in the

                             DVD depicts the legend of Huike, a would-be disciple, who

                             offers his severed left forearm as proof of his sincerity.   In

                             2004 Sesshū's painting "Huike Offering His Arm to

                             Bodhidharma" was designated a National Treasure. Used

                             with permission of Kyōto National Museum and Sainenji

                             Temple in Aichi-ken.

座禅   Zen meditation (seated with the legs crossed)

中庸   the middle way (course); moderation; the Doctrine of the

                             Mean

糧（かて）	nourishment (food; bread); 心（こころ）の糧（かて）、 spiritual nourishment
させていただく	to receive the favor of being allowed to make it (food; nourishment to sustain my life)
同事（どうじ）	同（おな）じこと; the same thing. (See the Sōtō sect explanation of this term in the box at the end of the transcriptions, p. 286, and on p. 292.)

Segment 2

表面的（ひょうめんてき）	superficial; apparent
儀礼（ぎれい）	etiquette
精神的（せいしんてき）	spiritually, emotionally
喩（たと）える	compare to; liken to
神木（しんぼく）	a sacred tree. (In Lesson 2, Segment 3.3, a farmer talks about a sacred tree near his house, and in Lesson 11, Segment 2.1, *shimboku* are mentioned in the context of animism.)
大地（だいち）	the vast earth, Nature
神・道	（しん・どう）the way of the *kami* . The priest explains that Shintō is made up of *shin* (kami) and *dō* (the way), just as Butsudō is made up of *butsu* (Buddha) and *dō* (the way).
仏道	ぶつどう the way of the Buddha Cf. 仏教（ぶっきょう）, Buddhism

本来<ruby>ほんらい</ruby>   fundamentally, essentially

Segment 3

僧侶   Buddhist priests, monks

役割を果たす   to carry out/perform/play a role

Verb (dictionary form) べきだ one should/ought to (do the verb)

寿命   one's life span

幸せ   happiness; a blessing; good fortune

条件   a condition   (What we would like for ourselves should

be predicated on equal opportunities for everyone,

everywhere.)

現実（のもの）にする   to make this a reality (referring to the condition

mentioned above)

地球上に   on the earth; on this planet

差別   discrimination

テロ   （テロリズム）terrorism

宗教戦争   religious wars

隔たり   difference, disparity

分け隔てる   to set apart, distinguish, separate

敬う   to respect, honor, revere

実践する   to put into practice

宗教家 _{しゅうきょうか}　　　men and women of religion

Segment 4

般若心経の読経 _{はんにゃしんぎょう　どきょう}　　*Prajñaparamita Heart Sutra* (sutra of the heart/essence of perfect understanding). The "Heart Sutra" is widely regarded as the essence of Buddhist teaching and the heart of the thirty-eight books of *Prajñaparamita* (Perfection of wisdom) literature, composed in India between 100 B.C. and A.D. 600 (Conze, 10).

経 _{きょう}　　　sutra; a scriptural narrative, especially a text regarded as a discourse of the Buddha

読経する _{どきょう}　　　to recite/chant a sutra　（お経を読む）

Hori, the head priest, chants the *Prajñaparamita Heart Sutra,* to which his discussion is an apt introduction. The sutra explains that *dharma*, things, have no separate, independent existence. Each thing exists because of all other things. In the words of Vietnamese Zen monk Thich Nhat Hanh, "Form is empty of a separate self, but it is full of everything in the cosmos." The chanting is enhanced by a torrential rain.

❖　　Text from Sōtō sect poster:

同事 _{どうじ}　　　The Sōtō sect website offers the following definition.

協力して事をなすこと _{きょうりょく}, doing things cooperatively

むやみに　　　recklessly, thoughtlessly

争う _{あらそ}　　　to fight, quarrel, dispute

傷<ruby>きず</ruby>つける   to harm, wound

曹洞宗<ruby>そうとうしゅう</ruby>   Sōtō sect of Zen Buddhism

Related Themes: Compare the priest's words here with the speaker's discussion in Lesson 11, Segment 2, of animism and the philosophical views informing the *anime* of Miyazaki Hayao.

話し合いましょう

１）地球上には、国や人種、あるいは宗教の違う様々な人々が暮らしています。その一人ひとりが明るく元気に生きることができるために、私たちは個人として何ができると思いますか。

人種<ruby>じんしゅ</ruby>   a race; an ethnic group

２）僧侶や、あるいは宗教家という立場にいる人は、現代社会においてどのような役割を果たすべきだと思いますか。自分の意見を述べてください。

第１９課　　日本語さまざま、その一

Diversity in the Japanese Language, Part I

The conversations in our final two lessons address elements that contribute to linguistic diversity within Japanese. Keep in mind that these are the personal views of the speakers, none of whom are linguists by profession.

Taniguchi Yōko, a graduate student in anthropology, begins with a discussion of some of the geographical factors contributing to the development of dialects, and some of the social factors that affect speech level and style. Sachi Yoshio, a retired schoolteacher, shares with us some of the distinctive features of Kansai-*ben*, a dialect particular to the Osaka-Kyoto area. You will encounter many variations of Kansai-*ben* as you travel through the region. MORI Sōya, an economist and president of the Japan Association of Sign Linguistics, explains that just as there is a standard form of spoken Japanese, so there is a standard Japanese Sign Language. Also like the spoken language, each region has its distinctive features; he illustrates some of these regional differences.

Lesson 20 opens with singer Yamazaki Mayumi, raised in Gumma-ken, and pianist Sasaki Yasuko, born and raised in Akita-ken. Yamazaki explains how, even within the same prefecture, one will find different ways of speaking according to place and profession. Sasaki illustrates this further by discussing linguistic differences in Akita between those who make their living by the sea and those in the mountains. Each region may have not only distinct vocabulary, conjugations, and speech styles, but also greetings あいさつ that are unique to local culture. Sasaki provides an example from Akita. Off-camera she further notes that in the cold climate of Akita people tend to speak without opening their mouths wide, giving their words a muffled effect, as if you were hearing them through the snow.

Odajima Mamoru, born and raised in Hokkaido, refers to his native prefecture as a "melting pot" of dialects, from which emerges a common form of speech. Hokkaido was aggressively "settled," from the 1870s onward, by Japanese from diverse regions. Odajima knows that his Ainu neighbors have lost their language—not in the melting pot of Japanese dialects, but through a more deliberate process of cultural annihilation. In *Our Land Was a Forest: An Ainu Memoir*, Kayano Shigeru writes: "The Ainu have not intentionally forgotten their culture and their language. It is the modern Japanese state that, from the Meiji era on, usurped our land, destroyed our culture, and deprived us of our language under the euphemism of assimilation" (translation by Kyoko and Lily Selden; 153).

Japanese dialects have also declined in use due to the dominance of metropolitan culture over the cultures of peripheral prefectures, and due to the mobility of contemporary society. The Ministry of Education dictates that students speak in standard Japanese—the dialect of middle-class Tokyo (Sugimoto, 71). Because dialects of the periphery tend to be disparaged, fluency in both local and standard dialects is a gift not fully recognized by the individual or society at large. Local dialects are beginning to be appreciated through regional literature and cinema. Miyazawa Kenji (1896-1933) of Iwate-ken, once snubbed for his use of Tōhoku-*ben* and local settings, is now one of Japan's most highly regarded writers.

Taniguchi Yōko closes our conversations with an amusing story about the miscommunications that often arise in her family because each member grew up in a different part of the country and retains many of his or her regional speech characteristics.

Why is it important to preserve languages, or to preserve dialects within a language? As you listen to the following speakers, consider this question from a variety of perspectives. Language is a fundamental component of cultural identity. Linguistic and cultural diversity add color to our world. A language or dialect is an invaluable resource in that it contains within it a specific knowledge of place—its natural and cultural history. Above all, to lose linguistic diversity is to restrict our freedom to think in different ways.

Segment 1　　　　　　　　　　　　TIME CODE　2:14:40

Q 同じ日本語でも多様な話し方と言葉遣いがあると思いますが、それについて少しお話し下さいますか。

Segment 1.1

ええと、ひとことに日本語といっても非常に多様な言語だと思っています。それは、ぁのぅ、まず、日本といっても、その北から南まで細長く、まぁ、本州、九州、四国、北海道、沖縄、あともっと小さな島々が、こう、ばーっと細長く分布していて、で、海とか山とか川が非常に多いです。で、そういうことも手伝って、ま、地域的なその言語の差異というのが生まれるような状況がありました。で、一山越えたり、あと一つ川を向こうとこっち側とではもう全然（言葉遣いと）言葉遣いも違うし、あとはその生活習慣も違うということがありました。

Segment 1.2　（続き）　　　　　　　　TIME CODE　2:15:28

で、それと、あとは、ぁのぅ、日本語は、そのだれが（日本）言葉を使うかによって、（ひとの）その人の属性によって、まぁ、非常に、まぁ、多様性があります。例えば、女性であるか、男性であるか、あるいは、ぁのぅ、耳の不自由な方は、ぁのぅ、手話を使って話したりします。で、まぁ、男性と女性の言葉の違い、あとは、ぁの、年齢によって、まぁ、違うってこともあ

りします。で、女性は、まぁ、小さいころから男性よりも、ぁのぅ、やわらか

く話しなさいとか、あと言葉遣いも乱暴にあまりしないようにっていうふ

うに言われて、例えば、男性と女性が一緒に向き合って話してる場面を見

るとよく分かるんですけれども、もう、しぐさからその目線やら、その使

ってる言葉遣い、特に語尾に表れるんですけれども、それが非常に、ぁの、

異なって見えてくると思います。あと、年代差でいうと、ぁのぅ、年上の人

と年下の人が向き合って話してる場面では、年下の人は年上の人に対して、

ぁの、尊敬語を使ったり、謙譲語を使ったり、あと丁寧な言葉を（使っ、

使い）使うということがあります。

Segment 1.3   TIME CODE 2:16:38

Q 高校生の場合は？

高校生に限らず若者全般に言えるんですけれども、その仲間意識（が非常

に）が強くて、で、仲間にしか分からないような言葉を新しく作り出した

りします。で、高校生なんかは、特にそれが激しくて、もぅ、私はもぅ、

ぁのぅ、二十八歳なんですけれども、私は高校生の時にもやっぱり同じよ

うに、ぁの、ま、自分の仲間内でしか分からないような言葉を、こぅ、わざと

縮めたり言ったりするというようなこともしましたけど、今、私がもう二

十八になってから、今の高校生たちを見ると、もう全然何言ってるのか分

からないっていうような状況もあります。

Segment 1.4   TIME CODE 2:17:16

Q　高校生の言葉は時々日常会話に入ってくることもありますか。

ええと、例えば、ぁのぅ、「気持ちが悪い」っていう言葉を、ぁのぅ、「キモ

イ」っていうふうに略して言ったりする言葉があるんですけど、それは、

まぁ、私が考えるところ、まぁ、若者とか高校生がはじめに使い始めたんじ

ゃないかと思うんですが、今では私でも使いますし、三十代ぐらいの人

も普通に「ちょっとキモイよね」っていう言葉を使ったりします。｛そう

ですか。｝はい。と、それと、ぁのぅ、ええと、「キモイ」は、ぁのぅ、関東の

方でよく使われるんですけど、関西の方の人に聞いた話だと、その関西

の方では「気持ち悪い」を「気色悪い」って言ったりするんですが、それ

を略して「キショイ」っていうふうに言ったりもするそうです。

Segment 2   TIME CODE 2:17:56

Q　関西弁についてお話しくださいますか。

えぇ、関西弁と標準語の違いを例にあげて言います。えぇ、標準語では「ありがとう」というところを関西弁では「おおきに」、あるいは、えぇ、「これしてくれませんか」というのを「これしてくれへんか」とか、えぇ、「そんなことできません」ということを「できまへん」とか、そういう例があります。えぇ、そのように、えぇ、関西弁は、標準語と比べてやわらかい感じがします。どうしてやわらかく*言い方になったかというと、まぁ、二つあげられると思います。一つは、風土として、えぇ、こう、人々がこうのんびりこう過ごしてきたというのが一つと、もう一つ考えられるのは、えぇ、関西は、お商売人が非常に多い、商売人言葉というのがものすごくこう広がったという、その二つが、えぇ、独特の関西弁を生んできたんじゃないかなあと思っております。

*The speaker may have started to say やわらかくなったかというと.

Segment 3 TIME CODE 2:19:07

Q 日本では全国で統一した手話法がありますか。それとも手話は地域によって少しずつ違うのでしょうか。で、もし違うようでしたらその例を少しあげていただけますか。

日本では、ぁのぅ、聞こえる人たちの音声言語もそれぞれ地域で違っていたりするけれども、ぁのぅ、通じる、ええ、一つの言葉として音声も通じていますが、手話もそれと同じです。日本の各地で手話もそれぞれ少しずつ違っていますが、でも、標準的に通じる手話というものがあります。

標準手話というものがあります。聾者はその標準手話とそれぞれ地域で少しずつ違う手話を身につけていると思いますが、例えば、どのように違うかと言いますと、自己紹介をする時にまず自分の名前を言います。そしてこのあたりの関東の場合には名前という手話をこのように使うのです

が、関西の場合には名前という手話はこのような形の手話を用います。

まったく形が違います。また、例えば、悪いことをしてしまって、すま

なかったと謝る、謝り方の手話ですが、関東の場合にはすみませんとい

ったものを使いますが、北海道や東北の地方では今やっているようなすみ

ませんという手話を、このような形の手話です。関東はこうです、とい

ったようなその手話の形の違いというものがあります。

単語と文法ノート

On the DVD Lesson 19 opens with images of guardians of the road 道祖神, who, it is

believed, protect travelers in this world and on the path to the next from evil spirits and

other dangers. *Dōsojin* also may be found at village borders. The images often take the

form of a man and a woman.

Title

| さまざまな | various; all sorts of; diverse |

Segment 1

| 多様な | diverse |
| 言葉遣い | language; manner of speech; use/choice of words |

Segment 1.1

| 細長い | long and narrow |
| 分布する | to be distributed |

差異 (さい)　　　　difference(s)　（差）

状況 (じょうきょう)　　　conditions; circumstances

越える (こ)　　　to cross; to go over (across, beyond)

向こう側 (む・がわ)　　　the other side

生活習慣 (せいかつしゅうかん)　　　customs of daily life

Segment 1.2

Note:　The deaf community signs in Japanese Sign Language (JSL), which is an independent language.　Please see Lesson 1, Segment 3 vocabulary.

属性 (ぞくせい)　　　an attribute

多様性 (たようせい)　　　diversity

不自由な (ふじゆう)　　　inconvenienced, restricted.

　　　（耳の不自由な　hearing disabled）

手話 (しゅわ)　　　sign language

年齢 (ねんれい)　　　age

やわらかい　　　soft, gentle

乱暴 (らんぼう)　　　rough, rude, violent

向き合う (む・あ)　　　to face each other

場面 (ばめん)　　　scene

しぐさ　　　one's gestures

目線 (めせん)　　　one's line of sight; one's gaze

やら	and, or
語尾	the end of a word or a sentence
表れる	to appear; to show up
異なる	to be different; to vary
年代差	differences between the generations
尊敬語	honorific expressions
謙遜語	humble expressions
丁寧な	polite

Segment 1.3

Xにかぎらず	This is not limited to X, but . . .
若者全般	young people in general, young people as a whole
仲間意識	peer/group consciousness; feelings for their peers
激しい	strong; fervent; keen
縮める	to shorten; to reduce; to abridge

Segment 1.4

| 日常会話 | everyday language, speech |
| 略す | to abbreviate, shorten |

関東 （かんとう）	the Kantō Plain, on which are located Tokyo and the prefectures of Ibaragi, Tochigi, Saitama, Gumma, Chiba, and Kanagawa
関西 （かんさい）	the Kansai region, centered around the cities of Kyoto, Osaka, and Kobe

Segment 2

関西弁 （かんさいべん）	Kansai dialect
標準語 （ひょうじゅんご）	the standard language of a nation; standard Japanese (based on the middle-class spoken language of Tokyo)
比べる （くら）	to compare
やわらかい	soft, gentle
感じがする （かん）	to feel, have a feeling that
風土 （ふうど）	climate; the natural features of a region
のんびり	freely and easily; calmly; peacefully
過ごす （す）	to pass the time; to live
商売人 （しょうばいにん）	merchant; shopkeeper
独特の （どくとく）	peculiar, unique to
生む （う）	to give birth to

Segment 3

統一する （とういつ）	to unify; to standardize

<ruby>音声言語<rt>おんせいげんご</rt></ruby>	a spoken language
それぞれ	each; respectively
<ruby>地域<rt>ちいき</rt></ruby>	region
<ruby>通<rt>つう</rt></ruby>じる	to be understood
<ruby>各地<rt>かくち</rt></ruby>	in each district
<ruby>標準手話<rt>ひょうじゅんしゅわ</rt></ruby>	standard sign language
<ruby>聾者<rt>ろうしゃ</rt></ruby>	a deaf person
<ruby>身<rt>み</rt></ruby>に<ruby>付<rt>つ</rt></ruby>ける	to learn/acquire knowledge, skills
<ruby>自己紹介<rt>じこしょうかい</rt></ruby>	self-introduction
<ruby>用<rt>もち</rt></ruby>いる	to use, make use of, employ
<ruby>謝<rt>あやま</rt></ruby>る	to apologize

(Discussion questions for Lessons 19 and 20 come at the end of Lesson 20.)

第２０課　日本語さまざま、その二

Diversity in the Japanese Language, Part II

We continue the discussion begun in Lesson 19.

Segment 4.1　　　　　　　　　　　　　TIME CODE　2:20:36

Q 同じ県内でも、話し方や言葉遣いが違う場合があると聞きました。山崎さんは群馬県のご出身ですが、群馬の場合はいかがでしょうか。

はい、そうですね。私は、ぁのぅ、桐生に嫁いでくる前は同じ群馬でも西の方にね、生まれたんですけども、例えばそこでは、ぁのぅ、ダンベイっていうお菓子がね、ぁのぅ、甘い和菓子、小豆の入っった甘いお菓子なんですけども、ダンベイ饅頭っていうんがあるんですね。で、それは、例えば、標準語ですと「そうでしょう」っていうのが「そうだんべい」「そうだんべい」っていうんですね。が、それが、ぁのぅ、桐生に嫁いできてからは、その「そうでしょう」っていうのが「そうだが」っていうんですね。だから、ぁのぅ、地方によって、地方っていうか同じ県内でも、で、それを先生にお話ししたら、秋田では「んだんだ」っていうんで、ずいぶん違うと思います、はい。

Segment 4.2   TIME CODE 2:21:36

Q 桐生にいらっしゃった時、女性の話し方にかなり驚いたとおっしゃ

いましたが、その経験についてお話しくださいますか。

それもありました。ぁのぅ、桐生に嫁いだころに、ぁのぅ、初めてこうパン屋

さんに買い物ね、パン買いに行ったんですけども、あまりにも周りがすご

く声が大きいのと、それからなんかきつく感じたので、パンが買えなかっ

たんですね。で、それをあとで聞きましたらば、桐生は、ぁのぅ、ご存知の

ように織物の町で、機械がもう一日中ガチャンコンガチャンコン動いて

るので、女工さんたちがその機械に負けない声の大きさじゃないと話し声

ができないので、すごく声が大きいと後で聞きまして、それから私も負

けじと大きな声でパンを買うようにできましたけども、はい。

帯を織る機械の音

Segment 4.3   TIME CODE 2:22:42

Q では、秋田県はいかがですか。

秋田県は、ぁの、群馬と違って海があって、それから山がありますので、

海は、ぁのぅ、やっぱり漁師さん、魚をとる人が、ぁの、多く住んでいます

ので、やっぱり、ぁの、漁師さんの言葉ってのはわりと男性ぽくて荒々し

いんですけど、山の 樵 さんが住んでいる山の方はやっぱりゆったりとした、ぁの、やさしい話し方します、同じ秋田弁でも。ずいぶんぁの、こう違ってると思いますけれども。

Segment 4.4　　　　　　　　　　　　TIME CODE　2:23:11

Q 挨拶の言葉にはその場所の風土がよく 現れますが、秋田あたりにも独特な挨拶の言葉がありますか。

秋田は、ぁの、日本でも、ぁの、有数のお酒のおいしいところなので、ぁの、必ずこぅおもてなしをする時は、ぁの、お酒を 必ずふるまいますので、その時にまた、ぁのう、「この次に遊びにいらして下さい」ってのを、そういうふうな言い方じゃなくて、「また飲みに来いや」って言うので、やっぱり 私も群馬に始めて来た時、そういうふうにして言ったら、皆さんやっぱり 驚いてました。それがやっぱり文化の違い、群馬とまた違っています、はい。

Segment 5　　　　　　　　　　　　　TIME CODE　2:23:48

Q 北海道には方言がありますか。

ぁの、実はですね、よく、ぁのう、よそから、まぁ、本州とかですね、よそから来た人は「北海道は言葉がきれいですね」っていうこと言います。で、

それはその東京なんかのような、いわゆる標準語に近いということを言ってるんですね。で、私はまあ、北海道で生まれて育ちましたから、ええ、私たちの子供のころってのは実は方言の坩堝だったんですね。あのぅ、親の出身の地方の言葉を同級生たちはいろいろ持ってるわけですね。そうすると、まず、学校で何が起こるかというとですね、通じない、その土地だけでしか通じない親の方言を使うと皆ワーと囃したてる。「何だそれ、それなのおかしい」って分からないわけですよ。で、たぶん標準語ってのは、まぁ東京を中心に、まぁ、標準語化されてくんだと思うんですけど、北海道も同じなんですね。いろんな地方から人が集まったために、共通語が必要になってくるんですね。そのために、こぅ、必然的にというかね、結果的にその標準化していく。それは、標準語の生まれてきたですね、ええ、東京中心に生まれてきた理由と北海道と同じだと僕は思ってます。

Segment 6   TIME CODE 2:24:54

Q ちょっとしたアクセントの違いで言葉の意味が違ってくる場合もありますが、谷口さんのお宅でもそういうことは時々あるそうですね。

これは私が幼いころから経験した非常に面白い点なんですけれども、私は六人家族で、私と弟は東京で生まれ育っていますけれども、私以外の四人家族はみんな出身地が違います。祖父は西日本の、あのぅ、方の

岡山県というところで生まれ育って、で、祖母は静岡県、で、父は九州の鹿児島県、で、母は、ぁのぅ、ま、十八歳のころまでは大阪で生まれ育ちました。ということで、もうみんな出身地が違っていて、しかも、ぁのぅ、（自分）物心つくころまでずっとその違う出身地に暮らしていて、もう大人になってから東京に来たっていう経緯があるので、非常に言葉がみんな違っているのが非常に面白い点です。で、あるエピソードなんですけれども、ぁの、これは最近の話なんですけど、と、父は、ぁのぅ、（じゅう）二十三歳か四歳くらいまで九州にいました。それから、ぁのぅ、就職して東京に来たんですけれども、もう東京に来てから三十年たつんですが、まだ鹿児島の言葉がずっと残って、アクセントもそうなんです。で、ある食事時に父がお箸をさがしていて、で、私だったら「おはしない？」ってふうに聞くんですけど、「おはしは、おはし、おはしどこ」っていうんです。で、私はそのアクセントの違いに最初気がつかなかったので、「ハシってなに、オハシってなに」、っていうふうにずっと聞いていて、彼は「おはしだよ、はしだよ」って言って、「何だろう何だろう」ってずっと考えて、「ああ、そうか、お箸か」っていうふうに、ぁのぅ、気がついたっていうことがありました。アクセントがちょっと違うことで、同じ言葉でも、ぁのぅ、ぜんぜん意味が分からなくなってしまうっていう、そういうエピソードもあります。

注：東京では「お箸」というと、「は」にアクセントがつきます。

東京には、日本各地からの出身者がいますが、谷口さんの家族ほど多様

な地域の出身者がいる家族は少ないでしょう。

単語と文法ノート

Segment 4.1

県内   within a prefecture

出身   to be from

嫁ぐ   to marry (into a family)

お菓子   a sweet; candy

和菓子   a Japanese sweet

小豆   azuki beans (used to make sweet bean-paste or bean jam)

饅頭   a bun with a bean-jam filling

だんべい   This expression is a contracted form derived from

                       にてあるべし (should be the case; perhaps), which

                       became であるべし. Then the "r" and "sh" dropped out,

                       producing であんべい. At this point a vowel contraction

                       took place, giving us だんべい.

Segment 4.2

きつい   harsh (in this context)

ご存知のように   as you know (polite)

織物   textiles

機械   machine

負けじと   without giving in, without yielding

帯   sash for kimono

Segment 4.3

漁師   fisherman, fisherwoman

                     Cf. 猟師、hunter

男性ぽい   masculine; mannish

〜ぽい   ＝　らしい

荒々しい   rough, harsh, violent

樵 さん   a woodcutter

ゆったりとした   calm, unhurried, leisurely

やさしい   gentle, kind

秋田弁   Akita dialect

Segment 4.4

挨拶   a greeting, salutation

有数の   prominent, leading, greatest

持て成しをする   to entertain someone; to receive someone (at one's home)

振舞<ruby>振舞<rt>ふるま</rt></ruby>う   entertain, もてなす ; treat, ごちそうする

Segment 5   Segue photos courtesy of Odajima Mamoru.

<ruby>方言<rt>ほうげん</rt></ruby>   a regional dialect

<ruby>実<rt>じつ</rt></ruby>は   actually

よそ   some other place   ほかの<ruby>場所<rt>ばしょ</rt></ruby>

<ruby>坩堝<rt>るっぼ</rt></ruby>   a melting pot; a crucible

<ruby>出身<rt>しゅっしん</rt></ruby>の<ruby>地方<rt>ちほう</rt></ruby>   the region/part of the country (they) came from

<ruby>同級生<rt>どうきゅうせい</rt></ruby>   classmates (same class; same level in school)

<ruby>通<rt>つう</rt></ruby>じる   to be understood

<ruby>囃<rt>はや</rt></ruby>し<ruby>立<rt>た</rt></ruby>てる   to jeer at; to hoot

<ruby>集<rt>あつ</rt></ruby>まる   to gather

<ruby>共通語<rt>きょうつうご</rt></ruby>   a common language

<ruby>必要<rt>ひつよう</rt></ruby>   necessary

<ruby>必然的<rt>ひつぜんてき</rt></ruby>に   necessarily; inevitably

<ruby>結果的<rt>けっかてき</rt></ruby>に   as a result; consequently

Segment 6   Segue watercolor courtesy of the speaker's maternal grandfather, Ishihara Taikan   石原大幹。

アクセント   the reference is to "pitch-accent"

<ruby>幼<rt>おさな</rt></ruby>い   very young; infant

経験^{けいけん}する	to experience

経験する　　　　　to experience

出身地^{しゅっしんち}　　　　one's hometown; one's birthplace

育つ^{そだ}　　　　to grow, be reared

祖父^{そ ふ}　　　　my grandfather (humble)

祖母^{そ ぼ}　　　　my grandmother (humble)

物心つく^{ものごころ}　　　　to begin to take notice of things

暮らす^く　　　　to live

経緯^{けいい}　　　　circumstances; details, particulars

就職する^{しゅうしょく}　　　　to find work

注^{ちゅう}　　　　(explanatory) note; an annotation; 注釈^{ちゅうしゃく}

各地^{かくち}　　　　each place; various places/districts

出身者^{しゅっしんしゃ}　　　　someone from a certain place

話し合いましょう

１）ある地域^{ちいき}でしか通用^{つうよう}しない方言^{ほうげん}、あるいは独特^{どくとく}の言^いい回^{まわ}しが消^きえていく過程^{かてい}で、同時^{どうじ}にどのようなものが失^{うしな}われていくでしょうか。近頃^{ちかごろ}では動植物^{どうしょくぶつ}の多様性^{たようせい}が重視^{じゅうし}されつつありますが、言語^{げんご}の多様性^{たようせい}が失^{うしな}われることについてはどのような意見^{いけん}をもっていますか。

通用^{つうよう}する　　　　to be accepted; to be valid; to be in general use

ほうげん 方言	a (regional) dialect
どくとく 独特の	peculiar to; characteristic of; unique to
い まわ 言い回し	an expression; a turn of phrase
き 消える	to vanish
かてい 過程	a process, a course
うしな 失 う	to lose; うしな 失 われる to be lost (passive)
たようせい 多様性	diversity
じゅうし 重視する	to consider/regard as important

2）日本の留学生たちに、故郷の方言について聞いてみましょう。

3）自分の故郷には、その地域に独特の言葉遣いはありますか。

Verb Conjugation Table

Ikita Nihongo uses a five-base conjugation system for modern Japanese verbs.

	Nickname		Common suffixes
First base	Plain negative	未然形	ない、れる (られる)
Second base	Continuative (pre-ます)	連用形	ます、たい、やすい
Third base	a. Dictionary form; conclusive	終止形	
	b. Attributive	連体形	ことにする
Fourth base	Conditional	仮定形	(literary, 已然形)　ば
Fifth base	Imperative	命令形	

For further detail see the conjugation tables in a standard Japanese dictionary such as *Kōjien* 広辞苑 (岩波書店).

For a review of basic conjugations and definitions of grammatical terms see:
Makino, Seichi and Michio Tsutsui. *A Dictionary of Basic Japanese Grammar.*
　　　Tokyo: The Japan Times, 1989. Note especially Appendix 1, "Basic
　　　Conjugations."
——. *A Dictionary of Intermediate Japanese Grammar.* Tokyo: The Japan Times, 1995.
　　　Note especially "Grammatical Terms," pp. 13-29, and "Conversational
　　　Strategies," pp. 46-54.

References and Suggested Reading

Students may benefit from using *Ikita Nihongo* in conjunction with a general text on Japanese society, such as Yoshio Sugimoto's *An Introduction to Japanese Society,* cited a number of times below. Students will also enjoy Shigeru Miyagawa's CD-ROM, *Star Festival, A Return to Japan.*

Websites are current as of May 2006.

Lesson One
For current statistics and related essays and reports, see the Ministry of Health, Labor, and Welfare 厚生労働省 website, www.mhlw.go.jp (Japanese and English), and the Bureau of Statistics 統計局 website, http://www.stat.go.jp (Japanese and English).

Clark, Gregory. "Japan's Migration Conundrum." *Japan Focus* 217. http://japanfocus.org/217.html Online.

Cohen, Joel. "Human Population Grows Up." *Scientific American,* September 2005, 48-55.

McNeill, David. "Time Running Out for Shrinking Japan," *Japan Focus* 173. http://japanfocus.org/173.html Online.

Miyazaki Tetsuya, et al. "What Can We Do About the Baby Bust?" *Japan Echo,* February 2006, 14-19.

Sugimoto, Yoshio. *An Introduction to Japanese Society.* Second edition. New York: Cambridge University Press, 2003. See Chapter 3, "Geographical and Generational Variations," and Chapter 6, "Gender Stratification and the Family System."

Lesson Three
Although we focus in Lessons 2 and 3 on single family homes, residences range from small, uniform units in public or company apartment complexes to personally designed condominiums; and from the "three generation" home in which elderly parents have a separate floor to institutional senior homes. On the truly micro scale, many a low-budget salaryman, upon missing the last train, has found a home for the night in a "capsule" sleeping space, available at some urban train stations!

Kawashima, Chūji. *Japan's Folk Architecture.* Tokyo: Kodansha International, 1986.

Nitschke, Gunter. *Japanese Gardens.* Cologne: Taschen, 2003.

Takashina, Shuji. "Relativity in Japanese Architectural Space." *Japan Echo,* October 2000, 55-60.

Ueda, Atsushi. *The Inner Harmony of the Japanese House.* Tokyo: Kodansha International, 1998.

Lesson Four
Dunn, Charles J. *Everyday Life in Traditional Japan.* Tokyo: Charles Tuttle, 1969.

Koizumi Kazuko. *Traditional Japanese Furniture.* New York: Kodansha International, 1986.

Munsterberg, Hugo. *The Folk Arts of Japan.* Tokyo: Charles Tuttle, 1958.

Smith, Bruce, and Yoshiko Yamamoto. *The Japanese Bath.* Salt Lake City: Gibbs-Smith, 2001.

Yanagi, Sōetsu. *The Unknown Craftsman, A Japanese Insight into Beauty.* New York: Kodansha International, 1972. Reading Yanagi will cultivate a deeper understanding of 用の美.

Lesson Five

ERS (Economic Research Service), USDA. "Japan: Basic Information." http://www.ers.usda.gov/Briefing/Japan/basicinformation.htm Online.

Gender Equality Bureau, Cabinet Office 内閣府男女共同参画局. "Women in Japan Today, 2004." http://www.gender.go.jp/english_contents/women2004/statistics/s02.html Online.

JA グループの紹介. (http://www.nokyo.or.jp/ja-group/ja01.html) Online.

Ministry of Agriculture, Forestry, and Fisheries 農林水産省 http://www.maff.go.jp/eindex.html (English and Japanese) Online.

Richardson, Bennett. "Sticky Situation for Japan's Rice Policy." *Asia Times Online,* August 6, 2005. http://www.atimes.com

Yamashita, Kazuhito. "New Growth for Farms." *Asia-Pacific Perspectives,* February 2005, 20-21.

Yamazaki, Yasuyo. "The Untapped Potential of Japanese Agriculture." *Japan Echo,* June 2004, 50-52.

Lesson Six

Bestor, Theodore C. *Tsukiji, the Fish Market at the Center of the World.* Berkeley: University of California Press, 2004. A fascinating study!

Earle, Sylvia. "Deep Trouble," in *Tidal Seas/Coasts,* Vol. 4 of *The Blue Planet, Seas of Life* (DVD). British Broadcasting Corporation, 2001. We learn how an insatiable appetite for sushi, particularly bluefin tuna, affects our marine ecosystem and individual species.

Iwamura, Nobuko. "Crisis in the Kitchen." *Japan Echo,* April 2004. www.japanecho.com Online.

Kishi, Asako. "Good Eating in an Age of Abundance." *Japan Echo,* October 2001. www.japanecho.com Online.

Lesson Seven

Faiola, Anthony. "Japanese Women Live, and Like It, on Their Own: Gender Roles Shift as Many Stay Single." *Washington Post Foreign Service,* August 31, 2004, A01.

Statistical Research and Training Institute, Bureau of Statistics, Ministry of International
Affairs and Communications 総務省, ed. *Statistical Handbook of
Japan, 2005.* http://www.stat.go.jp/english/data/handbook/c02cont.htm Online.

Sugimoto, Yoshio. *An Introduction to Japanese Society.* Second edition. New York:
Cambridge University Press, 2003. See Chapter 6, "Gender Stratification and the
Family System."

Tachibanaki Toshiaki. "The Rising Tide of Poverty in Japan." *Japan Echo*,
October 2005, 47-50.

Yamada, Masahiro. "The Expectation Gap: Winners and Losers in the New Economy."
Japan Echo, February 2005, 9-13.

Lesson Eight

Arita Eriko. "Postwar Labor Scene Still Grim for Working Women." *The Japan Times
Online,* August 5, 2005.
http://www.japantimes.co.jp/cgi-bin/makeprfy.p15?nn20050805f1.htm.

Brasor, Phillip. "Little Progress on Japanese Gender Equality." *The Japan Times Online*,
February 13, 2005.
http://www.japantimes.co.jp/cgi-bin/makeprfy.p15?fd20050213pb.htm

Ministry of Health, Labor and Welfare 厚生労働省、「働く女性の実情」
http://www.mhlw.go.jp/houdou/2005/03/h0328.7a.html .

Sugimoto, Yoshio. *An Introduction to Japanese Society.* Second edition. New York:
Cambridge University Press, 2003. See pp. 161-165 on career
women and part-time workers.

Weathers, Charles. "Equal Opportunity for Japanese Women—What Progress?"
Japan Focus 411. http://japanfocus.org/411.html Online.

今森光彦『おじいちゃんは水のにおいがした』偕成社、２００６.
http://www.imamori-world.jp/imamoribook/imamoribook020.html

まど・みちお『まど・みちお画集—とおいところ』新潮社、２００３.

Lesson Nine

Asada, Shizuko. "Confessions of Troubled Elementary School Teachers." *Japan Echo*,
April 2005, 35-37.

Kariya, Takehiko. "The Baby Bust and the Lowering of Academic Standards."
Japan Echo, June 2001, 20-22.

Kondō Motohiro. "Rethinking Japanese Education—Again." *Japan Echo*, April 2005,
27-29.

Lewis, Catherine C. *Educating Hearts and Minds: Reflections on Japanese Preschool
and Elementary Education.* New York: Cambridge University Press, 1995.

"Public Schools Failing Parents." *Asahi Shimbun Online*, October 8, 2005.
www.asahi.com/english/

Sakakibara, Eisuke. "First Reform the Educational Bureaucracy." *Japan Echo*,
June 2001, 23-26.

Satō, Manabu. "Japan's School Crisis: A Trail of Misguided Reforms." *Japan Echo*,
    April 2005, 30-34.
Yasuda, Yuki. "High School Graduates Who Cannot Find Work." *Japan Echo*,
    April 2003, 56-62.

Lesson Ten

Ministry of Education, Culture, Sports, Science and Technology 文部科学 省 (MEXT).
    "School Education." http://www.mext.go.jp/english/statist/04120801/005.pdf
    Online.
Sugimoto, Yoshio. *An Introduction to Japanese Society.* Second edition. New York:
    Cambridge University Press, 2003. See Chapter 5, "Diversity and Unity in
    Education."

Lesson Eleven

Japan Society for Studies in Cartoons and Comics 日本マンガ学界.
    http://www.kyoto-seika.ac.jp/hyogen/manga-gakkai.html Online.
"Miyazaki Hayao 宮崎駿." http://www.net.nausicaa.net/miyazaki/ Online.
    Official Studio Ghibli site for information on Miyazaki's *anime* and *manga*.
Napier, Susan J. *Anime from Akira to Howl's Moving Castle, Revised and Updated:
    Experiencing Contemporary Japanese Animation.* New York: Palgrave
    MacMillan, 2005.
Tanaka, Yūko. "Tracing the Premodern Roots of Manga." *Japan Echo*, October 2004,
    55-60. This article may also be found on the Internet at www.japanecho.com

Lesson Twelve

Boufford, David, Yasushi Hibi and Hiromi Tada. "Japan."
    http://biodiversityscience.org/publications/hotspots/Japan.html   A publication of
    the Center for Applied Biodiversity Science, Conservation International.
Carnegie Council. "Interview with Yukiko Kada, Japan Team Leader, Environmental
    Values Project." http://www.carnegiecouncil.org/viewMedia.php/prmID/156
Dauvergne, Peter. *Shadows in the Forest: Japan and the Politics of Timber in Southeast
    Asia.* Cambridge: The MIT Press, 1997.
"Japan's Secret Garden," Nova #2716. *Nova Online.*
    http://www.pbs.org/nova/transcripts/2716satoyama.html
Kada Yukiko et. al. "From *Kōgai* to *Kankyō Mondai*: Nature, Development, and Social
    Conflict in Japan." Forging Environmentalism: Justice, Livelihood, and
    Contested Environments. New York: M. E. Sharpe, 2006.
Katō, Sadamichi. "The Three Ecologies in Minakata Kumagusu's Environmental
    Movement." *Organization & Environment*, Vol. 12 No. 1, March 1999, 85-98.
Short, Kevin. *Nature in Short.* Weekly column in *The Daily Yomiuri*.
    http://www.yomiuri.co.jp/index-e.htm Online.
Takeuchi, Kazuhiko *et al.*, eds. *Satoyama, the Traditional Rural Landscape of Japan.*
    Tokyo: Springer-Verlag, 2003. This is an English translation of the Japanese text
    listed below, 武内和彦 *et al.*, 編. The concepts are clearer in the original.

Yabe, Mitsuo. "Trees and Forests, Part of the Cultural Fabric of Japan." *Nipponia*, No. 24, March 15 2003. Note the opening photograph by Imamori Mitsuhiko depicting a contemporary *satoyama* district in Otsu, Shiga-ken. The online site contains further articles and photographs illustrating points mentioned in this lesson. http://web-Japan.org/nipponia/nipponia24/en/feature/feature01.html (English and Japanese).

今森光彦『里山を歩こう』岩波書店、２００２．

小田島 護『大雪山のヒグマ』山と渓谷社、１９８２．

武内和彦 *et al.* 編『里山の環境学』東京大学出版会、２００１．

田端英雄『里山の自然』保育社、１９９７．

Lesson Thirteen

International Lake Environment Committee. One Hundred Years of World Lakes by Utilizing Now and Then Photographs 今昔写真でみる世界の湖沼の１００年。Kusatsu, Shiga Prefecture: Lake Biwa Museum, 2001. (English and Japanese)

Lake Biwa Museum. *A Guide to the Lake Biwa Museum, Lakes and People: Toward a Better Symbiotic Relationship*. Kusatsu, Shiga Prefecture: Lake Biwa Museum, 2003.

今森光彦『里山物語』新潮社、１９９５．

嘉田由紀子『生活世界の環境学、琵琶湖からのメッセージ』農山漁村文化協会、１９９５．

嘉田由紀子『水辺ぐらしの環境学――琵琶湖と世界の湖から』昭和堂、２００１．

深町加津枝 et al. 編「里山と人・新たな関係の構築を目指して」『日本造園学会誌』Vol. 61 No. 4, March 1998.

前野隆資写真、嘉田由紀子解説『琵琶湖・水物語』平凡社、１９９６．

Lesson Fourteen

Dower, John. *Embracing Defeat: Japan in the Wake of World War II*. New York: W.W. Norton, 1999.

Hein, Laura, and Mark Selden, eds. *Censoring History: Citizenship and Memory in Japan, Germany, and the United States*. New York: M.E. Sharpe, 2000.

Ienaga, Saburo. *Japan's Past, Japan's Future: One Historian's Odyssey*. Translated by Richard Minear. Lanham, Maryland: Rowman and Littlefield, 2001.

――. *The Pacific War 1931-1945*. New York: Random House, 1978.

「子どもたちに伝えたい戦争の悲劇」『東京新聞』2005 年 8 月 14 日、p. 8.

Lesson Fifteen

Kensho, Takashi. "Music Education in Japan, 1868-1944."
　　　http://www.u-gakugei.ac.jp/~takeshik/mused1868j.html Online.
童謡、唱歌へのいざない. http://www.aba.ne.jp/~takaichi/douyou/izanai.html.
野ばら社、編『日本のうた』野ばら社、１９８２.
読売新聞文化部『唱歌・童謡ものがたり』岩波書店、１９９９.

Lesson Sixteen

Dalby, Liza Chrihfield. *Geisha*. Berkeley: University of California Press, 1998.
Sugimoto, Yoshio. *An Introduction to Japanese Society*. Second edition. New York:
　　　Cambridge University Press, 2003. See Chapter 9, "Popular Culture and
　　　Everyday Life."

Lesson Seventeen

Tokeshi, Jin'ichi. *Kendō: Elements, Rules, and Philosophy*. Honolulu: University of
　　　Hawai'i Press, 2003.
梅崎邦奉「剣道について」相生剣道クラブ、２００４年６月２９日.
　　　Unpublished manuscript.
新渡戸稲造『Nitobe 武士道を英語で読む』宝島社、２００４. Nitobe
　　　Inazō's *Bushidō* was first published in 1900 by the Leeds & Biddle Co.,
　　　Philadelphia.

Lesson Eighteen

For an excellent photo dictionary of Japanese Shintō and Buddhist figures, see
　　　www.onmarkproductions.com/html/buddhism.shtml.
Conze, Edward. *Buddhist Wisdom Books*. New York: Harper & Row, 1958.
Kitagawa, Joseph. *Religion in Japanese History*. New York: Columbia University Press,
　　　1966.
Nhat Hanh, Thich. *The Heart of Understanding: Commentaries on the Prajñaparamita
　　　Heart Sutra*. Berkeley: Parallax Press, 1988.
Reader, Ian, Esben Andreasen and Finn Stefansson. *Japanese Religions Past and
　　　Present*. Honolulu: University of Hawaii Press, 1993.
Sōtō Zen website. www.sotozen-net.or.jp (English and Japanese text)
ひろ・さちや『仏教と神道』新潮選書、１９８７.

Lessons Nineteen and Twenty

Kayano Shigeru. *Our Land Was a Forest: An Ainu Memoir*. Boulder, Colorado:
　　　Westview Press, 1994.
Sugimoto, Yoshio. *An Introduction to Japanese Society*. Second edition. New York:
　　　Cambridge University Press, 2003. See Chapter 3, "Geographical and
　　　Generational Variations."

About the Author

Karen Satsuki Colligan-Taylor, professor emerita, Japanese Studies, University of Alaska, Fairbanks, grew up in the suburbs of Tokyo. She received her Ph.D. from Stanford University, focusing on the evolution of environmental literature in Japan. In 1989 she participated in the Baikal Forum, a traveling forum of scientists, journalists, and writers studying the effects of lake-water quality on local residents in Russia, Armenia, Kazakhstan, Mongolia, and Japan. In 2001 she received the Miyazawa Kenji Shōreishō, a literary award, for her translations of selected tales by agronomist-poet Miyazawa Kenji (1896-1933). These translations have been published in single volumes and in *Masterworks of Miyazawa Kenji* (co-authored with Sarah Strong, 2002) by the International Foundation for the Promotion of Languages and Cultures in Tokyo. Other book translations include *Rowing the Eternal Sea: The Life of a Minamata Fisherman*, by Oiwa Keibo and Ogata Masato (Lanham, Maryland: Rowman and Littlefield, 2001), and *Sandakan Brothel No. 8: An Episode in the History of Lower-class Japanese Women*, by Yamazaki Tomoko (New York: M. E. Sharpe, 1999). Her articles on environmental issues and nature writing have appeared in a number of Japanese academic journals, books, and newspapers, and she has translated medical papers on Minamata disease. Colligan-Taylor established a Japanese program at Whitman College, Walla Walla, Washington, and a Japanese Studies major at the University of Alaska, Fairbanks. She currently divides her time between research in Japan and writing at her home in rural southeast Alaska.

DVD 写真クレジット

第1課　　　　撮影：カレン・テイラー
第2課　　　　撮影：小田島護
第8課　　　　「まど・みちお」撮影：伊藤英治、『まど・みちお画集、
　　　　　　　　　とおいところ』新潮社、2003.
　　　　　　　「ぞうさん」、『まど・みちお画集、とおいところ』
　　　　　　　　　新潮社、2003.
　　　　　　　A Guide to the Lake Biwa Museum. 滋賀県立琵琶湖博物館、
　　　　　　　　　2003, pp. 23, 77.
第11課　　　宮崎駿監督作品『もののけ姫』(1997) プログラムガイドの表紙;
　　　　　　　『千と千尋の神隠し』(2001)VCR の表紙、© スタジオジブリ.
第13課　　　「沖島」撮影：前野隆資　　提供：滋賀県立琵琶湖博物館。
　　　　　　　「海津」撮影：石井田勘二　　所蔵：高島市教育委員会、
　　　　　　　　　提供：滋賀県立琵琶湖博物館.
第14課　　　写真提供：石井和、カレン・テイラー
第16課　　　写真提供：楠岡泰、柳澤智子、カレン・テイラー、ロン・リード
第18課　　　国宝「達磨大師二祖慧可断臂図」雪舟筆
　　　　　　　　　提供：愛知県斉年寺、京都国立博物館
第20課　　　撮影：小田島護
　　　　　　　水彩画：石原大幹　　提供：谷口陽子